The Amazing Life of
Ormond McGill

**A new type of magic and hypnotism book in
which a thoughtful professional
reveals secrets of a lifetime**

Ormond McGill
Dean of American Hypnotists

Crown House Publishing Limited
www.crownhouse.co.uk

First published by

Crown House Publishing Ltd
Crown Buildings, Bancyfelin, Carmarthen, Wales, SA33 5ND, UK
www.crownhouse.co.uk

and

Crown House Publishing Company LLC
4 Berkeley Street, 1st Floor, Norwalk, CT 06850, USA
www.CHPUS.com

British Library of Cataloguing-in-Publication Data
A catalogue entry for this book is available
from the British Library.

10 Digit ISBN 1845900014
13 Digit ISBN 978-184590001-4
LCCN 2003102130

Printed and bound in the UK by
Cromwell Press
Trowbridge, Wiltshire

This book is an autobiography. It is dedicated to my beloved wife, Delight. This autobiography is an original. It has to be, as it is about you, and you are the only one exactly like yourself in the entire universe.

Contents

Biographical Foreword

Lifetime of a Magician/Hypnotist

Ormond McGill is a name to conjure with for those who know hypnotism. I use the word "conjure" as he is a magician in addition to being a hypnotist, and has combined those arts into stage shows of outstanding merit. His exciting magic/hypnotic shows have been witnessed by thousands throughout the United States and internationally in Canada, India, Hong Kong, Taiwan, Japan, Korea, Philippine Islands, French Polynesia, Australia and New Zealand.

Ormond was born in Palo Alto, California, June 15, 1913, and started his performing career in grammar school showing his classmates the ever popular "Wine and Water Trick", which was made possible by a chemistry set received as a Christmas gift.

While attending high school in Palo Alto, the budding entertainer took the Tarbell Magic Course by correspondence, which, at that time, was being nationally advertised. Work in the high school manual training shop made possible the construction of various pieces of apparatus which resulted in his first full evening magic show, presented for the high school in 1928. It was the start of a career in show business which has continued for 70 years plus. During those high school days, Ormond became interested in hypnotism. An interest which eclipsed even the young performer's interest in magic. Hypnotism became the feature of his shows, which, through the years, have been billed as "The Concert of Hypnotism".

During the 1930s, in addition to attending college, the developing magician/hypnotist performed at California summer resorts. It was also during that period that his work as an author began, (he will tell more about that in subsequent chapters of his auto-biography).

While attending the Pacific Coast Association of Magicians Convention in San Diego in 1940, Ormond met Arnold Furst who subsequently became his personal manager and booked his shows on many tours throughout the western United States and overseas.

The year 1942 marked a milestone in Ormond's career as it was then that he launched his original Spook Show, under the title "The Great London Hypnotic Seance". The show played the Fox and United Artists Theatres throughout the Pacific Coast and midwestern states, as well as in Famous Players Theatres across Canada, as far east as Quebec. He adopted the stage name of Dr. Zomb, for that phase of his career, and he continued playing theatres as Dr. Zomb. The name of the show was changed to "Seance of Wonders", but the name Dr. Zomb stayed with him, being used as a subtitle even in his overseas tours, as "The Man Called Dr. Zomb".

In 1943, Ormond married a girl named Delight. She was exactly her name, he says, and she became his "Girl Friday" in numerous performances.

An outstanding showman, Ormond McGill is also the author of numerous books on hypnotism, magic, and other things. In 1947, he began the writing of his now famous *Encyclopedia of Genuine Stage Hypnotism*. It has gone through half a dozen printings, and become recognized as the "bible" of stage hypnotists. An enlarged edition called *The New Encyclopedia of Stage Hypnotism* was recently published in the UK by Crown House Publishing. Already it has gone through six printings, and hit "best seller" acclaim.

The year 1955 found the McGills touring in Australia, Japan and Korea, on a tour arranged by Arnold Furst. And, in 1958, in association with motion picture producer, Ron Ormond, they made a tour of the Orient, both filming and performing in the Philippines, Hong Kong, Taiwan and India. On returning from this trip, Ormond, in collaboration with Ron, wrote the book *Into the Strange Unknown*, which was later rewritten and expanded into the book *Religious Mysteries of the Orient*, published by A.S. Barnes & Company, Inc. in 1976. Ormond McGill and the late Ron Ormond were the first men to bring Western attention to the "psychic surgery" of the Philippines.

In 1969, Ormond and Delight made a pioneer tour to Tahiti and other islands of French Polynesia with the first magic/hypnotism show to play these remote islands of the South Pacific. On returning to the States, the couple designed their new show of "South Sea Island Magic" which combined with "The Concert Of Hypnotism". During this period, Ormond, also, had featured roles in two movies produced by Ron Ormond Films, Inc.: *Please Don't Touch Me* and *Sacred Symbol* with John Calvert (The Falcon).

The 1970s proved a time of writing five books: *The Secret World of Witchcraft, Religious Mysteries of the Orient, The Mysticism and Magic of India, How to Produce Miracles,* and *Entertaining With Magic.* These books were published by A.S. Barnes & Company, Inc. for public sale. *How to Produce Miracles* was also produced in a popular paperback edition by Signet. It was a busy time in which the couple managed to squeeze in their last overseas tour for Kerrig-Odeon Theatres in New Zealand.

Then, in 1976, tragedy entered Ormond's life. His beloved Delight died. Ormond's thought was to end his career then and there, but friends stepped in and encouraged him to continue on. Friendship with renowned illusionist, Lee Grabel resulted in his being booked to play sponsorship shows for the National Federation of the Blind, to raise funds for that worthy organization. The association lasted for 20 years. The last show for NFB was in 1999.

In 1981, in addition to performing hypnotism on the stage, Ormond McGill turned attention to teaching classes as a state-approved Hypnotherapy instructor at the Hypnotherapy Training Institute of Northern California (HTI). He developed some revolutionary techniques. He has written of some of these in the Hypnotism section of his autobiography, and also in *The New Encyclopedia of Stage Hypnotism.* Besides teaching at HTI, the conventions of the American Council of Hypnotist Examiners (ACHE) and the National Guild of Hypnotists (NGH) annually engage his services. In recognition of his contribution to the field of hypnosis, he has become internationally recognized as "The Dean of American Hypnotists". He wears the mantle well.

Ormond McGill is recipient of numerous awards and citations including recognition by the New Hampshire House of Representatives, and the prestigious Dr. Rexford L. North Award. Likewise he is on the Faculty of the Hypnotherapy Training Institute, Northern California, and the advisory board of the American

Council of Hypnotist Examiners (ACHE) and the National Guild of Hypnotists.

However, I believe the finest tribute to this man is the aura of friendship he radiates to everyone. Outside the field of hypnotism, his book *Grieve No More, Beloved: The Book of Delight*, written after Delight's passing in 1976, has brought comfort to hundreds of people who grieve the passing onwards of someone they loved. It is known as a handbook of life after death, as channelled through Ormond by his wife, Delight, in spirit.

In writing his autobiography, Ormond McGill takes you on a journey through this lifetime from his birth in 1913 onwards into current space and time (2003), and along the journey you will learn some clever magic you can perform, innovative hetero-hypnosis and self-hypnosis methods you can use, and much more.

I close now this brief biological outline of Ormond McGill, and let Ormond tell his own story, in his own way, with magic and the magical-like sprinkled along the way.

Charles Mignosa
San Jose, CA
2003

Timeline

1913	Ormond Dale McGill born on June 15 in Palo Alto, California, USA.
1920	Started school at age of seven.
1925	Performed first magic trick in front of classmates in 5th grade in grammar school.
	Saw magician Herman Hansen perform at Pantages Theatre in San Francisco.
1926	Family moved to Berkeley, CA, for a year.
1927	Family returned to Palo Alto. Started high school.
	Took Tarbell Course in Magic. Saw magician Ralph Richards perform at Liberty Theatre in San Jose, CA.
1928	Saw magician Charles Carter (Carter the Great) perform at the Columbia Theatre in San Francisco.
	Presented first full evening Magic Show at Palo Alto High School Auditorium.
1930	Played some shows with magician Mandu.
1931	Graduated from Palo Alto High School.
1932	Saw magician Maurice Raymond perform with Franchon & Marco Revue at Fox California Theatre in San Jose.
	Joined Mystic 13 Magic Club as a charter member.
	Saw Howard Thurston perform at the Orpheum Theatre in San Francisco.
1932–1934	Attended San Jose State College majoring in psychology.
1932–1940	Performed shows during summer season at vacation resorts: Yosemite, Lake Tahoe, Russian River.

1934	Attended "El Wyn Midnight Spook Party", the first Spook Show Ormond ever saw, at the Fox Stanford Theatre, Palo Alto. Was offered to take a unit of the show on tour. Refused due to college commitments.
	Saw Chinese Magician Long Tack Sam at Fox Stanford Theatre, Palo Alto.
1935	Met and became friends with Chatauqua magician, Edwin Brush.
	Designed and presented his first Midnight Spook Show "The Great London Hypnotic Seance", developed with theater manager, Hal Honoré. Presented at Fox Sequoia Theatre, Redwood City, CA.
	Adopted theatrical name of "Dr. Zomb".
	Met Delight Beth Olmstead.
1935–1954	Presented Dr. Zomb Midnight Shows throughout Western USA and Canada with show titled "The Séance of Wonders".
1937–1938	First writing on magic/hypnotism published as a monthly column in *TOPS* magazine for Abbott Magic Company, Colon, Michigan.
1939	Offered an opportunity to manage an Abbott Magic Shop in Buffalo, New York. Offer refused due to success of playing Midnight Shows.
1940	Met Lee Grabel in an elevator of the Golden Gate Theatre Building in San Francisco while on the way to meet his theatrical agent Lou Emmel. Became close friends.
	Met magician Arnold Furst while attending Pacific Coast Association of Magicians Convention (PCAM) in San Diego, CA. Arnold subsequently became Ormond's manager and booked many tours throughout Western United States and overseas. Visited Thayer's Magic Studio in Hollywood.

1943   Married Delight Olmstead on September 29,1943 in Santa Monica, California. Lived in Los Angeles for two years.

Met fellow hypnotist Gil Boyne in Hollywood.

Wrote *Radio & Night Club Mindreading*, his first book on magic, for William Larsen, Sr. of Thayer's Studio of Magic.

1944   Dunninger Radio Show era. Saw Dunninger perform in person at Shrine Auditorium in Los Angeles.

Performed many hypnotism shows at the Hollywood Canteen for service men of World War II.

Met motion picture producer Louis Berkoff. Became technical advisor on magic for Berkoff picture *The Strange Mr. Gregory* starring Edmund Lowe, as a magician.

Wrote *How To Produce Miracles* introducing miracle-type magic to magicians. First published by Barnes and subsequently by Signet.

Appeared on Art Linkletter's *People Are Funny* Radio Show, as a performing hypnotist. A pioneer performance.

1945   Appeared on Art Linkletter's television show *Life With Linkletter*, as a performing hypnotist.

Delight and Ormond left Hollywood to return to live in Palo Alto, near their parents.

1947   Began writing now famous *The Encyclopedia of Genuine Stage Hypnotism*, the "bible" of stage hypnotists, presenting his work from 1927 to 1947. Published by Abbott's Magic Company of Colon, Michigan.

1950   Wrote *Atomic Magic*, a book suggesting sci-fi themes for the performance of magic, which was published by Magic Inc. of Chicago.

Abbott's Magic Company published three titles written by Ormond: *21 Gems of Magic*, *Fooling The Public* and *Psychic Magic*.

1951   Wrote books *A Better Life Through Using Conscious Self-Hypnosis* and *Dental Hypnosis* for Dr. Rexford L. North, director of Hypnotism Center of Boston.

1952   Launched first full evening show "East Indian Miracles".

1955   McGills toured overseas playing shows booked by Arnold Furst in Australia, and for the US Military in the Philippines, Okinawa, Korea and Japan.

1958   In association with motion picture producer Ron Ormond, the McGills made a tour of the Orient, both filming and performing in the Philippines, Hong Kong, Taiwan and India.

1959   Ormond wrote, in collaboration with Ron Ormond, *Into the Strange Unknown*, telling of their adventures in the Orient. Later, Ormond rewrote and enlarged this book, titled *Religious Mysteries of the Orient*. Published by Barnes, Inc.

1959–1976   Ormond became a seashell dealer, providing rare shells for collectors. During this period the McGills presented many shows for schools in natural science. Booked under the direction of James L. Gray.

1963 onward   Ormond featured in two movies produced by Ron Ormond Films Inc.: *Please Don't Touch Me* and *Sacred Symbol* with John Calvert (The Falcon).

1969   Ormond and Delight made a pioneer tour to Tahiti and other islands of French Polynesia with the first magic/hypnotism show to play these remote islands of the South Pacific.

On returning to the States, the couple launched their new show entitled "South Sea Island Magic".

1970   The McGills went on their last overseas tour for Kerridge-Odeon Theatres in New Zealand.

Wrote *The Art of Stage Hypnotism* presenting his work from 1947 to 1970 published by Lloyd Jones Magic Limited of Oakland, California (now out of print).

1970–1979   Wrote five books: *The Secret World of Witchcraft, Religious Mysteries of the Orient, The Mysticism and Magic of India, How To Produce Miracles* and *Entertaining with Magic* published by A.S. Barnes & Company Inc. *How To Produce Miracles* also published in paperback by Signet.

1973   Compiled chapters not included in *Into the Strange Unknown* into a new book entitled *The Secret World of Witchcraft*. The book has been used as a text for anthropology classes.

1976   Delight died August 28, 1976.

Met fellow magician Charles (Chuck) Mignosa. Became close friends.

1977   A revised and copyrighted edition of *The Encyclopedia of Genuine Stage Hypnotism* enti-tled *Professional Stage Hypnotism* published by Westwood Publishing Company.

1981   Joined staff of Hypnotherapy Training Institute of Northern California (HTI), to teach hypnotherapy with Randal Churchill and Marleen Mulder, directors. Teaching continues.

Wrote *Hypnotism and Meditation*. Published by Westwood Publishing Company.

1982	Played shows booked by Robert Cook sponsored by Kiwanis Clubs.
1983–1999	Fund-raising shows for National Federation of the Blind. Performed as a team with friend, Charles Mignosa.
1986	Wrote *The Magic and Illusions of Lee Grabel*. Illustrated by the popular magician Patrick Martin.
1987	Started teaching annually for the American Council of Hypnotist Examiners (ACHE) Conferences.
1990	Association with The National Guild of Hypnotists, Inc. attending annual Conventions and presenting workshops (continues).
	Ormond McGill and Marleen Mulder invited on an international teaching tour to instruct hypnotherapy at seminars in New Zealand and Australia. Other tours followed.
1995	Honored by acclaiming "1995 The Year of McGill" by National Guild of Hypnotists (NGH).
	Patented his new invention "The Love Clock". *Grieve No More, Beloved: The Book of Delight* was published by the Anglo American Book Company.
	State of New Hampshire declared Congratulations to Ormond on 60 years as a showman and author.
1996	Awarded honorary PhD in hypnotherapy by St. John University of Louisiana.
	An enlarged edition of the *Encyclopedia of Genuine Stage Hypnotism* was published in the UK as *The New Encyclopedia of Stage Hypnotism* by Crown House Publishing Ltd (became a bestseller).

1997	*Seeing The Unseen* was published by the Anglo American Book Company presenting for the first time his original Transcendental Hypnotism Induction Method.
1998	Hypnotic demonstrations and stage show presented at Hypnotherapy Training Institute (HTI) on his 85th birthday televised by BBC (UK).
	Development of Serenity Resonant Sound, as Theta/Delta background for hypnotic induction. Developed with sound engineer Joe Worrel.
1999 onward	Presented Stage Hypnotism workshops in Boston, London and Las Vegas with Jerry Valley & Co.
2003	Publishing of *Secrets of Dr. Zomb: The Autobiography of Ormond McGill* and *Secrets of Stage Mindreading*.

Preface

Every life is individual and different, yet there are universal similarities, so reading an autobiography or a biography can be of value to one's personal life. Each person serves the other in increasing the value of a lifetime.

This is my autobiography and it, also, gives you instructions in the arts of magic and hypnotism as an autobiographical sharing.

This autobiography, with its Biographical Foreword and Timeline, spans better than three-quarters of a century, and tells of enchanting things I have found of value to myself. I share them with you.

Ormond McGill
Palo Alto, CA
2003

Introduction

This autobiography tells of my life from 1913 to 2003. In a way, it is a different kind of autobiography as it is also a Magic and Hypnotism book. It tells of my life adventures as a professional magician, hypnotist and transcendental author.

When one has used up their "three-score-and-ten", and even more, it is high time to take stock of oneself, determine what is to be left to posterity, and write an autobiography of their life – if such is ever to be.

So, since I have reached 90, I have gathered things I cherish and am presenting them here. Have fun tossing these ideas about. Remembering . . .

While you will find much that is magical within these pages appreciate that the greatest magic of all is you!

As is my motto: "Join the crowd, but while you do it be an original as then you have value." An original Van Gogh will sell for over a million dollars. A good copy of a Van Gogh will bring about fifty if you are lucky.

Part One

Conception of a Magician/ Hypnotist

Chapter One

A Magician is Born

Somehow I always knew I was just a visitor on this planet; however, my birth certificate affirms I was born on June 15, 1913 at 5.15 p.m. in Palo Alto, California, USA. According to astrology, this makes me a Gemini (the Twins), as being a person with a sort of dual personality, as it were.

My mother was a relatively small woman with flashing brown eyes. Her maiden name was Julia Battele. She was born in Florida, spent her girlhood in Omaha and then moved to San Francisco where she met my father, Harry A. McGill, and said, "I do."

My father was a gentle, soft-spoken man, who often told of having gone through the San Francisco earthquake of 1906. Harry and Julia teamed up together to live their lives. And they did until death bid them apart. Their union resulted in the birth of me in 3D space.

Harry joined the American Telephone and Telegraph Company (AT&T) in Berkeley, California, while living in San Francisco. He worked in that East Bay City for 15 years, and then was appointed telephone manager in Palo Alto. His work included the entire district from Redwood City to Mt. View.

Harry and Julia performed the magic of conceiving me one night in La Honda, a vacation spot in the West Coastal Mountains. Today, it takes less than an hour to get to La Honda from Palo Alto. It was a full day's trip by horse-and-buggy in 1912. Nine months later I was born in a brown shingle house on Fulton Street in Palo Alto. That makes me a native son of the town. A native son of Palo Alto is rare these days, as it has grown from a community to a thriving city adjacent to Stanford University.

Palo Alto in Spanish means "tall tree" or an approximation thereof. The old redwood tree still stands by the Southern Pacific Bridge, at the entrance to the city. Palo Alto is known as an educational center. Today it lies in "Silicon Valley", a capital of the electronic industry.

Many famous people lived there who contributed to world progress. Novelist Mary Robert Rhinehart wrote her stories there. Artist Swinnerton, creator of "Little Jimmy" and "The Canyou Kids" had his studio there. DeForest discovered the vacuum tube in Palo Alto, which revolutionized radio. Two young men, starting in a garage, advanced to Apple Computer fame. Hewlett Packard, from a small beginning in the town, became a billion dollar industry in electronics. And, of course, Stanford University nurtured many a prolific mind. Truly, Palo Alto was a creative place to grow up in. A few childhood memories stand out . . .

I recall my mother mentioning that she named me Ormond, using the last name of a friend she had known in Omaha. She also gave me the middle name of Dale. I have used this very seldom. Mostly, Ormond McGill is quite enough for identification.

I recall my father saying, "There is something different about Ormond." What the difference was I haven't the slightest idea. Maybe he had a premonition that I would grow up to be a magician/hypnotist if that can be called "something different".

Most assuredly, I have always had a yen for the mysterious, which Einstein expressed so magnificently in saying, "The most beautiful and profound thing we can experience is the mysterious. It is the source of all true art and science. He to whom emotion is a stranger, who can no longer wonder and stand rapt in awe, is as good as dead for his eyes are closed."

I recall my father going frequently to Army Station Camp Fremont in Menlo Park, a neighboring town to Palo Alto, to collect nickels from the pay telephones during World War I. My birth and his job kept Harry out of the service, but he did his share. He would bring the sacks of nickels back to the car (we had an old Overland at the time) to be counted later in his office. Frequently, slugs were used to make the phone calls instead of nickels. The nickels used, at that time, were "Liberty Heads". Wish I had kept them; they are worth far more than a nickel now!

Occasionally I would go with my father to help carry the bags of nickels. One night, on returning to the car, a dog was sitting on the front seat – an Eskimo dog of the most affectionate nature. Somehow he had the good sense to sit in that car, as it would give him a happy life with people who liked dogs. He was obviously a dog of value, so we advertised for his owner to claim him. None showed up, so we kept him and named him "Sport". He was the first dog I knew who became my friend. Also, a few other animals joined my family from time to time. I have always had a soft place in my heart for animals.

Another childhood event I still vividly recall was seeing fairies dancing in a bush across the street from my home on Forest Avenue (we moved there shortly following my birth) in Palo Alto.

The strange illusion of the "dancing fairies" is still clearly etched in my memory. I did not understand it then anymore than I understand it now. I saw a number of what appeared to be dainty little people dressed in flowing white garments, dancing amidst rose bushes. They vanished shortly, and I have witnessed nothing like it ever again. Possibly it was the imagination of a child, as I was quite an OZ book reader. All I can say is that it remains as definite an experience as any I have marveled about in this lifetime. In any event, it provides a nice memory of childhood days, and, in its way, was my first encounter with magic.

Some memories are not so pleasant. One that especially stands out in my mind is of an experience at an amusement park in La Honda, California, when I was bitten by a monkey. A small chimpanzee was chained to a post and people were allowed to feed him pieces of apple. When it was my turn, I held out a piece to him, and, in my childish excitement, dropped it as he was about to take it. I reached down to pick up, and the monkey, thinking I was trying to take it away from him, grabbed my arm, pulled my hand to his mouth, and bit deeply into my right forefinger. Blood poisoning set in. Fortunately, my mother knew how to use flaxseed poultices to draw out the infection and my arm was saved, but it is not an experience I would care to repeat. I still carry the scar on my right forefinger.

I started school at the age of seven, one year later than most kids did, but it worked out all right. Palo Alto had a good school system. In 1923, my father changed jobs and we moved to Berkeley for a year. In Palo Alto, my scholastic work was average; in Berkeley, I was a "genius", as they were a year behind in the curriculum. It was fun while in Berkeley but not much fun when I returned to Palo Alto, as I was a year behind my classmates. It took some private tutoring to catch up.

It was to my classmates, in the fifth grade of grammar school, that I did my first magic trick. I have always had an interest in chemistry, so the trick I did was the popular one of "Wine and Water". It was an ambitious trick for a kid to do, but my father helped me prepare it. I learned it from a book on chemical magic; the effect and "how to do it" go like this:

A glass pitcher half-filled with water is shown along with five empty glasses. The magician pours water into the first glass, wine into the second, water into the third, and wine into the fourth. Then, he pours the contents of the first and second glass back and forth, and they both become wine. He pours the contents of the third and fourth glasses back and forth, and they both become water. The first and second glasses of wine are poured back into the pitcher, making a pitcher of wine. The third and fourth glasses of water are poured into the pitcher, and the wine visibly changes to water. The pitcher seems filled with water, as it was at the beginning of the trick. For a surprise climax, the magician then pours water from the pitcher into the fifth glass, and it changes to milk!

It was a good trick then and still is. Years later I saw it performed by a famous magician billed as "Think-a-Drink Hoffman", as the opening effect in his vaudeville act at the Golden Gate Theater in San Francisco.

Here's how to do it using harmless chemicals:

From a drug store, get a bottle of strong phenolphthalein solution. Fill a second bottle half-full with powdered tartaric acid; then, fill the bottle to its top with water. Fill a third bottle half-full with potassium carbonate and make a solution by adding water. The chemicals for performing the trick are now ready. You also need five glasses and a clear glass pitcher with enough water in it to fill four of the glasses.

To prepare for the exhibition, arrange the glasses in a row on the table, and into the first glass place one-half teaspoon of potassium carbonate solution; into the second glass place a few drops of phenolphthalein; into the third glass place a teaspoon of the tartaric acid solution; into the fourth glass place a few drops of phenolphthalein; and into the fifth glass place one teaspoon of the phenolphthalein solution.

You are now ready to perform the trick.

Pour water from the pitcher into the first glass, filling it about two-thirds full. The water mixes with the clear solution of potassium carbonate in the glass and looks like water. Pour the contents of this glass back into the water pitcher. This makes a mild solution of potassium carbonate in the pitcher. Again pour the "water" from the pitcher into the first glass and place it on the table as a glass of water.

Then, pick up the second glass and pour the "water" from the pitcher into it; a chemical reaction occurs and the glass appears to be filled with wine.

Pick up the third glass and pour the "water" from the pitcher into it; it mixes with tartaric acid, but as no visible reaction occurs it passes for a glass of water.

Pick up the fourth glass and pour the "water" from the pitcher into it. The visible results, on your table, will be two glasses of water and two glasses of wine that appear to have been poured from a pitcher of water alternately.

Now comes more magic. Pick up glasses No. 1 and 2 and pour the contents back and forth between them. The result appears as two glasses of "wine." The "wine" is poured from the glasses into the pitcher, which results in the contents of the pitcher turning red. You show it to the audience as a pitcher of wine.

Now, pick up glasses No. 3 and 4 and pour the contents back and forth. The result appears as two glasses of "water". The "water" is poured from the glasses into the pitcher, and a chemical reaction occurs which appears to change the "wine" in the pitcher back to water.

To climax the trick, pour the "water" from the pitcher into glass No. 5, and you end up with what appears to be a glass of milk, as the concentrated phenolphthalein forms a milky solution.

The trick went over great with my classmates, and their acceptance gave me the confidence to perform more magic in the future. Really, it was rather bold of me to perform the trick, as I was a shy child. So shy, in fact, that when my folks visited friends I would prefer to stay out on the porch until refreshments were served. Refreshments have a remarkable way of curing shyness.

Shy as I was, I never seemed too bothered standing before a group; possibly, it was an inborn sense of theater, as I liked to dress up in costumes and pretend to be different characters.

I recall being a clown, a policeman, a cowboy, and an Indian. I even recited some poetry before a church audience and won a prize. Then, magic came along in the form of a Gilbert *Mysto Magic Set* under the Christmas tree, and a magician was born.

Chapter Two

Early Adventures in Magic

It was not until I started high school that my "career" in magic really took off. I was 14 at the time. The year was 1927, and the Tarbell Home-Study Course in Magic was being nationally advertised in all the major magazines. I wanted to take the course. My folks were a bit concerned that it might interfere with my studies, as I was just entering high school. However, Principal Walter Nichols assured them it would be the best thing in the world for a boy to have magic as a hobby.

Walter Nichols, what a fine man he was. We became good friends over the years; he even stooged for me one night during a "Stunt Show" at Palo Alto Union High School ("Paly Hi" as it is affectionately known). He pretended to become hypnotized and walked zombie fashion from his seat in the audience onto the stage. It caused a sensation at the school that some remember to this day. Some remember Walter Nichols through his work in the literary field; his book, *Trust A Boy* has become a classic.

And so, I took the Tarbell Course in Magic, and it provided a quantum leap. While in high school, the Manual Training Class gave me a chance to make equipment in the shop, and I finally presented my first full evening magic show on that Paly Hi stage.

I will never forget my presentation of "Sawing A Woman In Half" during that show. I tried to saw the box in half using a standard tree-cutting saw which had large notches between the teeth. The notches kept catching on the sides of the box during the sawing, and it took a full half an hour to cut it through. The girl used in that illusion ended her career as a magician's assistant then and there!

As word got around that I was a Tarbell student and was putting on magic shows, invitations from various magic clubs came in inviting me to attend shows put on by their members. I attended and made some new friends interested in magic. By and large, magicians are a friendly group and, contrary to popular opinion, are not adverse to sharing their "secrets" and helping out a new-comer. They helped me.

Many of the members must have been Tarbell students too, as I recall much patter being exactly as it was given in the course.

Tarbell's patter was often recited word for word as though his patter were some sort of sacred text. I did that too, at the start, until I finally had the good sense to patter my own way rather than repeat verbatim what I had read.

While many of his students, of those days, seemed to precisely use his patter line, Tarbell himself never said to do that. He emphasized the importance of being natural and being yourself when performing magic. Good advice! If you want to be outstanding in any field, you must be an original, not a copy. It was advice I eventually heeded, which led to developing my personal style of presentation; in my case, a leisurely one.

Some early adventures in magic, however, were not particularly leisurely ones, such as the time I was asked to present "something of an exciting nature" from an aeroplane during a 4th of July Show. This was way back in the late 1920s, and the Palo Alto Airport, at that time, was located just south of town off of El Camino Real. The planes used were one-motored biplanes.

I thought about it and finally decided to try a "Mailbag Escape", The apparatus for this consisted of a canvas mail bag large enough to hold a person. Along the top of the bag were grommets, and a metal bar was laced back and forth through these, a padlock being then fasted on each end of the bar making the person inside the sack a prisoner. Escape seemed impossible to the spectators who didn't know that the steel bar had been carefully machined so as to unscrew at its center. To escape, all one had to do was unscrew the bar, push it out of the grommets, get out of the bag, replace the bar through the grommets, and screw it up tight again. Usually, the stunt is performed behind a screen on stage; this 4th of July I decided to do it from the cockpit of an aeroplane as it flew over the heads of the assembled crowd.

To increase the mystery, I was handcuffed before being placed in the mail bag. Getting out of the cuffs was easy, as I had a duplicate key in my pocket.

Locked in the mail bag, I was deposited inside the plane. These early planes had an open cockpit, so that was convenient. Then, the plane took off and circled the airfield. Within the cockpit, I went to work and freed myself from the bag, replaced the bar, and tossed the locked mail bag out of the plane. It fluttered to the ground empty. The plane landed and I got out and took my bow. The stunt went over fine and garnered me some publicity. It made me appreciate a master such as Houdini.

In my early adventures in magic, I found I had a liking for sensational publicity stunts, so I dreamed up a way to perform the dangerous "Catching a Bullet in the Teeth" trick. This is legendary amongst magicians as being hazardous since Ching Ling Soo was killed performing it.

I knew the trick was dangerous, but I wanted to try it. When you are young and frivolous, you do all kinds of "nutty" things which you would never think of doing, as advancing years make you more cautious.

Anyway, I figured out a way to do the trick. I performed the feat a number of times and got away with it. (Obviously, or else I would not be writing these memoirs.)

As I designed the effect, a standard 22-bolt action rifle was used. A 22-caliber bullet was selected from a box of cartridges and carefully marked with a knife to identify it. The bullet was then loaded into the rifle. I took my position boldly across stage; the rifle was aimed and shot at me by a man from the audience. On the report of the rifle, my head jerked back and I staggered. Finally standing erect, it was seen that the bullet had been caught between my teeth. An assistant brought forward a plate, and the bullet dropped from my teeth onto the plate with a clatter. On being examined, the bullet still had the mark which had been placed on it. The mystery was complete.

How was it done? Very simply, by a method that really worked surprisingly well considering how brazen it was:

The man who did the shooting was a stooge who had been instructed to aim the rifle off to the side of my head and shoot into a sack of sand placed backstage in the wings. To the audience, the slight

11

side-aiming of the gun was not noticed, as only a small displace-
ment of the barrel caused it to give a wide berth to my head, as the
bullet whizzed across stage into the sack of sand. From the spectators'
point of view, the gun seemed to be aimed and shot directly at me.

A duplicate head (lead part) of a 22 cartridge was used, the head
being carefully removed and marked (scratched) with an "X". This
marked bullet head I secreted in my mouth between my lower gum
and cheek. It remained perfectly concealed until I was ready to
bring it forth by my tongue and grip it between my teeth during
the course of the trick. I could even talk without interference.

In the presentation of the effect, several spectators were invited on
stage to help in the demonstration. Among these was my stooge
who knew how to fire the rifle to the side of my head. The rifle was
examined by the committee and then handed to the marksman. A
box of 22-caliber bullets were then dumped on a plate, and one
selected. One of the groups was told to mark the selected bullet for
later identification. No one knew how to mark a bullet, so I boldly
took out a pocket knife and, while all watched, made an "X" with
the knife on the lead head of the bullet. In doing this, I duplicated
the "X" of the bullet concealed in my mouth. A bold procedure but
it worked effectively. No one ever questioned this maneuver, and I
simply asked them to look at it so that they could identify the
bullet later. Sometimes it pays to be bold in magic. You can get
away with many things if you work with confidence and do not get
suspicious of yourself.

The marked bullet was then taken by one of the committees and
placed in the rifle ready for firing. The loaded rifle was handed to
the man who was to do the shooting. On stage, he was told to fire
the rifle directly at my mouth, as I was going to attempt to catch the
bullet in my teeth.

The rest was pure showmanship. The marksman took his position
at one side of the stage, while I took mine at the opposite side,
standing erect and bravely facing possible execution. The trick held
the audience breathless, as it had been explained that others had
been killed performing the feat. It was a sensation!

At the report of the rifle, I jerked my head back and staggered forward, which gave me the opportunity to bring the bullet from my

jaw to the teeth. Finally, standing upright with lips stretched back in a mirthless grin, the bullet could be seen caught between the teeth. My assistant brought a plate, and I dropped the bullet onto it with a clatter. On being examined by the committee, the "X" mark was noted.

During my early adventures in magic, "The Bullet Catching Trick" was a featured presentation. However, I would not recommend that others try it, as there is always the possibility that something could go wrong. Frankly, I would not do it today. Life is too precious. Magic is lots of fun; but sometimes, a bit dangerous too.

For a young magician, every show is an exciting adventure. While working at a Russian River summer resort, I had added some hypnotism to my show and wanted something sensational to finish on. A carnival man came to my aid.

The name of the man I cannot recall, but he was an unshaven wanderer who happened to stop by the resort and wanted a meal. We talked a bit about magic and hypnotism. He told me he had performed a hypnotic stunt in a carnival, in which, while apparently hypnotized, he made himself rigid and allowed his body to be suspended between two chairs. A large block of rock was then placed on his midsection and was cracked in two with a sledgehammer. He said he could do it. I was willing to try. It sounded just like the sensational stunt I wanted to close the show with at the resort that evening.

Accordingly, we searched out a large block of rock and a sledgehammer. He said no rehearsal was necessary. Just place his body suspended across the chairs, rest the stone on his stomach, and smack down hard with the sledge to crack the rock in two with one swift blow. I said, "Okay." To myself I said, "I sure hope it works."

At the show that night, I introduced the man. He apparently placed himself into a hypnotic trance and became stiff as a board. For all I know, he may really have hypnotized himself; he sure was stiff. With the help of a couple of fellows, we placed him across the back of two chairs, and carefully centered the block of rock on his stomach. I held my breath as I came down with the sledgehammer. I came down hard, and, to my relief, the block cracked into two, and the halves dropped to the stage. We lifted the man to his feet;

13

he opened his eyes and took a bow. He seemed perfectly okay. We gave him a wonderful meal before he went on his way.

How is the feat accomplished?

There is no trick to it other than to do it. A well-muscled man can make himself rigid enough to support his body across the space between two chairs, and the block of rock absorbs the blow of the sledgehammer. It is inertia that does the work. As long as the blow with the sledge is swift and sure, it will crack the rock, and the rock absorbs the force of the blow. The stunt surely did make a spectacular climax to my show that evening.

One time, way back, I got the bright idea that I would include a "Buried Alive" stunt in my show. I was booked to play in two theaters on consecutive nights: the Fox Sequoia (Redwood City) and the Fox San Mateo. To conclude my show the first night in Redwood City, I announced that I was going to allow myself to be buried alive, and that the following night my coffin would be dug up, and I would be revived on the stage of the theater in San Mateo, at the start of the show.

A stout wooden coffin was brought on stage. I appeared to "entrance" myself, became stiff, and was placed within the coffin. The lid was then screwed on. The coffin was taken from the stage, down the aisle, and carried out of the theater to a lot across the street. All had been arranged, and a waiting grave had already been dug.

As the feat concluded the show, the audience trailed out of the theater to witness the burial. All were curious to see the ordeal. Horror always does hold a theatrical fascination.

Theater ushers picked up the coffin and carted it off stage; it was too large to go down the steps, so the only way to handle it was to go via a backstage route, then out and down the aisle, and over to the lot with the grave waiting to receive it. The theater crowd was so excited that no one bothered to take in details. So as the ushers carried the coffin around they switched the coffin I was in for a duplicate coffin in the wings (it was weighted with a dummy inside) and continued their journey out of the theater to the grave. A large crowd tagged along.

Arriving at the grave site, the coffin was lowered into the hole and covered with dirt. All the rest of the night and the next day it remained buried. Persons were stationed to watch over it.

At the appointed hour, it was dug up and placed in a truck to take to the San Mateo Theater for the "revival".

Meanwhile, backstage at the Sequoia Theater, I was let out of the coffin, and kept out of sight. When opportunity allowed, the now empty coffin was taken backstage of the San Mateo Theater, and I went along with it. Prior to the show, I was again placed in the coffin backstage.

Then, came show time that night; the coffin in Redwood City was dug up and taken by truck to the other theater. Again to get it on stage, it had to be carried via a backstage route, and was switched for the coffin I was in. Brought on stage before the expectant audience, it was rested on sawhorses. All that remained to be done to start the show was to open the coffin, and the showmanship of the revival.

The effect was great, and the publicity filled two theaters to capacity. I enjoyed the experience, but I have never tried it again. Why trust your luck a second time?

The principle of conjuring used in accomplishing my theatrical "Buried Alive" feat is known as *screening*. On first consideration, it seems impossible that spectators will not suspect the artifice. But they do not because in everyday life we are constantly temporarily losing sight of objects until they reappear and fill in these short gaps mentally as a continuation of appearance. For instance, if while watching a child play ball we lose sight of a hand, it would be ridiculous to conclude that the child had suddenly become one-handed. Upon that psychology was based the success of this "Buried Alive" illusion. The principle can be successfully utilized in performing many magic effects.

* * *

As one looks at photographs of a person from babyhood, childhood, and onward to adulthood, it is wonderful to speculate on the changes which occur in the body. Every 7 years, each cell in the

body has been replaced, and you wear a new body. It is like tossing aside an old suit of clothes and putting on a new one. And yet,
somehow, the stream of memories of all that happened to the individual remains intact, and each person knows that he (or she) is the
same despite what is reflected in a mirror. In high school, I knew
this to be so for this lifetime. Now, it seems, for many lifetimes.
If ever there was magic!

Think about it. Every moment you live, something inside your
body dies and something is reborn anew. Life appears as a continuum. Reincarnation? Regeneration? Time has scant meaning. Even
the stars proclaim this: a star is born, it exists for eons of time, and
eventually it dies. More eons pass, and again it is reborn. Mankind
is a miniature of the universe.

Chapter Three

Magic Clubs and Other Things

The first Magic Club I joined was the Mystic 13 in San Jose, California. The year was 1932, and my friend, A. Caro Miller, was the club's first president. I was among the early members.

Magic Clubs provide a wonderful opportunity to develop friendships, talk magic, and watch other magicians perform. The interchanging of magic is the real joy of a magic club.

There is an unwritten "law" that the secrets of magic are to be kept secret. In general, most magicians respect that "law". Of course, the question of exposé in magic is pretty much an arbitrary one. There is no point in being a blabbermouth in explaining magic tricks just because someone asked you how such and such was done. On the other hand, there is no need to be too much concerned over the exposure of a trick either. It certainly is not a world catastrophe. Years ago when Camel Cigarettes ran a series of national ads in which the exposure of some choice magic tricks was the theme, many magicians thought the "end" had come. Not so! Magic remained just as popular as ever as entertainment. Entertainment is the real secret of magic, not the tricks.

If a person really wants to know how a trick is done, almost any public library has a number of books on conjuring that will tell them. I suppose that even this book, which explains many tricks, will in time reach the shelves of some public libraries. My other books have. Persons who have enough interest in magic to do some research deserve to know. However, that's a far cry from the magician being a blabbermouth. One must be a bit diplomatic.

I recall a friend asking me how "The Linking Rings" operate. I said, "Just go to the library and they have a book that tells all about the trick." Two weeks later, I met the person again, and the same question was asked. I gave the same answer. To this day, the person hasn't bothered to look it up, and he still doesn't know how the trick works.

A humorous way to handle a request for an explanation of a trick is this one which some magicians use:

The person asks, "How did you do that trick?" The magician replies, "Very well!" This brings a laugh and settles the matter.

Other friends in magic, among the early members of the Mystic 13, were "Cig" Miller (father of the famous stage and screen star, Marilyn Miller), Harry Canar (a great card man), Art Heisen (who built my "Sacrificial Cremation" illusion), Everett Lyda (for years, secretary of the Club), Fred Faltersack (a fine magical craftsman who created numerous effects for me), Harry Shaw, Fred Tuttle, Joe Garofalo, Ted Slater, and Walt Cunningham, to name a few. Walt Cunningham is still in there pitching; the others have moved on to "The Great Theater in the Sky".

Everett Lyda and I invented a trick which we put on the magic market. We named it "On the Spot". It advertised:

> Get "on the spot" and you'll never be on the spot! Six clever tricks with 12 tricky red and black spot cards: a spelling mystery, a follow-the-leader effect, a number divination, a transposition trick, and a surprise climax in which every card turns up a different colored spot card.

All the sets we made sold out. The original trick used printed cards, but you can easily make your own.

From a magic store, get a pack of blank playing cards, and from a stationery store, get a group of colored-marking pens. Twenty-seven of the blank playing cards from the pack are used to make up the set for the trick. On seven of these, mark a large Red Spot. On another seven, mark a large Black Spot. On the remaining ten cards, mark a large spot of a different color on each. The set of "On the Spot" cards is ready, and you can perform the trick. The directions went like this:

Arrange the Red and Black Spot Cards in two packets. For one packet, place a black-spot card on your hand face downward. On top of this, place the 10 assorted colored-spot cards (in any order). On top of this, place a red-spot card. Put this packet in your right hip pocket, with the black-spot card against your body so that you can instantly locate either the red or black card of this packet, as desired.

The other set of six red-spot and six black-spot cards are stacked in this order: place five black cards (spot side downward) on the palm of your hand; on top of these, place two red cards, then one black, and lastly four red. Cards are now ready to go for the first effect.

"On The Spot" Spelling Trick

Explain how the spots on the cards respond to the name of their color when it is spelled out. Then, start spelling: remove one card from the top of stack and place it on the bottom. Spell out each letter, viz. R–E–D; then turn up the fourth card, and it is Red. Then, spell B–L–A–C–K and turn up the next card, and it is Black. Continue this spelling through the entire stack, putting reds and blacks as they appear in opposite piles until you finally have six red-spot cards and six black-spot cards separated – having been magically spelled out alternatively. Follow immediately with the next effect:

Follow-The-Leader "On The Spot" Trick

Pick up the six black-spot cards, place them face down in your left hand, and on top of these stack the six red-spot cards. Mention that you have six red-spot cards and six black, as you count out *eight cards* face down on the table. Casually show the four black cards which remain in your left hand and deliberately pick up the cards you have counted out on the table and place them directly on top of the cards which remained in your hand. By this simple maneuver, you have unobtrusively stacked the cards so that they lie in this order from the top of stack downward to palm of hand: Black, Black, Red, Red, Red, Red, Red, Red, Black, Black, Black, Black. Your set-up is now complete, and the rest of the routine works automatically.

Divide the cards into two piles of six cards each, side by side on the table. Now, turn both piles face up, being careful not to expose cards of opposite colors in piles. Comment that you have a pile of red cards and a pile of black cards, as you take the two face-up cards and place each just above its respective pile. These you explain are "Leader Cards", and will serve to identify where the red and black card piles are respectively. Then, turn the two packets face downwards on the table.

Next, reverse the position of the two face-up "Leader Cards", so that the red card is now over the pile where the black was originally and vice versa. Turn top card of each pile up and throw it on top of "Leader Card", showing that the cards match and apparently have followed the leader. Reverse "Leader Cards" again and show that the top cards of each face-down packet still matches the "Leader Cards". Reverse "Leader Cards" again and place top card of each pile face down on top of its respective "Leader Card". Now, reverse the "Leader Cards" along with the face-down cards you have placed on them; suddenly, flip the latter over showing that they still match the "Leader Cards". Finally, reverse the "Leader Cards" once more and show that the last two cards still follow the leader and match colors.

You will find it an exciting bit of magical business, as the colored spots seem to follow their leader back and forth.

Number "On The Spot" Divination

Have a spectator shuffle the pack of six red-spot cards and six black-spot cards until it is obvious that no one could possibly know the location of any of the respective colors. Then, take the shuffled cards and deal eight cards slowly face down on the table forming a large pile, and place the remaining four cards, forming a small pile, face down beside it. Next, ask a spectator which color he prefers – red or black? As soon as he tells you, instantly you announce that there are *two more* Red-Spot Cards in the larger packet than there are Black-Spot Cards in the smaller packet. Verify this divination by counting the cards face up on the table, proving you are correct. Continue right on for more divination:

Deal three cards from the larger packet onto the smaller after both packets have been thoroughly shuffled again and turned face down on the table. This gives you seven cards in the former smaller packet and only five cards remain in what was the larger. Once again ask a spectator which his favorite color is this time and, whichever he says, announce immediately that there is now *one more* Black-Spot Card in the larger packet than there are Red-Spot Cards in the smaller packet. Each packet is checked again, proving your prognostication is correct.

How does the trick work? Never mind. Just perform it as described, and it comes out correctly for you every time.

Red and Black "On The Spot" Transposition

For this effect in the routine, pick up six of the cards (three red and three black). Hand over a red- and a black-spot card to a spectator with the request that he place them face up on the table about a foot apart. Meanwhile, you glance at the cards in your hand and arrange them in this order: red, black, red, black. Square up the four cards and hold in left hand.

Now, apparently pick up the top card of the cards in your hand and show it as a black card – actually, what you do is make a "double lift" so that it is the second card the spectators see. You name the card "Black" and replace both cards (as one) on top of the stack. Remove the real top card this time and place it face down on top of the face-up black card on the table, as you state, "Black onto black!"

Then, show the black card on bottom of stack in your left hand. Turn stack downward and apparently take the bottom card off. What you really do in this action is to perform the "glide" so that the red card, which is second from bottom, is actually removed as you name the card "Black" and again drop it face down on the black card on the table, as you repeat, "Black onto black." By these simple sleights, you have apparently placed the two black cards on the table and have the two red-spot cards remaining in your hand. Actually, just the opposite is true. Follow right along with your patter and comment, "And the two red-spot cards I place on top of the face-up red-spot card." Place the two cards in your hand face downward on the face-up red card.

Now comes the magic!

You comment, "Watch the cards change places—black onto red, and red onto black!" Pick up the red and black face-up cards, one in each hand, and criss-cross your hands, which brings these cards to opposite sides. Flip them over so that they fall face downward on the respective cards on the table, give a snap with your fingers, and suddenly turn over both packets showing they have magically transposed their positions. It is an effective bit of business, this criss-crossing of the visible colored cards, showing that the others have criss-crossed in a similar manner.

Next, pick up all 12 of the cards and hand them over to a spectator to shuffle, explaining that you want them to be completely mixed so that you could not possibly tell where any red- or black-spot card might be, as you are going to try to pick out red from black while the cards are held behind your back.

Receive the shuffled cards face downward, and place them behind your back. Immediately, they are out of sight behind you, place the shuffled stack of red- and black-spot cards in your right hip pocket and exchange them for the packet of varicolored spot cards you had secreted there. Bring these cards out and hold behind your back, as you proceed with the trick. This action only takes a second. It appears that you merely placed the shuffled stack behind your back. To keep the spectators' attention busy while you make this switch, explain that your fingers are so sensitive that you can tell by the sense of touch whether a card is red or black. To prove it, ask someone to tell which color they would like to have you produce without looking.

A spectator names a color and you immediately bring forward, from behind your back, a card of the requested color. You can do this as you know you have a red card on top of the switched packet and a black card on its bottom.

You are now ready to present the climax of the trick. Follow right on and bring the packet of cards from behind your back and deal them in a row, face downward, on the table. Tell a spectator you will give him a chance to see how well he can guess which cards are red and which are black. Tell him to run his hand along the row of face-down cards and point to a card he thinks is red. When he points to one, remove this card from the row and place it aside on the table still face down. Have him now point to a card he thinks is black. Remove this card from the row and place to one side. Continue in this manner having him point to cards he thinks are red and black until you have two piles of six cards each.

All set for the climax, ask the spectator if he wouldn't be amazed if he were to find that he had actually been able to sort out the colors by correctly guessing. When he acknowledges, tell him to turn the cards over and see how he did. Finding the cards are all different colors comes as a big surprise!

Practice this trick and get it down smoothly. The next time you are asked to perform some magic, do this trick, and you'll never be on the spot!

Chapter Four

Conception of a Hypnotist

My first interest was magic. Then, hypnotism also came along to occupy an important position in my life. It happened when the Danish hypnotist, DeWaldoza, came to town. I was in high school at the time. The show was presented under sponsorship of the Masonic Lodge. I was in the audience eager to see what demonstrations he might be performing. It was a packed audience largely composed of Stanford University students from the psychology department.

DeWaldoza came on stage and commented that his show would be in two parts. Part One would consist of demonstrations in mind-reading, and Part Two of demonstrations in hypnotic suggestion. The show got off to a phenomenal start.

The Danish hypnotist invited two Stanford students to come forward. One was told to take an object from his pocket. It was a comb. The second student was instructed to blindfold the hypnotist.

The first student was then told to hide his comb with any person in the audience and then return to the stage and concentrate on where it was hidden. DeWaldoza explained that he would attempt to locate the hidden object. It seemed impossible, but he did it using "contact mindreading". He gripped the hand of the student who had hidden the object, went down from the stage with the party, and dashed down the aisle. He came to a stop before a seated spectator. After a moment's pause, he reached out his hand into the pocket of that person and found the comb. The experiment was a great success.

He then repeated the demonstration with two other volunteers with equal success. Removing the blindfold, this expert explained how it was possible to accomplish such feats by paying careful attention to unconscious movements of the body. He termed it "muscle reading". DeWaldoza was an honest performer who, working before a university audience, did not try to garb his work in mumbo jumbo. He got real entertainment out of being instructional. He invited six persons on stage to learn how to do it. I was one of the six, the youngest.

All on stage took a seat and were handed a pendulum (a fish weight tied to the end of a string). Each person was told to hold the pendulum as still as possible while thinking of it swinging. Each pendulum of the group started to swing (some more than others) in response to the thought. DeWaldoza explained that this demonstrated visually how a thought in the mind causes an unconscious movement of the body muscles in response to the direction of the thought. He then showed how this operated over the entire body by performing a posture sway experiment.

One at a time, the volunteers were invited to stand, close their eyes, and concentrate on the idea of falling backward. DeWaldoza stood behind and caught each person, as he responded.

DeWaldoza then asked if one of the group would care to try the experiment in contact mindreading he had performed. I volunteered.

The performer explained that all I had to do was to follow the impulses of my body responses exactly as I had done in responding to the sensations of falling over backwards.

A blindfold was placed over my eyes. An article was hidden in the audience. DeWaldoza said he would grip my hand and concentrate on where the article was, but that he was not going to lead me; I would have to lead him. I was to respond to whichever way I felt like moving: forward, backward, right or left, stop and go ahead. I understood, and he gripped my right hand.

Immediately, I felt an impulse to go to the left side of the hall. Reaching the wall, I advanced down the side seats of the audience. Suddenly, I felt like stopping, so I did. Although I couldn't see a thing, I knew I must be standing before some seated person in the large audience. DeWaldoza said, "Now comes the fine work. Hold your left hand out and let it move wherever it feels like going." I did as instructed and felt my hand almost seem to move on its own. I leaned forward, reached into a pocket, and removed an object. It was the object that had been hidden. There was a burst of applause. The blindfold was whipped off my eyes, and DeWaldoza was smiling at me.

That was my first adventure with contact mindreading. It was fascinating and concluded the first part of the hypnotist's performance.

I have recently written a book as a companion book to my *The New Encyclopedia of Stage Hypnotism*, titled *Secrets of Stage Mindreading* which gives full instructions of how to do Contact Mindreading, such as DeWaldoza performed. The book even advances to the performance of noncontact mindreading, plus an Appendix of "Self-Hypnosis For Mindreading". The book is published in the UK by Crown House Publishing, Ltd. (the same company who published this autobiography).

A Show of Suggestions

The Second Part of DeWaldoza's show was devoted to demonstrations of hypnotism. His presentation was unique as he did not entrance his subjects, but worked entirely with "waking suggestion." In other words, he did not induce formal hypnosis but performed with volunteers in their waking state.

This matter of hypnotism versus suggestion has puzzled many thoughtful people. I look at it this way. Both hypnosis and suggestion have a right to be recognized in their own right; however, both are intimately related. Hypnosis is the state of mind that suggestion induces. A state of mind of heightened suggestibility. Suggestion is the means employed to induce and control that state of mind.

DeWaldoza's demonstrations on "waking suggestion" went like this. An introductory test was performed on the entire audience. DeWaldoza addressed the audience and told them to try an experiment in suggestion all together, in which their hands would become so firmly locked together they would not be able to take them apart. He explained that people differ in their responsiveness to suggestion, and that the better they were able to concentrate the more effect they would experience, and those that succeeded would be allowed to come on stage and learn how to use the power of suggestion.

The entire audience raised their hands in the air and interlocked their fingers. The suggestions were given, and many found their hands locked so tightly that they were unable to separate them. Those persons were invited to come forward to the front of the hall, and DeWaldoza unfastened their hands. They were then given an invitation to have a seat on the stage. DeWaldoza used this method to get the most responsive subjects for his show. Those with locked hands were invited on stage as the experimental committee.

Following the "Hand-Locking Test", it was explained that some might feel that the inability to unlock their hands was caused by muscle cramping. To prove this was not so, the test was performed on the group on stage of fastening their fingertips together so that they could not separate them until the suggestive influence was removed.

Next, the group were told to hold their hands beside their ears and shake them vigorously. When all the hands were shaking, the knees of various subjects were told to bounce up and down along with the shaking. Gradually, the test was concluded as the shaking subsided. It was an exciting demonstration of waking suggestion.

The subjects were then told to open their mouths as wide as they could, and that the jaw was stuck, so they could not close their mouth. The results were hilarious as the subjects tried in vain to close their mouths. Snapping his fingers beside the ear of each person in turn, the jaws snapped closed.

A subject was brought forward and his left leg caused to become so stiff he could not bend it. He was led walking stiff-legged about the stage until the influence was removed.

DeWaldoza asked for a volunteer to have all pain mastered and a needle passed through his cheek. A volunteer secured, "suggestion insensibility" was induced in the cheek, and a large needle passed through. In the test, the needle was sterilized and the process was painless. The subject walked down the aisle, so the spectators could see up close that the penetration was genuine. Returning to the stage the needle was removed. There was no blood.

A test in the control of speech and a name amnesia demonstration was next presented. This was a combination of suggestion influences, in which the effects were developed one upon the other, resulting in a striking demonstration. A subject was brought forward and seated center stage. First, his mouth was stuck together so that he could not open it. The influence was removed and he was caused to stutter and finally be unable to pronounce his own name and, eventually, although speech had been returned, he could not remember his own name. The influence was removed. It was an excellent demonstration of the compounding effects of the power of suggestion.

Possibly DeWaldoza's most amusing and impressive demonstration of suggestion in the waking state, with a solo subject, was a combination of heavy water, shaky pouring, bitter taste, and becoming drunk on a glass of water. An empty glass and a pitcher of water were placed upon a table at the side of the stage. The subject approached the table and was told to grip both the glass and pitcher. It was suggested that they had become so heavy he could not lift them from the table. After vainly trying to lift them, the influence was removed.

It was then suggested that he pick up the glass and the pitcher, and that his hands would become so shaky he could not pour the water from the pitcher into the glass without spilling it. The water spilt about the stage, to the delight of the audience. The hypnotist calmed the subject so that he could pour the water into the glass, and it was suggested that the water tasted so bitter he would spit it out when he tried to drink it. The subject responded vigorously to the bitter water. Then, it was suggested that the glass actually contained gin, and the subject was told to drink it. He became drunk and drunkenly staggered about the stage. Directly continuing, it was suggested that the subject would see a white mouse on the stage, and that it was coming towards him and crawling up his leg. The subject's antics were a riot of laughs. Finally, the test was concluded and all returned to normal. It was a wonderful demonstration of suggestion in the waking state.

The "Show of Suggestion" was climaxed with a group experiment in which everyone on stage participated. Each person was requested to stand up in front of their chairs and close their eyes. DeWaldoza suggested that they would fall over backwards, and that when they hit the seat of their chair, their eyes would become stuck together and they would not be able to open them.

The entire committee of volunteers responded as a group, falling into their chairs and having their eyes stuck tightly together.

DeWaldoza went to each person in turn and released the influence. As each subject's eyes opened, he or she was dismissed from the stage. The bewildered looks of the volunteers, as the session in waking suggestion ended, provided an impressive finale.

After the subjects had returned to their seats in the audience, DeWaldoza asked the spectators to applaud the volunteers who had been on stage and thanked the audience for sharing the evening with him. The show was over.

Watching the DeWaldoza Show hatched my interest in learning about "The Power of Suggestion". I immediately sent ten cents off to Johnson Smith & Company to purchase a little book on hypnotism. It gave the following *modus operandi* of how to give suggestions and perform the Danish hypnotist's experiment of "Drawing a Spectator Over Backwards" and how to "Lock a Subject's Hands Together". I followed these instructions.

Drawing a Person Over Backwards

Have a person stand away from all obstructions, with his back towards you. Tell him to stand erect, with his head up, his heels together, and let his hands hang loosely by his sides. Tell him to relax his muscles and close his eyes.

Place your hands on his shoulders and sway him gently back and forth an inch or two. If he is relaxed, his weight will follow your pull easily. If his muscles are tight and you feel resistance, remove your hands from his shoulder and tell him that he is not truly relaxed, and that he should just let every muscle hang loose and limp this time. Have him assume the former position and close his eyes again.

Now form your right hand into a loose fist and rest your right index finger at the base of his skull. Ask the person to lay his head back on your hand. The exact position of your right hand is not important, except that it must comfortably support the person's head when he lays it back. No pressure – merely a support, like a pillow.

With the person's head resting on your right hand, lay the fingers of your left hand on his forehead. Now, gently and slowly, tilt his head a little further back. Do not cause any discomfort; you simply want his head an inch or so farther back than he placed it. Tell the person now to think of falling backwards.

Keeping your left hand on his forehead, hold the position for about 30 seconds. Then, say in a calm voice (not loudly but positively) "When I draw away my hand you will slowly fall backwards. As you feel yourself falling, just let yourself go. I will catch you."

Now, while slowly touching the person's forehead with your left fingertips, draw your left hand across the forehead to the left, above the ear and back to near the neck, where your left hand is removed from contact. The exact point of lessening contact is not important. What is important is that you use only the fingertips, and move them while retaining contact and drawing them back and away.

Now, say positively and with conviction, "You are falling backwards. You are falling backwards. You are falling backwards." The mind is used to performing in groups of threes, so repeat the falling backwards suggestions three times while removing your right hand slowly from the person's head in an almost imperceptible manner.

While you are withdrawing your right hand, most people will slowly fall backwards in time with your slowly moving hand. Then, your right hand is suddenly removed from the nape of the person's neck after his body has swayed backwards 3–5 inches.

Immediately, catch the person when he (or she) falls and return him (her) to his (her) feet.

Locking a Person's Hands Together

Have a person stand facing you. Tell him to put his hands together and interlace his fingers. Demonstrate what you mean. Tell him now to make his arms stiff and squeeze his hands together tightly.

Take his hands between your hands gently, and have him look steadily into your eyes. You gaze steadily at a point between his eyes (the bridge of his nose). After 5 or 10 seconds of this intense gazing, start pressing his hands together between yours, moving your hands to a slightly different position after each press, and keep this up until you remove yours. Make the pressure firm but gentle, while he keeps looking into your eyes.

While keeping your gaze firmly between his eyes, slowly state, "Think now of your hands sticking together. Think of them sticking tight. Yes, your hands are sticking together. Your hands are sticking tight . . . tighter . . . tighter . . . TIGHT! . . . and you cannot get them apart no matter how hard you try. You can't get them apart." At this point remove your hands, but keep right on gazing and talking. "You cannot get your hands apart. They are stuck tightly together. You cannot separate your hands try as hard as you can. You cannot. Try. Try hard. The harder you try the more they stick. You cannot get your hands apart. You cannot!"

Give these suggestions in a low tone, but positively. Put firm conviction in your voice, and when you get to "tight . . . tighter . . . tight!" put even more force into each word. As you proceed, put more and more force into your voice, more power, and keep your voice low-pitched.

As soon as the person tries to get his hands apart and fails, you clap your hands together sharply and say in a snappy commanding voice, "All right. Come back now. Now, you can take your hands apart." Snap your fingers a time or two and say, "You just did fine. You performed this experiment wonderfully and well."

Always praise the person for his or her success in performing all such experiments showing "the power of suggestions".

Following these instructions in this little ten-cent book on hypnotism I purchased, and what I learned by watching DeWaldoza's show was a milestone in my career as a magician/hypnotist.

It started me on my way to study hypnotism, which ultimately became an integral part of my performance. I used many of the Danish master's tests. I wrote full details for performing the DeWaldoza Show in my book, *The Encyclopedia of Genuine Stage Hypnotism* published by Percy Abbott in 1947. The book has become recognized as the "bible" of stage hypnotists and gone through five editions.

While visiting with Percy Abbott at his magic plant in Colon, Michigan in 1958, he told me, "You and I will pass away, but there will always be an *Encyclopedia of Genuine Stage Hypnotism*." Percy died some 2 years later.

It seems I have yet awhile to go, as in 1997 I wrote an enlarged version of the book titled, *The New Encyclopedia of Stage Hypnotism* published in the UK by Crown House Publishing Ltd. As with the first book, this book has gained worldwide recognition.

Chapter Five

School Days

School days usually come along early in life and can continue on and on. So, I will go into the matter of education a bit in this Chapter.

Education is unquestionably of great importance. I rather look upon it as the accumulation of information, some of which will be useful. However, I am much more interested in knowing than I am in education. Education is tuition. *Knowing* is intuition.

As a native son of Palo Alto, California, I graduated from grammar and high school in that city and then went on for a couple of years at San Jose State College (now San Jose State University). At the time I attended San Jose State, there were 3000 students; today there are ten times that many. It was a good college, and I majored in psychology.

As a psychology major, I took various courses in the field: general psychology, abnormal psychology, experimental psychology, etc. The psychology professor who impressed me the most was Dorothy Hazeltine Yates, Ph.D. She was interested in hypnotism, and did a bit of private practice in hypnotherapy. She authored a couple of books: *Psychological Racketeers* and *Psychology You Can Use* – this latter book dealt with practical applications of psychology for everyday living and included her hypnotic work training college athletes for better performance in sports.

Undoubtedly, it was our mutual interest in hypnotism that brought us closer than just teacher and student. I took a few one-to-one classes with her, wrote my term paper on hypnotism, and was invited to be included in her upper division class of psychotherapy.

Dorothy is dead now. Strange accident. As the years advanced, she retired from teaching and would find herself dozing even while talking. She had just completed writing a book on *Safe Driving For Older People*. The manuscript was in the back seat of her car ready to be mailed to her publisher when she had an accident. She went to sleep while driving her car and crashed into a store window. She was not badly hurt, but she died next day in the hospital. It was just too much shock for her to survive this personal refutation of the very thing she had stressed in her new book on safe driving. The mind can kill. Dear Dr. Yates, I remember her well. She played a part in my career as a hypnotist.

Having completed two years of college, I had a chance to go on the road with Mandu the Magician. Magic called, so I went. Meanwhile, I took some correspondence courses in commercial art and advertising.

A job came along handling advertising for Skaggs Drug Stores, during which time I met the girl I was to marry, Delight. She wanted me to return to college, so I took another year at San Jose State, majoring in art and advertising this time. It has always appealed to me to diversify interests, and my study of advertising made it possible for me to co-author a book with advertising executive, Fred Klycinski, entitled *Advertising for the Independent Business Man*. I completed writing the book, but never did anything with it. It still rests on my shelf. Maybe some day I will see about getting it published, as it does fill a niche in the business world. I will have to bring the advertising examples up-to-date. Advertising styles change so rapidly.

My junior years at college completed, Delight and I got married, so that wound up my formal education. That was way back in 1943. I never did get a "sheepskin" to hang on the wall, and it was not until 37 years later (1980) that my education picked up again when I met Patanjali – the greatest schoolmaster I have ever known. This is quite a story, as Patanjali has been dead for over a thousand years.

While teaching a class in hypnosis, a student gave me the book, *Only One Sky* by the Hindu guru, Bhagwan Shree Rajneesh. It told of the Tantra methods of meditation. I read the book and followed it up by visiting a metaphysical bookstore. I asked if they had anything further by Rajneesh on Tantra Meditation. They did. I bought a copy of *The Book of Secrets*, which professed to tell of the 112 methods of meditation which Shiva gave his beloved Devi some 5000 years before. I read the book from cover to cover, but it ended on meditation technique 24. Returning to the bookstore, I asked about this and was told that the complete 112 techniques were given via a five-volume set. I purchased the remaining four volumes and learned about the full 112 methods. These Tantra methods are said to be all the different kinds of meditation techniques there are in the world. They were great, but a lengthy ordeal to study. Then, inspiration dawned: why not condense them into one volume. Hindus seem to have a way of saying things in half a dozen different ways. That is fine for an eastern audience, but not so good for busy westerners.

I wrote to the Rajneesh Foundation in Poona, India, and asked permission to condense the five-volume set into one volume. Permission was granted, and I was informed they might even be interested in publishing my edition. I went to work with the help of my close friend, Chuck Mignosa (my associate in magic), and months later it was finished under the title, *The Way Out Is In*. I sent the manuscript to India and received a reply informing me that the old editorial staff had been replaced, and it had been decided they did not wish *The Book of Secrets* condensed, but that they did have a ten-volume set of Patanjali's Yoga they would like to have incorporated into one volume. They stated they would send these to me if I agreed. I said, "Okay."

Weeks later the books arrived, and I went through them and drew a blank. Somehow I just could not get inspired to work on the Patanjali material. He seemed too stiff and stern a disciplinarian for me. In other words, I could not identify with his consciousness, so I put the books on the shelf. They remained there for a year and a half.

One day, a year and a half later, I pulled one volume down and glanced through it. Suddenly, I knew Patanjali. Stern as his teaching was, I recognized the twinkle in his eye. I read and read, and came to know this great teacher. That is how this sage became my schoolmaster from way back in the past. In other words, I became conscious of him. He was just as close to me as anyone in my current lifetime. After all, how do you know anyone except that you are conscious of them?

And so, I condensed the volumes of Patanjali into one and reported to India.

Things had further changed in Poona, and I was advised I could do as I wished, but as far as they were concerned they were only publishing the words of Rajneesh as recorded from his sessions at the Ashram. Currently, I am rewriting it in a Western manner, titled, *How To Be a Mastermind and Operate the Universe.*

Possibly, you would like to meet Patanjali and hear a bit about what he has to say. Patanjali was a teacher of Yoga in northern India, around 319 B.C. Some call him, "The Father of Yoga". He did not discover it, but he did systematize it into a practice others could master, Patanjali's Yoga being a process of using the mind with brilliance and advancing consciousness from normal perception to superperception. There was nothing mystical about his teaching; he gave precise directions of what you should do. He gave instructions which, if followed, would cause the mind to function in its original crystal clarity, bringing enlightenment.

Patanjali is the Einstein amongst the Masters. He is the one master who has been able to express enlightenment and/or how to achieve enlightenment in a technical manner. Those who have studied Patanjali say he is great! Patanjali, himself, would never say he is great; he would simply say that he is a teacher, and by using yoga methods a person is able to discover their true nature. He would simply say that he gives precise processes which, if used, make it possible for anyone to discover their reality, which is neither great nor not great – *it is simply the case.* "Simply the case" is a favorite expression of Patanjali. That is the way of a scientist in uncovering truth. Patanjali is a scientist.

Patanjali describes Yoga as pure science. Via yoga, religion has been brought to the state of science. All religions call for belief, but yoga calls for no belief at all. Yoga simply tells you to experience, just as science tells you to experiment. Patanjali tells you to experience by experimenting. Experience and experiment are both the same to Patanjali; only their directions are different. Experiment means something you do outwardly; experience means something you do inwardly. In other words, experience is an inner experiment.

Being scientific makes Patanjali's Yoga especially interesting to people of the Occident, for Western people are the ones who have most advanced through science and technology. Western people are doers, and Patanjali's methods for finding enlightenment, via mental forms of yoga, are for those who like to do something.

It may be well to pause a moment and ask what is this goal called "enlightenment?" Actually, it is not a goal at all; it is just becoming aware of your true nature, becoming aware of what you really are. Enlightenment is just another word for increased awareness. Increased awareness is just another word for increased consciousness. Increased consciousness is just another word for cosmic consciousness. Cosmic consciousness is the consciousness of a Master such as Patanjali, and a way to discover that higher form of consciousness which links man with the cosmos – the totality of all that IS. That is why Patanjali's Yoga has been called the science of alpha and omega, *because the beginning is the end*.

"Alpha" means the beginning – the beginning of the spiritual journey, and "omega" means the end of the journey. Most seekers for enlightenment feel that the path they must tread will be long and arduous. Ordinarily, seekers on the path of Yoga are made to feel that the gap between alpha and omega must be tremendous and, in fact, many people like it that way. Then, they feel that if and when they reach omega they have accomplished a great thing. To all this, Patanjali merely smiles and commences his teaching by saying, "Now the discipline of yoga . . . ."

Education by Patanjali

Patanjali begins by presenting these sutras (a sutra being an Oriental term for condensation of teaching, an encapsulation of wisdom):

Yoga is the cessation of mind.
Through yoga the witness is established in itself.
In the other states than yoga there is identification with the
modifications of the mind.

In these three premises, Patanjali sums up his entire teaching and further adds, "If your mind has advanced sufficiently to come to realize that whatever you have been doing up to now was mostly senseless, that it was a nightmare at its worst or a beautiful dream at its best, then the path of yoga opens before you."

What is this path? What is yoga? Patanjali says, "Yoga is the cessation of mind."

Yoga is the state of no-mind. The word "mind" covers all – your ego, your desires, your hopes, your philosophies, your religions, your education, etc. Whatever you can think is mind; all that is knowable is within the mind. When there is no-mind, you are in the unknowable. Yoga takes you beyond the knowable into the unknowable.

What is mind? Ordinarily, we think that the mind is something substantial inside the head. Patanjali doesn't agree. He states that mind is just a function – just an activity for producing thoughts. Possibly you can understand this best through a little analogy: You walk and you say you are walking. What is walking? If you stop, where is the walking? Walking is nothing substantial; it is just an activity.

Mind is also an activity, but because you have given it a name (mind) it appears as if something substantial is there. You would come closer to the truth if you called it "minding" – just like "walking". It is an activity. And just as you can control the activity of walking, so can you control minding.

"Yoga is the cessation of mind", says Patanjali. In other words, when there is "no-mind" you are in yoga; where there is mind you are not in yoga. It is as simple as that. People tend to think of yoga in terms of stern discipline and of performing exotic exercises, and it is well that you perform the exercises as they are good for you, but unless they help you move beyond the mind to "no-mind" the postures are useless, for if the mind goes on thinking, you are not in yoga. The truth is that if you can advance beyond the mind, without doing any postures, you have become a perfect yogi. It has happened to many without doing any postures, and it has not happened to many who have been doing postures all their life.

All the Masters have told you the same thing, that if you would reach enlightenment you must move to no-mind, and men have developed many ways to try to reach this state, i.e., mantras, meditation methods, whatnot. You can sit for hours trying not to think, but then trying not to think becomes a thinking. The more you think about wanting to control the mind, the more active it becomes, and so you fail. By using Patanjali's Yoga you will not fail.

How then, do you master Yoga? Patanjali tells you how, and w
he says something appreciate that he means exactly what he ⌐⌐ˌ
and to reach yoga (the state of "no-mind") he says to simply bring
your mind to a stop. To do this, Patanjali tells you just to look and
do not specifically try to control the mind in any way. He is starting you on a great process here for obtaining control of the mind
(making it think when you want it to think and to stop thinking
when you don't want it to think), which begins by not trying to
control it at all.

And so Patanjali says just to look. Let the mind go; let the mind do
whatever it is doing. Don't interfere. Just be a witness; just be an
onlooker – not concerned, as if the mind doesn't belong to you. Just
look and let the mind flow. It is flowing because of past momentum, because you have always helped it to flow.

For all your life (for many lives if you wish to think in terms of
repeated incarnations), you have co-operated with mind, you have
helped it to flow. But if you don't co-operate with it, while the flow
will continue on for awhile, it will not be long before it stops flowing by itself. When the momentum is lost, the mind will stop. And
when the mind stops, you are in yoga, you are in control. You have
become master of your mind rather than your mind being the master of you – you have become a *mastermind.*

Then, a wonderful thing happens: *the witness is established in itself.*
This simply means that you, in becoming a witness to your thoughts,
have caused the mind to stop, and when the mind stops you drop
down to that place inside yourself where your real *self* dwells –
blissful and silent beyond the mind. You find yourself in the realm
of "no-mind", and you have attained yoga. Then, you have become
a witness – a seer. Then, you are not a doer, then you are not a
thinker, then you are pure being! When the witness becomes established in itself, you are pure consciousness. Then, you have
obtained enlightenment.

As Patanjali continues to explain, except in states of yoga you are
in mental states which identify with the modifications of the mind.
In other words, in all other mental states except in witnessing, you
are identified with the mind, and you become one with the flow of
thoughts. When you become one with the flow of thoughts, you are
not in yoga, and then mind becomes clouded and unclear, and you

41

can miss the truth. As an example, a thought comes that you are hungry, and the thought flashes in the mind. The thought is simply that there is hunger, but immediately you get identified with the thought, and you say, "I am hungry."

Patanjali also feels hunger, but he will never say, "I am hungry." He will say, "The body is hungry", or "My stomach is feeling hunger", or "There is hunger." He will say, "I am a witness of this thought which has been flashed by the stomach to the brain that the stomach is hungry," but Patanjali, himself, will remain a witness and thus is observing all in existence from a higher consciousness than does the average man.

This "higher consciousness" is "enlightenment". Remember this always, all identifications are of the mind, and they can bind you to misery. But if you transcend the identifications, you have transcended this world of misery and have entered the world of bliss.

It is the world of "the here and now" which Patanjali has told you how to enter in his very first instructions on Yoga. And it is here right now for you this very moment if you become aware of it. Just become a witness to the mind and you will have entered. Get identified with the mind, and you will miss. This is Patanjali's basic instruction.

One time, while I was writing Patanjali's instructions, I felt the ol' boy lean over and whisper in my ear, "Ormond, if you really want to be a great magician, hypnotist, or whatever, for heaven's sake do not try to become an extraordinary one. Most everyone tries to feel they are extraordinary, so it is very common to feel one is extraordinary. It is just ego talking, and for a performer that is disastrous, as audiences hate the egoist. A man who has really mastered his mind and/or his work is perfectly content in just being what he is, as he has discovered his true nature. The truth is that in recognizing he is ordinary, such a one becomes exceedingly extraordinary.

Chronologically, Patanjali came into my life during my latter years, but I consider him as belonging to my school days, as education is ageless. So I include him in this first part of my autobiography. Other than as an orderly way to keep track of events, time has no meaning to ones of enlightenment. Existence is recognized as a continuum. That is the meaning of eternity.

What Patanjali taught me was the greatest education I have ever had. It applies to everything in life.

Chapter Six

The Girl I Married

Delight Beth Olmstead was the girl I married on September 29, 1943. I never called her "wife". I always called her "sweetheart". The marriage lasted until she died 33 years later. We were even more in love then than when we first met.

My father often said he would give his right arm to have a marriage like ours. He married a second time after my mother died in 1962, but he couldn't find the supreme happiness that Delight and I enjoyed. Few people do. After all, glorious angels are rare. Mrs. Olmstead must have sensed her younger daughter's sterling qualities when she chose her name. Delight lived up to her name all her life. One time she told me it was a difficult name, as everyone expected her always to be delightful.

Our marriage came about like this:

Delight and I had been going together for 4 years. I wanted to marry her, but kept thinking that I should build up a good bank account first. Then, Delight took things into her own hands. A woman will often do that when she knows it's right.

A friend, Robert Bernhard, had taken a job as public relations man for an artist agency in Hollywood. Bob was a magician whom I met at Stanford University. He and I co-authored the book, *Fooling the Public*. We became close friends, and I did a show for him at Stanford's "Big Game" rally one year. Since his new job in Southern California gave him theatrical connections, he invited me to come south and offered to help advance my career. I decided to go and told Delight. She said she would go with me. It was while on that adventure in Hollywood that we got married.

As simple as that! We went to the private residence of a minister in Santa Monica after fulfilling requirements at the L.A. City Hall, and got married. Our folks were a little disappointed, as they had wanted a more elaborate wedding. Not Delight. She preferred to be free of ceremony. Being together was all that really mattered to her. If marriage helped the union, so much for marriage. We went to La Jolla for our honeymoon.

La Jolla, California, is a spot on earth that was very special to Delight. Her grandmother had lived in that beautiful seaside paradise which she often visited when a little girl. The charm of La Jolla goes unquestioned. The very name means "The Jewel". Delight always wanted to live there, but fortune was not that kind.

La Jolla was the perfect place for a honeymoon. We took long walks down the beach, explored enchanted nooks, and enjoyed the sunshine.

As it turned out, everyone in the family was happy that we got married, big wedding or not. They sent out this announcement to friends subsequently:

Mr. and Mrs. Ray C. Olmstead

announce the marriage of their daughter

Delight Beth

to

Mr. Ormond Dale McGill

on Wednesday, the twenty-ninth of September

Nineteen hundred and forty-three

Santa Monica, California

Relatives can be a riot in the concern they have over the propriety of "family". I rather suspect it is more concern over wagging tongues that might besmirch the family name than anything else. Moral codes are much looser these days than they were back in '43.

While we were honeymooning in La Jolla, a phone call came through from Delight's aunt. Somehow she had heard we had gone together on the L.A. trip. Her voice was full of righteous concern over the scandalous nature of our action. She was ready to scold when we cut her short by saying, "We are married." The scolding tone of her voice became all honey, "How absolutely wonderful, dear." Dear Aunt Margaret, we both loved her. She has long been dead, but I often think of that telephone call with a chuckle.

After La Jolla, we returned to Hollywood, discussed things with Bob Bernhard, and started about the business of earning a living as a magician. First, though, came the practical matter of finding a place to live. There was a war going on, and most apartment houses had a sign out saying "No Vacancy".

Luck favored as we found a place to live at the Casa Alta Apartments at 317 S. Olive Street in the heart of downtown Los Angeles. The Casa Alta was on "Bunker Hill" diagonally across the street from historic "Angel's Flight". We often took a ride on that trolley up the steep incline from the street below to our level. The fare was two cents. Things were reasonable in those days. You could get a good dinner for 50¢ and our apartment rent was $1.00 per day.

World War II went on, but finally D-Day came, and Germany gave up. Japan soon followed. I recall a newspaper hawker, standing on a corner in downtown L.A., yelling each time we passed him, "It won't be long now!" He was right!

For the first two years of our married life, Delight and I lived at the Casa Alta, spending a great deal of our time in Hollywood. To support ourselves, I did magic shows – mostly casual dates booked by local theatrical agencies. Calling upon booking agents for work has never been my idea of a good time. Often they would say, "Nothing today but keep in touch."

I kept in touch, and some bookings came through. Not much, but enough to keep "the wolf from the door". Delight helped out, too, by working as an elevator operator at a hotel. They liked her and offered the job of assistant manager. However, she declined.

It was while living at the Casa Alta that I wrote *How To Produce Miracles*, which years later was published by A.S. Barnes & Co., Inc., in hardback, and subsequently put out in paperback by Signet

Books. It was a book of special interest to psychic entertainers. The book was based on the premise that in every gathering, social or otherwise, when thoughts turn toward the mysterious they eventually lead to a discussion of miracles, in which someone will tell of seeing the apparently impossible performed. The book explains how to perform tricks of this type.

In the introduction I wrote, those long years ago, "This is not a book on conjuring; it presents a new entertainment form of mystery – Miracle Magic!"

I gave "miracle-magic" in half a dozen classifications: Mindreading, Hypnotism, Mesmerism, Yogic Powers, Spiritism, and Occult Phenomena. And it was fun illustrating the feats with surrealistic drawings. Surrealism is symbolic art expressing in simple line what Confucius said, "One picture is worth a thousands words." Thirteen rules were given for presenting miracle effect as a unique form of entertainment:

1. Miracle never accomplishes a pleasure response; instead, it must incite awe.
2. Miracle never meets the demands of the performing occasion; the occasion must be made to meet the demands of the effect.
3. Miracle is never volunteered to be presented; it must occur naturally as an objective illustration of a point raised in speculation.
4. Miracle is always presented seriously.
5. Miracle is always presented intellectually.
6. Miracle never is shown as an exhibition of the performer's skill; the performer's relationship to the effect is entirely that of the instrument through which the effect is made a manifestation.
7. Miracle calls for peak audience attention, the effect of miracle being in direct ratio to the expectation of the observer's attention.
8. Miracle is never the result of showing off personal power or the result of challenge; miracle is always aimed at amplification of discussion of the miracle.
9. Miracle must always seem impromptu in its presentation, and directly related to the subject of miracle under discussion.
10. Miracle is an isolated effect, the one example performed being the sole period of its survival.

11. Miracle is offered in only one phase of miracle nuclei on any occasion; in other words, only one miracle effect is presented before the gathering at any one time.
12. Miracle is never repeated.
13. Miracle is never discussed by the presenter after its presentation.

It is in the careful following of these thirteen rules of presentation of miracle-magic that the art form of this extraordinary type of entertaining is developed, and a lasting impression upon the spectators of having witnessed a miracle is produced.

The Miracle Pendulum

I included in my *How To Produce Miracles* one chapter devoted to The Pendulum. Books on Pendulum Power can now be found in Antiquarian Bookshops, but when I wrote about it in 1944 I was a pioneer. I included it in the book because it was a performable "miracle".

The Pendulum can be used as a prognostication device in answering questions. The method is simple.

Make a pendulum by tying a small weight to the end of a 12 inch length of thread. A light fish weight is fine. For a start, in getting used to using it, experiment with how it can indicate gender.

If you dangle it over the hand of a man it will swing back and forth. If you hold it over the hand of a woman it will swing in a circle. Test it for yourself.

For the purpose of prognostication, decide on how you wish the pendulum to respond in answering questions. For example, if the answer to a question is "yes" it is to swing back and forth; if "no" it is to remain motionless. Then decide on the question you wish to have answered.

When ready, speak the question out loud, and with a pencil or pen draw a line an inch long on a sheet of paper – this mark becomes associated with the question being asked. It becomes a "mark of representation".

Next, dangle the Pendulum over the mark. Do not try to move it consciously or guess the answer. Allow it to respond entirely of its own violation. In a moment, it will start to swing or not, depending upon whether the answer to the questions is "yes" or "no".

You will have lots of fun answering questions for people in social groups. Just sit at a table with the pendulum dangling from your fingers, and each time a question is asked by a spectator draw mark and allow it to respond on its own in answering questions. Question after question can be answered in this way. Obviously, for pendulum prognostication, the questions must be framed for a positive or negative response.

How does "The Prognosticating Pendulum" operate? Obviously, there is no magical power in a length of thread and a fish weight tied to its end. The magic resides in your mind. ESP powers are subconscious (subliminal) in nature, and the Pendulum affords a means of externalizing these subjective impressions. Remarkably, these answers often come out surprisingly accurate and perceptive.

Somehow it seems fitting that I would write about "Miracle Magic" during my first years of marriage with Delight.

Chapter Seven

Adventures in Hollywood

While living in Southern California, following our marriage, Delight and I had some interesting adventures in Hollywood, among them visiting Thayer's Studio of Magic. I had visited there in 1940 following the Pacific Coast Association of Magicians (PCAM) Convention in San Diego. Floyd Thayer had his studio behind his home at 429 S. Longwood Avenue at that time. It was a mecca for magicians. I met Thayer there. Ronald Hamblin worked behind the counter. Movie stars of that period interested in magic came in on occasion. Harold Lloyd, Chester Morris, and Orson Wells were frequent visitors. I got to know Floyd Thayer quite well, and also his wife Jenny. The friendship made possible the trading of a Thayer "Talking Vase" for an antique urn I had. Jenny liked the urn, while I liked the vase, so everybody was happy. The urn was a collector's item then. Thayer's "Talking Vase" is a collector's item now.

Floyd Thayer was a remarkable craftsman of magical apparatus. Each piece he made has become a valuable collectable for magicians.

In 1943, with Delight, I again visited Thayer's Studio of Magic; Bill Larsen, Sr. had traded his home in Glendale for the property, and now ran the business. Bill was a lawyer by profession, but magic won out for a time. He even opened a second shop in downtown Hollywood. Bill, Sr. and I became friends and, of course, I met the family and knew them well: Gerie, Bill, Jr., and Milton. Milton even assisted me in a few Dr. Zomb Spook Shows, which I later played in the area. Bill, Jr. and Milton went on to create and operate the famous Magic Castle in Hollywood which is now known worldwide.

As William Larsen, Sr.'s business expanded he needed more items to sell, so I turned out a few things for him. Among them was a book we titled, *Radio and Night Club Mindreading*. Dunninger was going great guns on radio at the time. This book told ways to make it possible for other magicians to perform a Dunninger-type act via radio. To add scope to the book, I also explained ways to perform a mindreading act in night clubs. The book sold well. Here are some extracts from it:

For success in the field of radio mindreading, the fundamental rule to bear in mind is that you must be *entertaining*.

These half dozen rules are basic to success in that field:

1. The radio mindreader must possess a good speaking voice and an understanding of the effective use of language.
2. The radio mindreader must have an innate understanding of human nature, coupled with the ability to size up people quickly and accurately.
3. The radio mindreader must have knowledge of mindreading methods – the "tricks of the trade".
4. The radio mindreader must possess a nature capable of daring audacity.
5. The radio mindreader must be alert to turning the unexpected to his advantage.
6. The radio mindreader must play to his radio audience more than to his studio audience, looking upon his studio audience as a part of his program that is going "over the air".

Consider mindreading mentalism as an introspective type of entertainment which does not provide much to see but does provide a great deal to think about. As its mystery develops within the mind of the listener, it is perfect for radio. The more simple and direct the visual counterparts, the more powerful the presentation. *Simplicity of modus operandi is the aim of the mindreader.*

These rules are as true today for the successful presentation of magical mindreading as the day I wrote them back in the 1940s.

The second part of the book explained how to perform a mindreading act in the middle of a night club floor. The method suggested was the use of a gimmicked clipboard to pick up questions from diners at their tables before the act. A girl assistant tends to this. The gist of the questions, secretly secured via the clipboard, is written (very small) on a card. This "prompter card" is palmed beneath the crystal ball used in the act. Looking through the crystal the small writing is magnified, giving the mentalist easy access to the questions.

The night club section of the book went on to explain how to earn extra money in the field with Palm and Card Readings at the tables: the "table hopping" way.

The first edition of the book Bill put out was in mimeograph. The second edition was printed. Both sold out. *Radio and Night Club Mindreading* got me started writing books on magic.

While in Hollywood, I called upon theaters to book my show. At one of these I met a manager named Louis Berkoff. Not only did he book my show, but we became close friends over the years.

Louis Berkoff was part of a Russian troupe who had starred in the Ziegfeld Follies. The entire family was in show business. Louis was a millionaire who owned two theaters in the area. Also, he had produced a motion picture. Meeting Louis Berkoff was fortunate for me, as he furthered my career in many ways, including arranging to have me hired as technical advisor for a film he produced about a magician. The film starred Edmund Lowe and was titled *The Strange Mr. Gregory*. Jean Rogers co-starred. I also got a small part in the film those long years back, which got me into the Screen Actors Guild. Louis Berkoff is now dead, but I remember him with fondness. I will see you later, dear friend.

My Hollywood period occurred during World War II when the famous "Hollywood Canteen" was in full swing. It was the entertainment center of Hollywood for servicemen. Through my friend, Robert Bernhard, I was introduced to Ted Lesser, a top agent who had been manager for Rudy Vallee. Ted got me an engagement in the "Canteen" for a tryout performance. It was so successful that I was invited back a dozen times. Military men are very responsive to hypnotic entertainment. The Hollywood Canteen proved an excellent showcase for my work. Also, it gave me a chance to meet some of the top movie stars of the times: Bette Davis, Hedy LaMarr, Sydney Greenstreet, Buster Keaton, and John Wayne were among those I came to know. Show business people have a way of liking show business people.

Hollywood Canteen

Affiliated With American Theatre Wing, Inc.

HOLLYWOOD, CALIFORNIA

OFFICERS
PRESIDENT—Bette Davis
1st VICE-PRES.—J. K. Wallace
2nd VICE-PRES.—John Garfield
3rd VICE-PRES.—Mervyn LeRoy
4th VICE-PRES.—Carroll Hollister
5th VICE-PRES.—Mrs. John Ford
EXEC. SECRETARY—Jean Lewin
TREASURER—Ray Marcus

COMMITTEE CHAIRMEN
BLDG. & ALTERATION—Alfred C. Ybarra
BUS. MGEM'T.—Jules C. Stein
CHECKERS—Paul Jaffee
DECORATORS—Casey Roberts

ENTERTAINMENT:

   HON. CHAIRMAN, Bob Hope
   CHAIRMAN, Kay Kyser
   CELEBRITIES—Ann Warner
   RADIO—Georgia Fifield
   VARIETY ARTISTS—Florine Bale

HOSTESSES—Doris Stein, Florence C. Cadrez
HOSTS—Mervyn LeRoy, Harry Crocker
KITCHEN EQUIP.—William Simon
MAINTENANCE—Paul Doyle
MUSIC—John TeGroen, Baron Moorehead
OFFICERS OF THE DAY—Edwin H. Knopf
PUBLICITY—Mack Millar
SNACK BAR—Mrs. John Ford
STAGE MGEM'T—George Ramsey
TREASURERS—Catherine Baldwin

DIRECTOR OF FOOD—Chef Milani
LEGAL ADVISOR—Dudley R. Furse

SPONSORS OF
HOLLYWOOD CANTEEN

Actors Equity Assn.
Affil. Property Craftsmen, IATSE Local 44
Amer. Fed. of Musicians, Local 47
Amer. Fed. of Musicians, Local 767
Amer. Fed. of Radio Artists
Amer. Guild of Musical Artists
Amer. Guild of Variety Artists
Amer. Soc. of Composers, Authors and Publ.
Artists Managers Guild
Asso. Motion Pic. Cost., IATSE Local 705
Association of Motion Picture Producers
B.S.E.I.U., Local 99
C., L. & R. F. D., Local 1247
Federated Amusement & Allied Crafts
Film Technicians, IATSE Local 683
Independent Publicists
Int. Photographers, IATSE Local 659
Int. Sound Tech., IATSE Local 695
Makeup Artists, IATSE Local 706
Mot. Pic. Hair Stylists, IATSE Local 706
Motion Picture Illustrators
M. P. Set Electricians, IATSE Local 728
M. P. Studio Grips, IATSE Local 80
M. P. Studio Projec., IATSE Local 165
M. P. Painters & Scenic Art., Local 644
Radio Writers Guild
Screen Cartoonists Guild
Screen Directors Guild
Screen Office Employees Guild
Screen Publicists Guild
Screen Readers Guild
Screen Set Designers
Screen Writers Guild
Society of Motion Picture Art Directors
Society of Motion Picture Film Editors
Society of Motion Picture Int. Decorators
Singwriters Protective Assn.
Studio Carpenters, Local 946
Studio Elec. Union, IBEW Local 40
Studio L. & U. Workers, IATSE Local 727
Studio Misc. Employees, Local 1104
Studio Transf Drivers Union, Local 399
Studio Util. Emp. Union, Local 724
L. A. J. P. & S., Local 78
V.C. U., B. S. E., Local 1f

ENDORSED BY
California State Federation of Labor
Hollywood Victory Committee
Hollywood Writers Mobilization
State Theatrical Fed. of California
U. S. O.

November 13, 1943

Ormand Magill
c/o Backhman & Co.,
8511 Sunset Blvd.,
Los Angeles

Dear Ormand Magill:

Please accept our gratitude for your entertainment of service men at the Canteen.

I am certain that each man who saw you here, will carry pleasant memories of Hollywood with him, wherever he goes.

Our best wishes and kindest regards.

Sincerely,

Bette Davis
President

1451 NORTH CAHUENGA BOULEVARD

PHONE HEMPST

"Thank you" letter from Bette Davis, President of the Hollywood Canteen, November 1943

The Hollywood Canteen shows landed me an engagement at the Trocadero Night Club on Sunset Strip. I opened there on a Saturday night, and the show was sensational. Sitting at a piano in the back of the room, Judy Garland got hypnotized. Everyone was thrilled. But show business is unpredictable. I presented the same show on Monday night and things did not go so well. On Saturday night, the place had been packed and people flocked up to be hypnotized. On Monday night, the crowd was small and no one wanted to volunteer. I decided it was best not to buck that difficulty, so I called the engagement off.

I have often reflected upon the matter. Night club entertaining with hypnotism has proved very successful for some performers such as Pat Collins. Had my show at the Trocadero repeated its opening night's success an entirely different pattern of life might have opened for me. I have frequently noticed that every so often a "cross-road" will seem to appear on the map of one's life. In other words, two paths open before you that lead in diverse directions. How to choose? Maybe it is best not to decide for yourself, but let the universe decide. As my dear friend, Lao Tzu, a Chinese sage who lived before the time of Christ, put it, "Go with the flow."

In case you may wonder how I could have a dear friend who lived before the time of Christ, all I can say is that I feel his consciousness close to me often, and seem to know him well. Perchance I knew him in a previous lifetime. Who is to say? If you have had such an experience yourself, you will understand. If you have not, you could never understand, so there is no need to mention it further, except to say, "How are we conscious of anything except to the degree of which we are conscious of it?"

In regard to Lao Tzu's idea of "Going with the flow", the following two-line verse came through from deep inside myself one time. I adopted it as a bit of personal philosophy:

LESS AND LESS TRY TO MAKE THINGS HAPPEN AND MORE AND MORE JUST LET THINGS HAPPEN.

Ted Lesser then booked me for Ken Murray's "Blackouts". It was a top stage show in Hollywood during the war years. Marie Wilson starred with Ken. I designed an act that Murray liked, in which I played the part of a magician in a haunted house scene. Lots of spooky stuff and illusions. Things looked good. The illusions were ordered from Abbott's Magic Company in Colon, Michigan. Finally, the illusions came, but the show never did play. With Japan's surrender the war was over, and "Blackouts" closed. It was a disappointment. However, one has to learn to take the good with the bad in show business. Just keep plugging away!

Art Linkletter

While in Hollywood, I had the good fortune to meet Art Linkletter. Art Linkletter is a famous name. He is one of the most respected men in show business. I am proud to call him friend, and the prestige of having presented hypnotism on his popular show added prestige to my own stage hypnotism shows.

In 1944, I was booked for an appearance on Linkletter's *People Are Funny* radio show. How do you present hypnotism on a radio show? Art's skill made it possible. It was a pioneer performance. I was asked to return.

When Art Linkletter went from radio to television, I was again invited to appear. As FCC regulations do not allow hypnotizing to be presented over the air lest some viewers become hypnotized, all hypnotic inductions must be performed "off camera".

Persons who prove to be effective subjects are used on the televised show, under the influence of a posthypnotic suggestion that "on cue" they will respond and enter hypnosis. The results are phenomenal.

More fun with Art follow in his *Life With Linkletter* programs, I used his name association frequently in my advertising. It is pure gold.

Also, while in Hollywood, just shortly after Delight and I were married in 1943, I met Gil Boyne. Gil became a close friend in the field of hypnotism.

At that time, Gil Boyne had just started his private hypnotherapy practice and was locally becoming known as an expert. Being located close to "Tinsel Town", he began to make inroads in working with motion picture personalities who sought his help. This association

John Guedel Radio Productions

Taft Building
Hollywood 28, California
HEmpstead 5186

March 31, 1950

Mr. Ormond McGill
6940 Longridge Avenue
Van Nuys, California

Dear Ormond:

I think Bob Brawn of the William Morris office,
CRestview 1-6161...212 North Canon Drive, Beverly
Hills would be the best bet for your television
project.

You did a wonderful job on "People Are Funny". We
have had hundreds of good reports on it and it should
be a natural for television.

Sincerely,

John Guedel

JG/gr
cc: Bob Brawn

Letter from John Guedel of John Guedel Radio Productions

opened the way for him to become technical advisor for *The Hypnotic Eye*, a movie featuring a hypnotist as its star. He introduced a novelty into the film by presenting from the screen a number of experiments in hypnotic suggestion the audience could try in the darkened theater.

After Delight and I left Hollywood, Gil and I corresponded occasionally. Then, I lost track of him until some years later when I played a week's engagement at the Ivar Theater in Hollywood, Gil showed up, and we renewed our friendship. He had advanced greatly in his profession, and now had a suite of offices for his work.

In addition to Gil Boyne's Hypnotism Training Institute, he has established the Westwood Publishing Company, which has become one of America's leading publishers of hypnotism books. He has published three of mine to date: *Professional Stage Hypnotism*, *Hypnotism and Mysticism of India*, and *Hypnotism and Meditation*.

After two years of activity in Hollywood, Delight and I began to feel we had had enough of "Tinsel Town". Also, our folks kept urging us to come back home, so we decided to follow our destiny elsewhere.

I wrote to an old friend, Hal Honoré, asking if he could book my stage show in his theater. Hal was the theater manager who had launched my original Dr. Zomb Show. Hal Honoré had become city manager for Mann Theaters in Eureka, California. He thought the idea was splendid and promoted a terrific campaign: Blindfold Drive, Window Sleep, Headline Prediction, Radio and Newspaper Interviews, Guest Speaker at Rotary, the works. Hal made Dr. Zomb a celebrity in Eureka.

Chapter Eight

The Language of the Eyes

Delight and I shared a lot of eye contact naturally, and it always reminded me of how I answered an ad in a 1932 issue of the *The Linking Ring* (official organ for The International Brotherhood of Magicians) and ordered "The Language of the Eyes". I'm glad I did as it presents a fascinating idea. I only saw it advertised once. I give it to you here. It is unlikely you will ever find it elsewhere.

Instructions for the Language of the Eyes

With the aid of this technique, you can convey messages to your partner secretly right in the presence of others. The messages are transmitted by means of the eyes, and can be received by the other person opposite within a distance of one to a hundred feet. While communicating in this language, you merely gaze calmly in front of yourself. Silence reigns, and yet you are "speaking".

In learning this language, start by pointing a finger at different locations which represent the letters of the alphabet. With growing proficiency this will be omitted, as the eyes alone are the sole means by which the language is "spoken".

Keep a sheet of paper in your left hand while "eye talking". Regard this as "Home". "Home" is used when a letter has to be doubled, such as the letter t in the word "better". Send b – e – t , then look at "Home", then continue "t"–e–r. Look quickly at "Home", and get quickly back to your spelling.

Numerals are conveyed the same way as are letters. According to their order in the alphabet: A is 1, B is 2, C is 3, D is 4, E is 5, F is 6, G is 7, H is 8, I is 9, J is 10 and/or zero.

As an example, the number "1929" is spelt (conveyed) as "AIBI"; the number "31007" is "CAJJG", etc.

Before transmitting a number, however, it is necessary to give your partner a "number" signal notifying that the following letters refer to numbers. This is done by sending the number signal "NN". Transmit the words to your message as usual, then send the signal with the eyes "NN". Continue then with the number.

If you have made an error in a word or sentence and wish to repeat it, send the "Mistake Signal", which is to look at your right hand and then aside to partner's waist. This signal conveys the meaning, "Mistake, I Repeat". Then start the spelling again.

When you and your partner have become expert at using this "Language of the Eyes", you can practice further together by reversing the roles (your partner being the transmitter and yourself the receiver).

Practice and persevere until you are both expert in both ways.

In practicing, keep the letter chart on hand until you both know it entirely by heart.

The Alphabet Chart for the Language of the Eyes

A   look at partner's head.
B   look at partner's head, then aside to head.
C   look first at partner's head, then aside to waist.
D   look first at partner's head, then aside to feet.
E   look at partner's upper waist.
F   look at partner's lower waist.
G   look first at partner's waist, then aside to head.
H   look first at partner's waist, then aside to feet.
I   look at partner's feet.
J   look at your right hand, then aside of partner's head.
K   look at partner's feet, then aside of head.
L   look at partner's feet, then aside to waist.
M   look at partner's feet, then aside to feet.
N   look at partner's right hand, then at waist.
O   look at your right hand, then at partner's head.

P   look at your right hand, then at partner's waist.
Q   repeat twice the letter K.
R   look at your right hand, then aside to head.
S   look at your right hand, then at partner's head, then aside to waist.
T   look at your right hand, then at partner's head, then aside to feet.
U   look at your right hand, then at partner waist, then aside to head.
V   look first at your right hand, then at partner's waist, then aside of waist.
W   look first at your right hand, then at partner's waist, then aside to feet.
X   look first at your right hand, then at partner's feet, then aside to head.
Y   look first at your right hand, then at partner's feet, then aside to waist.
Z   look first at your right hand, then at partner's feet, then aside of feet.

The "Language of the Eyes" is a rarity; it is almost a lost art which is why I include it in my autobiography. Once you master this language you will find you can "speak" to your partner almost as rapidly with your eyes as you can with your tongue. Don't grimace when you do it. *Just let your eyes do the talking*.

It takes diligence and practice to master, but once mastered with your partner, you have a skill few have.

Chapter Nine

Which Path to Take?

In many lives, there comes a time when two pathways open before one, for example, what career to pursue. For myself it was, should I go into commercial art and advertising, or pursue the arts of magic and hypnosis?

I had taken a correspondence course in commercial art with the Myer Both Company of Chicago. Also, I had taken advertising training with the American Institute of Advertising in New York. Both were excellent and I felt ready to launch into the advertising profession. That was Path One.

Likewise I had advanced as a professional in the field of magic and hypnotism. That was Path Two.

I submitted some of my art and advertising material to prospects in that commercial field, and was offered a job in the advertising department of Thrifty Drug Company, a prominent chain of drug stores in those years. It was a splendid opportunity to advance into a career along Path One.

I asked Delight which path I should take. Without a moment's hesitation she said, "Take Path Two. It leads to your destiny. Path One leads you into a profitable profession in the business world, but it is earthly. Path Two is far less substantial and at times can even be nebulous, but it leads into the realm of spirit. That is where you belong."

Without even a further question, I chose to take Path Two. That was back in 1944, one year following my marriage to Delight.

Chapter Ten

An Adventure with Dr. Zomb

During the 1940s, I might just as well have changed my name to Dr. Zomb, as I used it more than my own. It was perhaps the most professional period of my life, as it involved theater business. I always liked working for theater managers; we were kindred souls.

The Dr. Zomb Show was booked solidly by Fox West Coast Theaters, Fox Evergreen Theaters, Fox Intermountain Theaters, Mann Theaters, and United Artists. In the United States, the show played as far east as Illinois. In Canada, it enjoyed some successful summer seasons for Famous Players Theaters. Business in Canada was so good for the show that following the theater bookings I went out on my own playing auditoriums in the Provinces. Of these times, one special adventure stands out in my memory which I will share with you: my meeting with the Royal Canadian Mounted Police.

It was an exciting adventure. I was touring across Canada presenting a magic and hypnotism show, billed as Dr. Zomb. The show had just played in Banff, a popular resort city. The hypnotism demonstrations had been impressive.

The next day we moved on to another city, and so on throughout the week. One night, around midnight, there was a rap upon the door. Surprised at this unexpected visit, I gingerly asked, "Who is there?" A reply forthcoming, "Canadian Mounted Police".

Opening the door, a large man in redcoat and wide-brimmed hat stood before me, looking very much like Nelson Eddy when he played the role in the film *Rose Marie*, co-starring with Jeanette MacDonald.

The "mounty" inquired if I was Dr. Zomb. I admitted such was my stage name. He then explained his mission. The Canadian Mounted Police had been trying to locate me for days. It seems the next day after my Banff show, while at work, a girl became hypnotized and they couldn't arouse her from the trance. A fellow worker, in jest, came up to her and made hypnotic passes. She swooned away. On the spot, she dropped to the floor fast asleep.

Everyone at the factory swarmed about her, but no persuasion would arouse her.

As the story unfolded, it seems that the girl had not actually been hypnotized at my show, but had attended in the audience and was impressed. She developed a fine case of what has been called "Beatle Mania". It will be recalled how when The Beatles were on tour girls would swoon, as they sang. Psychologically, it was a way of getting attention, but the swooning was real. The mind can perform in strange ways when emotions are aroused. In my case, the girl had swooned herself into profound hypnosis.

One of the most notable characteristics of hypnosis is increased suggestibility, so the more the crowd of people gathered about her telling that they couldn't awaken her, the deeper into hypnosis she went!

That girl had become a center of attention at the place where she was employed; thus, mentally she preferred to remain in trance which made her important, while to awaken would cause her to lose the importance.

I explained these facts to the policeman. He understood.

Next day I was taken to the hospital to visit the sleeping girl. I had everyone leave the room. Five minutes later she was awake. She was fine. However, the episode took another turn.

The story of the prolonged hypnosis of the girl in Banff caught the wires. Newspaper and radio played up the story. It was even circulated in the States. Paul Harvey made quite a thing of it, in his syndicated broadcasts.

Delight and I both thought the incident would prove the end of our tour in Canada, as most certainly no one would want to volunteer to take the chance of sleeping for days. However, we had one further engagement booked at a theater in New London. We appeared on stage and did some magic. When the hypnotism portion was due, I asked for volunteers fully expecting no one would come up. Instead, it seemed as though half the audience clamored to get on stage. I made room for a stageful of volunteers.

Usually, I start my show with a relaxing test using a crystal ball: a peaceful and pleasant way to prepare the subjects for further experiences following some demonstrations in waking suggestion. An amazing thing happened!

I had scarcely held up the crystal before the crowd on stage, than half the group fell to the floor entranced. Even some people in the audience went to "sleep" in hypnosis. I had subjects sleeping all over the place, many of them lying outstretched on the floor. I had to step over them like so many logs. They didn't want to wake up, so I just left them sleeping and presented the show with those who had not "gone under".

The show went fine, and finally was over. Through it all the "sleeping" subjects slumbered on. After all, if a factory girl could garner national publicity by being hypnotized, here was a similar opportunity for themselves. The mind is a tricky monkey when it plays mischief upon itself.

How did I manage to awaken the sleeping persons?

I simply emptied the theater and told them they could sleep on the floor for as long as they liked; but, as far as I was concerned, we were locking the theater for the night, so they would be sleeping by themselves. If they wanted to keep on sleeping it was entirely okay with me, but no one would be around to see them sleeping, and the theater would not be unlocked until morning.

Immediately, everyone woke up. It almost seemed that they must have been pretending being hypnotized. Not really. The hypnosis was quite genuine, motivated by a desire for attention. When the possibility of attention was removed, there was no further motivation to remain entranced.

The mind operates like that on a subconscious level. The more you understand the "power of suggestion" the more you will understand that suggestion is a subconscious realization of ideas, not conscious realization.

Next day, Delight and I ended our tour in Canada and returned to our home in California. From a business point of view, leaving then was a foolish move, as we were "on a roll". The publicity we had garnered over the Banff incident could have packed theaters. However, from our personal point of view, it was for the best. As gentle people, we wanted to get away from the intensity of the situation. We wanted to go home.

On arriving home, we faced our parents. They were all curious as to what had happened. Dr. Zomb was news all over. Delight's mother even thought it must have been another Dr. Zomb, surely not Ormond! We explained, and the episode was closed.

Being Wanted by the Royal Canadian Mounted Police will be etched in my memory as an extraordinary adventure. It made me appreciate the tremendous power of suggestion.

Chapter Eleven

Publicity Miracles

Gathering publicity about yourself is what brings you to the attention of the public. Houdini was the great master of publicity. Through his publicity he became so famous that even though he passed onwards way back in 1926, he is still remembered by the general public as the greatest magician who ever lived.

I used two main publicity stunts to promote business for my Dr. Zomb show: "The Blindfold Drive" and "The Window Sleep". I will describe each along with modus operandi and details of their promotion. My dear friends, Donn and Erna, were assistants who helped me in my publicity stunts. They met, fell in love, and got married while performing publicity miracles.

The Blindfold Drive

This is a popular publicity stunt that many magicians have used. In the effect, a black cloth blindfold is examined and tied around the head covering the eyes and a good part of the face completely. Sight seems impossible. The blindfolded man then takes his position in a car and drives about the city. Usually, a police escort accompanies the driver.

My assistant Donn Wood (who later became known as "Merlin the Magician") was the driver in the demonstration, while I, as Dr. Zomb, appeared to direct the driver by telepathy from a following car. It was a publicity miracle I found effective to use in many cities. A great business booster for the Midnight Show.

During the 1940s and 1950s, it was not difficult for a theater manager to obtain permission from city hall to allow the drive. Today, with the tremendous increase in traffic it is a different story.

I performed the Blindfold Drive many times to advertise my show. The biggest splash I ever made of it was in Honolulu. I can still hear Al Karasick, manager of the Civic Auditorium, telling me, as we drove to the site for the start of the drive, "With all this publicity, this should better work or we bomb!" It worked brilliantly, and the auditorium was packed that night. Publicity in Hawaii was under direction of Buck Buckwack. Buck was the best P.R. man I ever worked with. He later became editor of the leading newspaper in Honolulu.

The Impossible Blindfold Drive

I have always admired the publicity value of this method of performing the Blindfold Drive, which was created by Louis E. Collins way back in 1928. It is an incredible method, yet few magicians I have mentioned it to seem to know of it.

Effect

Performer is blindfolded with a section of tire inner tube and a two-gallon bucket placed over his head. And the car to be driven has all the windows painted dead black with poster paint. Further, the performer has one of his hands handcuffed to the steering wheel, and all doors of the car are locked, with the performer inside and keyholes sealed. Under these impossible conditions, the magician drives the car through crowded streets and returns to the starting place where he may be examined by a public committee.

Modus Operandi

As soon as the blindfolded performer is locked inside the car, he slips off the bucket and slides the blindfold from his eyes just enough to enable him to see clearly, but not enough to disarrange the wrapping of the inner tube blindfold.

The driver has a small shoe polish bottle with cork and sponge attached filled with the black poster paint used to paint inside of car windows and windshield completely. This is concealed in the performer's breast pocket. As soon as the eyes are free, the performer moistens a finger of his free hand and carefully wipes a tiny speck of black paint from the windshield just level with the eyes, and at the extreme left side of glass. A spot the size of a fingernail is sufficient. The driver is ready to go, for that little "peep hole" gives enough vision to make the drive safely. Just take it slowly, never exceeding a five or ten miles per hour speed limit.

In making the drive, watch carefully and do not drive longer than 10 minutes, ending the drive at the place you started. As the car nears the end of the drive, get the bottle of black poster paint out of your pocket and be ready to daub the spot on windshield with paint, as soon as you come to a stop. Stop. Daub paint on peek hole and return bottle of paint to pocket. Shut off motor. Adjust inner tube blindfold over eyes, and put bucket over your head. Slump down in seat as though exhausted.

Outside the car, seals are broken and doors unlocked, and you are found impossibly blindfolded just as you were when the drive commenced.

Of his drive, the originator writes, "You will find this drive extraordinary. Performed in this manner, 'The Impossible Blindfold Drive' is more effective and talk producing as a short drive rather than a long drive. It is an event that will never be forgotten. Preserve the secret."

The Window Sleep

In my opinion, the classic publicity stunt of "the Window Sleep" is the best bally a hypnotist can use to bring in business. It proved box office dynamite for me during the period I was touring the theater circuits with my Dr. Zomb "Seance Of Wonders" show.

The theme of this publicity stunt is really very simple: a girl is hypnotized and left sleeping in a store window for several hours, being awakened on stage during the show. I presented it as a genuine hypnotism demonstration, usually starting around 3:30 in the afternoon so that the school kids would be out of class, and could get down to see it. Around 7:30 in the evening, the girl was taken by ambulance and placed sleeping on a couch in the theater lobby. During the show, the ambulance attendants carried her down the aisle onto the stage, and I awoke her from the hypnotic trance. The audience applauded her. I always used a local girl, it made her a celebrity in the city.

The girl used as a subject for "the Window Sleep" is usually hired by the theater. Using a local girl increases the publicity value of the stunt. As it is important to induce as deep a hypnotic state as possible so that the girl can sleep soundly during the several hours of the demonstration, suggestions are given that she will pass into a restful sleep, that all will seem quiet about her, that time will go by unnoticed, and that she will awaken feeling wonderful and well, just as she does when awakening from a normal sleep each morning.

So that "the Window Sleep" will be accepted by the public as an important event, it must be presented in good taste and with great care. The more prestige that can be invested about it, the better. I found that by tying it in with a radio broadcast (using local station) that the publicity value was greatly expanded. For its successful presentation, the following eight points should be maintained.

1. City License and Police Permission

Check at City Hall for any permits required to present a public demonstration feat of this kind. Also, arrange for permission from the police department and request that some police be on hand to handle the crowd. If you cooperate with them, they will cooperate with you – they like the publicity too. Advanced attention to these details can save possible conflicts at the time the demonstration is made public had not civic permission been obtained.

2. The Window

Have your personal manager, in conjunction with the local theater manager, line up the store window in which the hypnotized girl is to sleep. Try to obtain the best possible store located right in the heart of the city that has a large display window. Generally speaking, the more prestige the store has the more prestige the publicity stunt will acquire. As "the Window Sleep" will attract large crowds for the store, arrangements are easily made. Proprietors like to get crowds out to their store.

3. Setting the Window

The more attractively the window can be dressed for the demon-stration the better. A large bed should be in the center neatly made with crisp sheets and luxurious blankets. A sign with copy similar to this is then placed in the window.

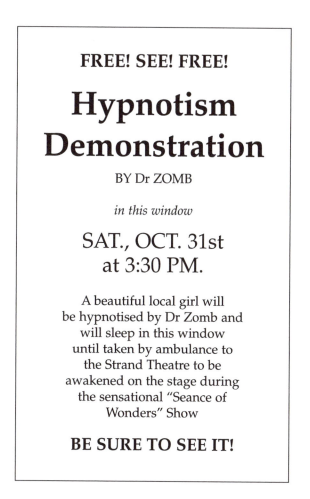

FREE! SEE! FREE!

Hypnotism Demonstration

BY Dr ZOMB

in this window

SAT., OCT. 31st at 3:30 PM.

A beautiful local girl will
be hypnotised by Dr Zomb and
will sleep in this window
until taken by ambulance to
the Strand Theatre to be
awakened on the stage during
the sensational "Seance of
Wonders" Show

BE SURE TO SEE IT!

Be sure to also have in the store window posters calling attention to the hypnotism show at the theater. After all, the basic purpose of the whole thing is to bring in business to your show. Always be alert to your advertising and publicity values.

4. Additional Advertising

Include a box, under your regular ads on the show, in the local newspapers, calling attention to the free hypnotism demonstration in the store window – giving date, time, and place. Also, such can be included in the show's radio announcements over the air. All this additional advertising of "the Window Sleep" will be appreciated by the store that has donated its window as it plugs the store at the same time. Such assures a large crowd being assembled to see the free demonstration.

5. The Hypnotic Subject for the Window Sleep

Use a local girl as the subject for the demonstration. Theater managers frequently use one of their usherettes for this purpose or else run a small classified ad asking for a girl interested in taking part in the hypnotic demonstration. She is paid for her services, and must sign a release form. Girls are to meet in the manager's office a couple of hours before the bally is scheduled to take place. At that time, the hypnotist will select the girl who proves most suitable as a hypnotic subject. Privately, in the office, the girls are hypnotized and the one most responsive is used for the demonstration. Often only one girl will be available, in which event the hypnotist must work with her carefully and entrance her deeply.

The "conditioning" of the girl to be used in the demonstration is important, as the sleep is to run several hours; the success of the hypnosis is vital, as were it to fail it would harm the success of the stage show.

Make it your rule never to enter the store window with an untried subject. By "conditioning" the girl for hypnosis in advance, the performer knows exactly what response he may expect and the demonstration will run smoothly.

6. Window Sleep Details

The length of the sleep should not run more than 5 hours. Longer sleeps have been done, but 5 hours will be found long enough to give full effectiveness, and still not be too difficult for the sleeping girl. Arrange to start the demonstration around 3:30 p.m. This gives the school crowd time to get down to see the free window performance. You want them there, as they are potential customers for the show. Young people like hypnotism.

Have a P.A. System set up in the store window (mike inside window and speakers outside of store) so that the crowd can both see and hear what goes on, and you can talk to them. Music can be played over the P.A. in advance of the demonstration and continued on throughout the afternoon and early evening while girl is sleeping. Occasionally the demonstration can be dressed even more by having a young woman in a nurse's uniform in attendance in the window while girl is sleeping, and an ambulance can be parked out in front of store by the curb. Such "medical handling" builds interest.

In the store window, have both a heater and a fan so that you can regulate the temperature to the sleeping girl's comfort. Do everything possible to make her experience pleasant. Attention to such details are important for smooth presentation of this publicity demonstration.

7. Presentation of the Window Sleep

When you and the girl enter the window, be sure both of you are neatly groomed. She should wear an attractive dress, and you dressed in a business suit. Be professional. All must look high class.

At the appointed time, enter the window and start talking to the crowd over the P.A. Be sure to commence right on schedule. Once you are in the window, just take your time and let the crowd build while you talk to them about hypnosis and the interesting experiments they are going to see at the show. As long as there is something going on, the crowd will stay, and a crowd attracts yet a bigger crowd.

Commence by telling what you intend to do: how a local young lady, whom some may know personally, has volunteered to be the subject in this hypnotic experiment. Explain that you will hypnotize her, and she will be left sleeping in full view in the window until 7:30 p.m., at which time she will be taken from the window, via ambulance, to the stage of the Strand Theater (name of place you are performing that evening) to be awakened from the hypnotic sleep during the show. Whet the public's appetite to see the successful conclusion of the feat. Also, be sure to describe other sensational features they will see when they attend the stage show at the theater that night. Remember, business is business, and show business is a business.

Conduct yourself with dignity in the window. You have a wonderful opportunity for direct advertising here.

The girl is then introduced, and over the mike she is asked if she is willing to be the subject to be hypnotized. After she confirms, she is seated on the side of the bed. You proceed to hypnotize her. Take your time doing this. It is interesting to the watchers, and what they came down to see. In the hypnotizing process in the window, at no time touch the girl yourself. After she is hypnotized, have your assistant lower her to the bed and carefully cover her. Then suggest to the hypnotized girl:

"Adjust yourself in a position of complete comfort to yourself and sleep soundly now. You will sleep soundly and pleasantly, and nothing will bother you or awaken you until I awaken you on the stage of the Strand Theater tonight during the show. Any sounds you hear while you are sleeping in this window will but serve to deepen your sleep."

Leave the girl sleeping peacefully on the bed, turn to the crowd outside the window and comment over mike that you will return from time to time to check on the subject to see that she is sleeping safely. *Always show concern for the girl*. Then, leave the window and leave the store by the back exit. This is best as you can avoid conversation with watchers that way. It increases dramatic value to maintain your aesthetic distance as a hypnotist.

Occasionally, throughout the afternoon and early evening, drop into the window to inspect the sleeping girl. While there, you can give suggestions that she can move her body in any positions she desires for comfort. Stay but a few moments on each visit. Make your professional observations and then leave. The last time you come, say to the subject, "You have only an hour or so more to sleep now when they will come and move you to the theater. You will sleep comfortably in the lobby for awhile, and then I will awaken you on the stage. As they move you from the bed, it will send you down deeper and deeper to sleep in deep hypnosis, and you will not be disturbed in any way."

8. Concluding the Window Sleep

At the arranged-for time, have ambulance attendants come to the store window, place the girl on a rolling stretcher, and carry her to the waiting ambulance to drive her to the theater. She sleeps right on, and you need not be on hand for her removal from the window. Indeed, it is better showmanship not to be. Have the ambulance turn on its siren as it drives through the streets en route to the theater.

The girl is then driven directly to the theater in the ambulance and rolled on the stretcher into the theater lobby. During the show (I usually plan it near the middle of my performance), the attendants are requested to roll the hypnotized girl down the aisle and bring her on stage. You then awaken her giving these suggestions:

"At 3.30 this afternoon you were hypnotized in the window of (give name of store), and have been sleeping ever since. It is now (state time as you look at your watch). I am going to awaken you now from your long hypnotic trance, and you will feel just fine. And it is interesting that it will seem to you that you have been asleep for only a few minutes, while actually it has been hours. Hypnosis has the power to distort the sense of time. When you awaken you will feel wonderfully well, rested, and happy. And you will tell your friends how good you feel. They will marvel at your remarkable experience."

Awaken the girl from the hypnosis. Help her to her feet. Thank her and have the audience applaud the young lady for her part in the demonstration. Dismiss her from the stage, and your show moves on.

Effectively advertised and presented, "the Window Sleep" will be found to have excellent publicity value.

Other Hypnotic Publicity Stunts

In addition to the sleeping girl in the store window, I have, on occasion, tried other such ballies; all have proven effective.

The Hypnotic Bicycle Ride

For this bally, a bike is placed in the store window, mounted upright on a stand so that it will be solid and yet have the rear wheel supported so that it will revolve freely.

The subject is seated on the bike, hypnotized, and is commanded to commence a bicycle ride. It is suggested that he is taking a long, enjoyable ride in the country, and will travel on his bike up hill and dale until he awakened from the hypnosis. It is suggested that he will not become tired in anyway, that he will rest and coast when he wishes to, and will continue his bike ride entirely as he elects.

The hypnotized subject commences pumping the bicycle, and you leave him in the window peddling the hours away until he is removed, still in hypnosis, from the bike by attendants and is taken to the theater lobby, placed on a cot, covered with a blanket, and is awakened on the stage during the show.

The Hypnotic Fisherman

The subject is hypnotized in the store window, seated in a chair. In front of him, on the floor, is a bucket of water. He is handed over a rod to which is attached a length of fishline with a weight on its end. It is suggested that he is sitting on the bank of a stream and is having a wonderful time fishing. Suggestions are given that he will play with the fish every time he gets a bite, and will reel the fish in when he hooks it. He will then remove the fish from the hook and place it in his fishing basket, then re-bait the hook, cast out again, and thus catch fish after fish until he awakens on stage during the show.

When the subject is taken from the window and brought to the theater, place him at the side of the stage and he continues fishing all through the performance. Awaken him just before the climax of the show. It's a riot.

The Hypnotic Three-Ring Circus

When the store window is large in size and the subjects are available, all three of these demonstrations can be presented simultaneously. Use boy subjects for the "Bicycle Ride" and "Hypnotic Fishing", and girl for sleeping in the bed. Give the hypnotized girl the center spot, with the boy subjects stationed on each side of her in the window.

Another stunt I have found effective, as a hypnotic bally, is to hypnotize a good piano player and have him play tunes throughout the afternoon until dehypnotized on the stage. While playing my show at the Manila Grand Opera House in the Philippines, a hypnotized three-piece combo was used in the window. Very effective.

I recall an amusing incident that occurred while presenting "the Window Sleep" in Klamath Falls, Oregon. There was a group of gentlemen pranksters in that city, who called themselves "the Cave Men". They dressed as primitive men and did all kind of strange stunts, just for the fun of it. They played a prank on me.

The girl was sleeping peacefully in a store window. All was going well, so I left for awhile. On returning to the window, the bed was empty and the girl was gone! I was told that during my absence "the Cave Men" had carted her away. Trying to locate her was a bit of a job. I finally found her sleeping in another store window across the city.

The girl slept on, entirely oblivious to her manhandling. When she was awakened on the stage, she felt fine and was surprised to learn she had been moved.

What had happened had Klamath Falls buzzing. Business in the theater that night had them standing in line around the block.

One season, while touring Canada, Delight and I hired a young woman, named Erna, to tour with us. She asked for a job, so we accepted her. Eventually it led to her marriage with Donn. They have been a happy couple ever since.

Erna was a remarkable hypnotic somnambulist who could render her body insensible to pain. On occasion, I presented "the Window Sleep" leaving Erna sleeping on a bed of nails, Hindu Fakir fashion, as the feat is performed in India. Erna is the only person I ever found who could perform this amazing publicity stunt.

Chapter Twelve
Donn Wood & Erna

Donn Wood was a young man of 19 when he came to visit me. Donn lived in Los Gatos while I lived in Palo Alto, cities not overly distant from each other in Central California. He asked if he might join my show and be my assistant. Donn had a good knowledge of magic and hypnotism, and his reading of my then just published book, *The Encyclopedia of Genuine Stage Hypnotism*, by Abbott's Magic Company, had stirred his interest. I needed an assistant, so I said "Okay".

Donn stayed with me, sharing in my adventures as my assistant, for many years until he was drafted into the U.S. Army during World War II. The call of the Military had to be answered, so Donn had to leave us while Delight and I were touring our show in Canada. It was then that we met Erna.

As part of our Dr. Zomb Show advertising campaign, we often presented "The Hypnotic Window Sleep" to publicize the show. The theater manager would seek a girl willing to perform the stunt. Erna volunteered.

Erna did a fine job. She was good looking and slept like a baby when hypnotized. She slept for hours without even a quiver. Her sleeping so peacefully in the store window helped us pack the theater that night.

The midnight show concluded, Erna asked if she might go along with us and perform "The Window Sleep". It was a great convenience to have someone ready on hand to do the feat. So we agreed to have her travel with us. Delight and Erna became good friends, during the course of which Delight showed Erna a photo of Donn. Erna thought he looked like a cute guy and asked if she might write to Donn and get acquainted. She did, and Donn replied.

Donn's military work had him stationed in Seattle, and when we concluded our tour, we went there to visit some of Delight's relatives living in that big city. Erna came along. As Donn was stationed in Seattle, it was a perfect meeting place. They met and fell in love. When the war ended and Donn was dismissed from service, the couple married and still are.

After their marriage, Donn and Erna went out on their own and developed their own show. Donn took the stage name of Merlin.

Somehow Donn came to favor presenting a mindreading act along with hypnotic presentations. He had long admired the great magician, Alexander, who played the role costumed as a Hindu prince. Alexander had long retired, yet Donn managed to locate him. He and Donn became fast friends, and it was agreed that he might carry on the Alexander type of presentation. Donn did, and did it well. Shortly thereafter Alexander died, and he must have smiled at seeing his tradition carried on.

The show Donn and Erna created, as a loving team, presented a first act of mentalism and a second act of hypnotism. Worked fine. Donn and Erna toured the show for 20 years.

Finally, deciding "enough is enough", they closed the show and bought a home in Sequam, Washington State, not too far distant from where they had first met. Opening a restaurant followed. They run it successfully to this day, a continuous happy couple. Delight had proved herself a darn good matchmaker.

Chapter Thirteen

Spook Show Days

Spook Shows were popular as a Midnight Show in theaters from late in the 1930s into the early 1950s. Following our marriage, Delight and I toured playing many Spook Shows. However, for the beginning episode of my acquaintance with Spook Shows, I'll have to go back in time to 1934, when George Tecmeyer called me from his office. Tecmeyer was manager for the Fox Stanford Theater in Palo Alto, California. Having recently completed playing a consecutive series of 52 Mickey Mouse Club Saturday Matinees for him I knew it was about magic.

Arriving at his office, George told me of a stage show he had booked, which was to play at midnight a couple of weeks hence. He showed me the show's press material on his desk. It was El Wyn's Midnite Spook Party. He was quite excited about it, and felt it was a great idea to bring in extra revenue at the box office without interfering with regular hour picture playing. It allowed an opportunity to add to the theater gross receipts. Business is business.

Tecmeyer thought it might be something of interest to me, and an opportunity to make good money in show business. We went over the El Wyn advertising materials together.

The campaign was strong, and at El Wyn's Midnite Show the theater was packed. It was SRO both lower floor and balcony. It was a young audience with fellows out with their girlfriends plus a smattering of Stanford University students. The audience was expectant, as no one had the slightest idea what a Spook Party would be like that said, "If you come alone you'll be afraid to walk home!"

Following the conclusion of the last regular movie, the theater was dumped, and the huge crowd which had gathered out in front came in to see the midnight show. It was 12:15 a.m. before all were seated and the performance got underway. The theater darkened, and the horror film started. This ran 90 minutes, so it was 1:45 before it was Spook Party time.

The curtains opened upon a dimly lit stage with a dark blue backdrop upon which was painted a huge demon face. El Wyn entered, dressed in tuxedo and wearing a white turban. He did a good show.

El Wyn spoke about spirits and said there was an invisible ghost upon the stage, which he would prove existed. He placed a sheet of glass across the back of two chairs and rested a lamp chimney in its center. He commanded the ghost to move it. Slowly the chimney crawled across the surface of the glass and toppled into his hands. Replaced in the center of the sheet of glass the effect was repeated, and finally it toppled off the edge of the glass and crashed onto the floor.

Two washbasins were nested together and placed on the surface of the sheet of glass. The top basin was filled with water. The ghost was commanded to move the basins. The one with water rose into the air, tilted, and dumped its contents into the lower basin. The floating basin then returned to renest into the lower basin.

The modus operandi of these tricks was simple but effective. The objects were moved by thin black fishlines stretched across the stage wing to wing, which assistants manipulated.

This is a sketch I drew showing how the black fishline goes across the stage, each end held by an assistant, in the wings. The assistants can sweep the lamp chimney off the glass plate, by moving the black fishline forward from the wings. The black fishline is invisible to the audience where the effect is presented in red lights.

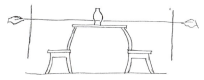

El Wyn's Floating and Water Pouring Basins operated on the same principle, i.e., black fishlines held by assistants in the wings of the stage.

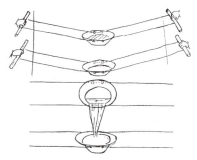

85

The stage lights came up, and El Wyn went into a series of effects, all of a "spirit" nature: Dancing Handkerchief, Winking Light Bulb, Walking Away from Shadow Illusion, Floating Table seance fashion. Spirit Writing on slates was then demonstrated. It was a true Spook Party.

Then came the blackout climax of the show in which the ghosts appeared. Luminous ghosts were seen on stage and skeletons danced. A large ghost flew out over the audience, and eerie heads staked the aisles. Some ghosts even appeared in the balcony. The entire ghostly sequence was presented in a totally black theater while creepy music blasted out over loudspeakers. The audience screamed and yelled. It was scary. The boys loved the way the "ghosts" made their girlfriends snuggle for protection.

The ghosts were accomplished by luminous cloth draped on assistants, and the skeletons were drawn with luminous paint on black costumes. Some of the ghosts wore cloth strips dangling from long black rods waved over the heads of the audience in the blackout theater. Meanwhile, hired boys, their faces smeared with luminous cream, walked up and down the aisles.

Finally, there was a pistol shot on stage, and all the ghosts cleared out on this cue. There was a burst of flash powder in the footlights, which caused the luminous painting of the demon head on the backdrop to glow eerily.

The front curtain closed. The creepy music stopped. The house lights came on, and the show was over. El Wyn never came back for a final bow. The audience marched out of the theater well satisfied they had had "the yell scared out of them" at the Spook Party.

During those days of the first spook show, the audience did not know what to expect, so El Wyn got away with his ghosts in the audience. In later years, as the kids got wise to the idea it had to be modified, as the ghosts got grabbed, and the luminous faces were tripped in the aisles. It became a hazardous situation, but at first it was great fun. Also, subsequent spook shows found it better to start with the stage show and allow the horror movie to come after. This really worked better.

I was introduced to El Wyn by Tecmeyer, and he offered me the chance to take out a unit of his show. I would have loved to have done so, but as I was attending college at the time I had to decline. However, my friend, Arthur Bull of Oakland, saw the opportunity and developed his own show. He worked under the name of Francisco's Spook Frolic. He took the name Francisco, from living so close to San Francisco. Francisco toured with his spook show, playing top movie houses for 12 years prior to his death. He did very well.

Other magicians such as Bill Neff, Mel Roy, Herman Weber, George Marquis, Ray-Mond, and the Baker Brothers with their "Dr. Silkini Show" got on the band wagon of spook shows and began touring the country. The Silkini Show made a deal with Universal Pictures to feature a Frankenstein Monster segment in their show. It proved great box office.

Bill Neff even had Bela Lugosi join him for a season. Spook Show business was booming throughout the late 1930s and through the 1940s.

Personally, I did not enter my Spook Show Days until 1941. College, working with a mentalist named Mandu, and performing my pantomime (drunk) act for booking agents in San Francisco kept me busy. It was while working in a defense job building transmitters for the Navy that I suddenly got an urge to try my hand at midnight shows.

I saw an ad in Bob Nelson's Catalogue (Nelson Enterprises of Columbus, Ohio) offering a Spook Show Advertising Kit. I sent for it. It contained ad mats, press stories, and told how to exploit a Midnight Spook Show. I took the material to my friend, Hal Honore, manager of the Fox Theater in Redwood City, and asked what he thought of the idea. He thought it was great!

First, we had to decide what stage name I should work under. It had to be a "doctor", of course, as every spook show performer was a doctor in those days. Lying on Hal's desk there happened to be the exploitation sheets of a movie which had just come out, called *I Walked With A Zombie*. I latched on to this and blurted out, "Why not call me Dr. Zombie?" We thought about it as the idea sounded properly spooky for a midnight show name. But Hal didn't quite like the "zombie" ring, so we finally decided on the name Dr. Zomb. The name caught on, and I worked my show under it for a full ten years.

Hal and I picked up some Spook Show admats from Nelson Enterprises in Ohio. Bob Nelson had used these in his own show. They featured "The Great London Ghost Show". As I performed hypnotism, we used the same mats and altered them to "The Great London Hypnotic Seance". I played my first Midnight Spook Show under that title, while dressed in a surgeon's gown, as Dr. Zomb.

To fit the advertising, I added some Spirit Seance effects to the show, while volunteers watched on stage. I later changed my advertising to "Seance of Wonders".

As the initial show, at the Fox in Redwood City, made money District Manager, Harry Seipel booked me in other Fox Theaters. Before long I found myself doing a lot of work for Fox, as well as for United Artists, and other theater chains.

That's how my Spook Show Days all started.

Using Thayer's "Altar of Sacrifice"
Illusion for a season, Dr. Zomb
burned up a maiden at every show.

Chapter Fourteen

East Indian Miracles

On Halloween of 1952, following a performance at the Orpheum Theater in Seattle, I said farewell to "The Seance Of Wonders". It was a fitting climax to nearly 12 years of touring as Dr. Zomb. I wanted to move on now and present my show under my own name.

Various magicians were working a full evening show under sponsorships such as Lions Clubs, Kiwanis, Rotary, etc. These Service Club groups all have charity projects for which they need funds. A magic show provides an evening of family entertainment which is an easy way for them to raise money, as all they have to do is furnish the auditorium and sell the tickets.

I entered the field.

The first full evening show I produced was called "East Indian Miracles". India – "The Land of Magic" – intrigued me. It seemed an ideal theme to develop a show around. There was an exclusive India Store in Palo Alto. Delight and I went shopping there.

A couple of 9 x 9 curtains, showing the Indian "Tree of Life", provided an effective background to the show, when set up against a black backdrop. Two 6-foot gold-gilded idol figures completed the set. Appropriate costumes, East Indian designed props in brass, and the tricks presented with Hindu-type patter and music developed into a stage show that was showy and different.

My close friend, Donn Wood, who later toured the nation as Merlin, with his own full evening show, helped me create and present the show, both on and off stage. The first act was magic given an oriental look. It was programmed as "The Physical Magic of the Fakir". The second act was hypnotism which I presented as "The Mental Magic of the Yogi". It was an appropriate show for "East Indian Miracles".

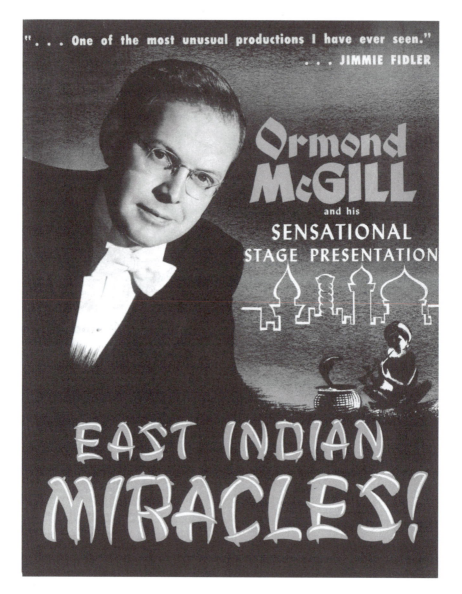

The advertising for the show was fittingly East Indian. The well-known columnist, Jimmie Fidler, caught the show and gave it a plug in his column, so I used his quote on my ads.

The show played well and I used it for awhile, but frankly it was just too much work for "one nighters" on the road, so in due time Delight and I retired it. It has remained at rest these many years, although some features I retained. One routine I always liked was the opening we designed of producing "fire balls" from a cloth bag. The effect went like this:

Center stage was a brass urn. The magician entered carrying a Hindu Carpet Bag. It was shown inside and out. A pass was made at the urn, and a flash of fire and smoke belched forth.

Reaching into the smoke a handful was caught and placed within the bag, immediately being withdrawn as a flaming ball of fire held on the performer's hand. It burned on the hand, was tossed in the air, and then deposited in a brass bowl held by assistant. Two further "balls of fire" were produced in the same manner. The flaming bowl was carried backstage by an assistant who put out the fire by clamping on a cover. The trick worked fine and got "East Indian Miracles" on its way. The modus operandi was simple.

The Hindu Carpet Bag was designed as an oversized "Egg Bag" having an inverted inner pocket in which the three "fire balls" could be held gripped in hand outside through the cloth, and the bag turned inside out and shown empty.

To produce the balls, all you had to do was release them, one by one, to drop into the bottom of the bag and set them aflame as they were removed from the bag. To produce the fire, a match-striking surface (sandpaper) was sewn inside the bag. The "fire balls" were turned from hardwood peppered with holes bored over their surface. In each of these little holes bits of asbestos wick was stuffed and clipped down flush to the surface of ball. Through the center of each ball, a matchstick size hole was drilled. In this, a wood kitchen match was placed leaving the head end of match extending.

Just before coming on stage, lighter fluid was sprinkled on the wicks. To produce a ball of fire, all you have to do is strike the match head on the sandpaper within the bag, and out comes the ball aflame. It will not burn your hand, as time is not allowed for that. The burning ball held flat on hand causes the flames to rise upward, so the underside does not get hot too rapidly. When it gets warm, simply toss in air, and then over into bowl held by assistant. All three "fire balls" are produced in this manner, the assistant then taking off the blazing bowl backstage to snuff out the fire. While the hardwood balls will become charred they are unharmed, and may be used over and over in performing the trick.

The center stage urn that produces the fire and smoke has a three-way flash pot within it, electrically operated from backstage. When I used it to make the urn belch forth fire and smoke, each time required, all Delight had to do in the wings was flick a switch. A mixture of flash powder and gun powder was used.

To climax the "Fire Balls Effect", I created the production of a giant "Fire Bowl" on a taboret. The method I used was based on the "Westgate Bowl Production" principle. It played like this.

Effect

A draped taboret (tripod) is on stage, on which a large brass cone (with open top) rests. The brass cone is shown empty and replaced on taboret. Reaching through the top of the shallow cone, the cloth is gripped and pulled directly upwards, and a large bowl of fire appears on top of the taboret.

Modus Operandi

The apparatus is arranged so the bowl can be lowered into the taboret, the bottom of the bowl resting upon cross supports between the tripod's legs. The taboret has a large opening in its top through which the bowl may be lowered or brought up, as desired.

The bowl used is made of brass, and has a handle across its top inside, so it can be pulled up as required, and on the bottom of the bowl is a catch arrangement, so when given a twist it will lock in position and remain resting on top of taboret.

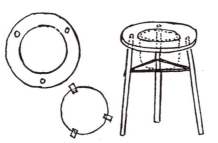

GIANT FIRE BOWL
in first position
under table.

Detail of table construction for
appearance of GIANT FIRE BOWL

Set up for produc-
tion of GIANT FIRE
BOWL . . . . Bowl
positioned beneath
tabletop covered with
cloth drape . . . .
Cone rests on top
draped tabletop as
illustrated.

GIANT FIRE BOWL
in second position when locked
in place on top of table.

Detail of locking arrangement of
fastening GIANT FIRE BOWL on
tabletop.

Fire Lighting Mechanism. Match inserted between two match striking surface,
encircled with rubberband. Striking mechanism attached to underside of draped
cloth over tabletop, and opposite end to inside of GIANT FIRE BOWL. Match
lights when table cloth is drawn through top of cone . . . other end of match
attached to inside of fire bowl -- falling back and igniting lighter-fluid soaked
wicking causing GIANT FIRE BOWL to become aflame.

Sketch I drew showing construction of my GIANT FIRE BOWL PRODUCTION ON TOP
OF TABLE . . . INCLUDING OPERATION, AND FIRE LIGHTING ARRANGEMENT

The cloth used to drape the top of the taboret is a 24" x 24" square of velvet. Attached to the center of the underside of the drape is arranged a "striker" for the match (cutout matchbox sides, clipped face-to-face encircled by rubber band). A match is attached to a length of wire (with suitable holder) attached to the inside of the bottom of the bowl, and around the bottom of the bowl is asbestos wick material, which is soaked with lighter fluid when used.

To set the effect for operation, the bowl is lowered down into the tripod, lighter fluid sprinkled on the wick material, a match placed in the "striker" underside of the cloth, and the cloth then draped flat over the top of the taboret. It appears simply as a skeleton tripod with a cloth drape. The shallow brass cone is then rested on the top surface of the tripod. The trick is ready to go!

When you want to produce the large bowl of fire, just pick up the brass cone and show it is empty, and then return it to the top of the tripod. Immediately, reach through the opening in the top of the cone, grip the handle inside of the bowl along with the cloth drape and lift both upwards. The catch projecting on the sides of the bottom edge of the bowl prevents it from rising higher than the surface of the taboret. The bowl is then given a twist, and the catches lock it firmly in position on the tripod's top (bowl appears to be resting on top of taboret). The action follows right on in a continuous movement, and the cloth is pulled directly up and out of the opening in the top of the brass cone. This pulling actions causes the match to light, and the burning match then drops back into the bowl, igniting the material. A blazing bowl of fire has been produced.

The effect of this action on the audience is that a shallow cone, with a large opening at top, is shown empty and replaced on the tripod; then, the drape is pulled through it and tossed aside. Immediately, flames appear to be coming out of the top of the cone which, on being lifted, reveals a large "Bowl Of Fire" produced on top of the skeleton tripod.

It is a startling production.

Fire effects fit well with East Indian Magic. Another one I created to use in this show was "Sacrificial Cremation". I always found the illusion of "Burning a Girl Alive" very effective; however, the coffin method was too large to conveniently troupe, so I invented this method. Abbott's Magic Company manufactured the illusion for me and put it on the market under my credit. It is still selling today, and produced the cremation effect in compact form: the magician appears to burn up the head of a girl.

"Sacrificial Cremation" is a mini-illusion based on "The Square Circle Production" (semi-black art production box principle), but is designed quite differently.

The apparatus consists of a four-legged stand with a half circle cutout on top, so the person kneeling beneath the top can rest their chin on the surface. Three cylinders of graduated sizes are used. These are made of metal and nest inside each other. They are large enough to easily go over a person's head, as the chin rests on the top of the stand.

The first cylinder (innermost one) is "the fire cylinder". This has a tray recessed about 2" from the top in which burning material is placed (asbestos wicking soaked in lighter fluid). This cylinder is covered with black felt; its rear side is flattened and a skull mask mounted in the center.

The second cylinder is unprepared, and fits easily over "the fire cylinder".

The third cylinder (outside one) has an opening cut in the front side, so a view of the interior can be had. The inside of this cylinder is lined with black felt to match the black of "the fire cylinder".

The last item required to produce the illusion is a torch, which is used to apparently set fire to the girl's head. The handle of the torch is brass tubing arranged to telescope with a spring inside to keep it extended; the tip of the torch is wrapped with asbestos wicking and soaked with lighter fluid. The effect to the audience is that when the torch is lit and placed into the cylinder, it goes in deeply, although actually it only touches the shallow "fire tray" in the center cylinder.

In performing the illusion, the nested cylinders rest on top of the stand, with the cutout front of the outer cylinder facing the audience. The skull mask of the "fire cylinder" faces the rear, inside, so only the black surface shows in the course of performing the illusion.

The unprepared center cylinder is first removed and shown. It is just a trifle higher than the other two, so it can be easily gripped to pull out. This allows the black surface of the "fire cylinder" to show through the opening of the front cylinder – the "black art" effect being that the audience has a view inside. It appears empty, viewed through the opening of the outer cylinder. The center cylinder is then replaced, and the outer cylinder is removed and shown empty. It is then replaced. The effect to the audience is that only two metal cylinders are used in the illusion, and both have been shown as unprepared.

A girl then comes forward and is introduced as "the victim of the Hindu Fire Sacrifice". Meanwhile, another assistant lifts the three-nested cylinders off the stand and gives a half turn to the group of cylinders he is holding. This brings the skull of "the fire cylinder" to the front when replaced. The girl kneels down and rests her head on top of the stand (half circle cutout allows her head to thus rest in the middle of the top of the stand). The three-nested cylinders are then placed over her head (her head goes inside of "fire cylinder", so she is completely protected). The torch is set aflame and pushed down inside of cylinders, apparently setting on fire the head of the girl. Actually, just the wicking in the tray of "the first cylinder" burns although the telescoping torch gives the appearance of being pushed way down inside of the cylinders, igniting the girl's head. Flames rise from the top of the cylinders. The effect is spectacular!

After the flames subside and smoke is rising, the inner unprepared cylinder is removed, which allows the skull face (now facing front) to be seen through the opening in outer cylinder. The effect causes a gasp, but it is obvious that the skull face is but an illusion, so no one takes it too seriously. Otherwise the effect would be too gruesome. After all, this is an entertaining illusion, not a murder!

The inner cylinder is replaced, and the assistant removes the three-nested cylinders (all together) from the girl's head resting on top of stand. She is okay. She rises and comes forward for a bow.

Occasionally, I would present this illusion using a person from the audience. In such an instance, the volunteer would be on stage helping in another trick on the conclusion of which it would be casually remarked, "You did so well in that trick that you have qualified yourself to be the victim in the "Fire God Sacrifice of India". That way you have a "captured" volunteer to perform with. Otherwise, I can assure you, willing volunteers for this effect are few and far between. The spectator used in the illusion will be completely in the dark (no pun intended) as to how the illusion works. Inside those cylinders all is very dark!

The second act of the show was provocative, as it presented a hypnotic show without once mentioning hypnotism. Every demonstration was presented as a demonstration performed by the Yogis.

It is interesting to observe how adaptable the hypnotism show can be; as long as the demonstrations are consistent in theme, hypnotic experiments can be presented under any causation. When I did my Dr. Zomb "Midnight Hypnotic Seance", the theme was Voodoo and Zombies. Worked fine! When I did my "East Indian Miracles" show, the theme of which was "the Physical Magic of the Fakirs" and "the Mental Magic of the Yogi", it too worked fine.

Whatever you believe in is magic.

Chapter Fifteen

South Sea Island Magic

The next full evening show I produced was called "South Sea Island Magic". It is a show I still present. Delight and I played our show in Hawaii several times. We felt at home there. We liked the people, the Island atmosphere, the Hawaiian music. One time while listening to "Hawaii Calls" on the radio, the orchestra played the tune, "South Sea Island Magic". It struck me as a perfect title and theme for a magic show. We got busy and designed the show.

We took fishnet and Hawaiian prints and used them for table covers. We decorated the magic apparatus Polynesian style. We converted "East India Miracles" into "South Sea Island Magic".

The show went on, and I used this introduction. Against the background music of "Song of the Islands", it is pattered:

> Imagine this scene, ladies and gentlemen: it is a balmly day, the fragrance of flowers is in the air, the soft sound of the surf is heard in the distance, and guests are gathered upon the verandah of an island house to watch the magician. You are the guests. So, come with me on an imaginary journey across the blue Pacific and witness South Sea Island Magic.

Delight and I played this show many times, under sponsorships in America. Then came an opportunity to take it to Tahiti. We were delighted, as it gave us a chance to delve deeper into South Sea Island lore. Our Australian magician friend, Ken Littlewood, had played Tahiti several times with an act in hotels there. He introduced us to a promoter, Louis Akamai, a German–Tahitian, who spoke fluent English, French, and Tahitian. Louis Akamai booked us for a tour. It was a pioneer tour of a magic show to

101

play the Tuamotu Archipelago. Taking our "South Sea Island Magic" out to play the south seas was much like taking "coals to Newcastle". But, it went fine. I doubt very much in these native islands people gave much thought as to whether it was South Sea Island magic or otherwise. To them it was just magic – a treat to be enjoyed.

Delight and I left the airport in San Francisco and made a direct flight to Papeete, Tahiti. We arrived at 5:30 a.m. Looking out as the plane pulled into the airport, we were amazed to see a band waiting, flags waving, and the airport jammed with people. We glanced at each other and commented, "Maybe the President of France is coming in."

As we disembarked from the plane, we found what all the fuss was about. It wasn't for the President of France, it was for us! Our show was the first full evening magic show to play these islands. We were celebrities. Louis Akamai was quite a promoter, and he had arranged for us to perform "The Blindfold Car Drive", right at the airport on our arrival. A car was waiting, and judging from the crowd assembled at this early hour, time has little meaning in Tahiti.

I dug into my suitcase and brought out my Magic Blindfold, so was all set to go.

We got out of the plane amidst music and fanfare, and were taken to a little French convertible of variable speeds. They showed me how to operate it, and I took a practice spin. The crowd gathered around. I brought out the blindfold and let various natives try it on. It was accepted as okay. Taking it back, I slapped it over my eyes, and it tied behind my head. I got behind the wheel of the car, and while local police cleared the way, I drove about the airport. Not too easy, as these people seemed to insist on hopping in front of the car, as a blindfolded driver drove the car. Oh well, no one got hurt. Ending the drive, I whipped off the blindfold and passed it out for examination. All okay. There was a stunned silence. Then an ovation. We were set for a great tour in Tahiti.

We played several spots on Tahiti, and then moved on to Moorea. They gave us some entertainment there. How those Tahitian girls can shake it up as the boys bang upon the drums.

Following Moorea, the show went to the Island of Raiatea, then over to Tahaa. The only way to get from Raiatea to Tahaa is by a small motor boat. I will never forget how it skimmed over the surface of the coral reef following winding channels.

Tahaa is a swampy place and big natives carried us to shore. The show was set for early next morning, and all the night boats arrived from all parts of the island. The sun had scarcely come up when the show started – to a packed house. Entirely SRO. Louis Akamai was our interpreter on all the shows, and he did a great job. Tahitians liked the magic and flocked up on stage to be hypnotized. They were a lively bunch of subjects. Everyone had a great time!

From Tahaa, we flew by seaplane to play on romantic Boro Boro, and then back to Tahiti for more shows there.

It was November of 1969 that we commenced our tour of these South Sea Islands. It was an amazing experience. Delight and I saw in the New Year of 1970 there. How little did I realize the heartache of her death that decade was to bring. But, at the time, when we left Tahiti our hearts were singing, our suitcases bulged with fine specimen sea shells we had collected, our necks were swathed in garlands of shell leis, and we left the airport of Papeete to return to the States amidst the smiles of many new friends we had made along the way.

The plane rose into a clear blue sky, and we saw the lush island of Tahiti drop away to become a dot in the ocean, and then fade from sight. We never returned again, and, without Delight, I never will.

How well I remember South Sea Island moonlight nights with Delight, as we walked along the lagoon, in the land where they called me, "La Roi de la Magic".

Chapter Sixteen

Military Daze

During my stage career, I went through four wars: World War I, World War II, Korea, and Vietnam without getting involved with the military, yet I held the rank of Colonel in the army for awhile.

Following touring in Australia, Arnold Furst booked me in the Far East Military Theater playing bases in the Philippines, Okinawa, Japan, and Korea. My rank came through at Clark Air Force Base which lies north of Manila. It made possible getting preferred air transportation and officer accommodations. Arriving in Tokyo, U.S. Army Special Services sent me on a tour of Korea.

It was 1955. The active Korean War was over, although border patrols still maintained vigil, and many military installations dotted that country. Plane loads of recruits came in daily, men assigned to Korean duty for two-year stints. Army life in Korea was on the rustic side. It brought me some unexpected thrills, not to mention chills.

I was transported by airplane from encampment to encampment to entertain the soldiers. The "flyboys" were young fellows and the planes old single-engine jobs. Somehow the pilots seemed to take a delight in using them to play leapfrog with each other high up in the air. They thought it great fun. I didn't.

Back in Japan, the "fun" continued on the ground this time, as I was booked to play the radar sites. These were stationed on mountain tops in Japan, and the only way to reach them was via narrow winding roads, the edges of which dropped off in sheer cliffs down to the ocean lying far below with waves dashing against jagged coastline.

What fun the truck drivers had making the trip up to the sites, speeding around blind curves with wheels just barely missing going over the brink into the drink. To me, at the time, it was as unnerving as the plane flights. Actually, the boys were darn good in both air and on land, otherwise I would not be here to share this autobiography with you.

Presenting magic in out-of-the-way places in the Far East Military Theater was anything but formal. The "theater" most often was the mess hall. If there was a stage, it was usually a raised platform at the end of the room. I had to design my show to be practical under such conditions, using very little equipment. A deck of cards came in handy.

One trick I worked up using a deck of cards was a demonstration of apparent ESP that a volunteer did. Besides the card the only apparatus the trick required was a large glass marble. In the presentation, I called it a "crystal ball" to aid in the experiment. It proved a hit:

Effect

A volunteer is invited on stage to try his hand at an experiment in ESP. A party comes up and takes a seat, and you explain you will give him the "crystal" which he is to use in attempting to name a selected card someone in the audience is concentrating on.

You go into the audience and have a card selected at random. No one sees the card but the person in the audience, who is instructed to concentrate on his card, step-by-step, thinking first of the color, then the suit whether it is a number card or a court card, and finally of the complete card.

The magic is to divine the card. While the volunteer on stage gazes into the "crystal," you work right along with the person climaxing in revealing what card is being thought of. ESP!

Modus Operandi

The effect develops in the minds of the spectators via your skill presentation. The modus operandi is nothing more than to "force" a desired card on the assisting person in the audience, so you secretly know what the card is, although no one knows that you know. The force is easy. Use this presentation:

"There is much interest in ESP these days. I would like to provide the opportunity for some person in the audience to test their own ESP talents. If possible, I would like some person to volunteer who feels they are somewhat psychic, and who may have had flashes of insights on occasion, such as somehow knowing who is phoning when the telephone rings. May we have a volunteer."

A person comes on stage and takes a seat facing the audience.

"Thank you for volunteering [sir or madam]. As mentioned, we are going to try together an experiment in ESP in which you will attempt to read the mind of someone seated in the front row of the audience. In this experiment in telepathy, you will function as the receiver, while the other person will be the transmitter. Who would you like to be the transmitter? Please point to some person seated in the front row, and that person we will use."

Volunteer points to person of his (or her) choice.

"Very good to [person in audience]. And you, sir, I trust, are willing to be the transmitter. For this experiment, we will use a deck of playing cards, as these are symbols we are all familiar with, and are easy to concentrate upon. We will use this deck of cards. Please look it over and shuffle thoroughly."

Take cards into audience and hand over to spectator to inspect and shuffle. As cards are returned to you, casually run through a few of the cards, as you comment, "Very good, you mixed them well." In this action, you spot the top card of the deck and remember it. "I will run through the cards and tell me to stop any place you wish, and we will use that card for the experiment."

Start pulling out cards in small groups at random below the top card, so when spectator tells you to stop, the card you know is still on top of the pack. Have person take this card, as his selected card. This "force" is simple and effective. Comment, "All right now, hold that card up before your eyes and concentrate on it. Try to visualize it in three stages: first color, then suit, then whether it is a number card or a court card."

Place remainder of deck in pocket and return to stage. Stand beside spectator seated there. Speak to the volunteer:

"At this moment in space and time you have no idea what card the transmitter is thinking of. Is that true?" [Volunteer affirms].

"Good. That means your mind is clear of any preconceived idea as to what the card might be, so whatever you receive about it will be entirely your own impressions. To help you do this, we are going to use a crystal ball [pick up "crystal ball" and display]. A crystal ball provides an oriental method of centering the mind and causing psychic visions to appear within the sphere. Using it will aid you in performing this experiment. Here, hold it in your hands and gaze into it."

Hand over "crystal ball" to volunteer to hold in his lap. Comment:

"We are ready now to commence this experiment in telepathy. I will try it right along with you, as perchance I have had more experience than you have with such things which will help your success. It will be interesting to see what percentage of success you do have. If you are ready, let us now begin."

To volunteer on stage: "Look deeply into the crystal now and tell me what you see or what comes into your mind as most promising."

To man in audience: "Think now of the color of the card you are transmitting. Think whether it is red or black."

To volunteer on stage: "What do you feel is the color of the card he is concentrating upon – is it red or is it black? What impression do you get?"

You are using a psychological forcing of the color upon the volunteer here in the way you say "Red or black". Name the correct color of the card first each time. If the volunteer names the color "RED", in this instance, pat him on the back and say, "Very good, you are doing great!" If volunteer names the color wrong, and says "BLACK", in this instance, continue right on and say, "You see black. Let me look in the crystal and see what I see. Hmmmm. I see the color red." To spectator in audience concentrating on the card, say, "Is red correct, sir?" Transmitter affirms. To volunteer on stage, simply say, "Quite alright. This is your first time to try this. Your success is a matter of percentage. Let us try for the suit now."

To transmitter in audience, say. "Think of the suit of the card now, sir. Is it a heart or is it a diamond?"

Again you are using a psychological force of choice by naming the correct suit first. If spectator names the suit correctly, appear greatly pleased and say, "Great. You see how you improve with practice." If volunteer names the wrong suit, simply say, "Let me try my hand at it again and see how I come out using the crystal. Hmmmm. Somehow I see a heart, it beats before me. Is that correct, sir?" Transmitter affirms it is. Continue right on . . . .

To volunteer on stage, "Look deep into the crystal and tell me whether you think it is a 'number card' or a 'court card'? What do you think it is, a numbered card or a court card?"

Again the psychological force of choice is used. If volunteer says, "Numbered card" (which is most likely as there are more number cards in the deck than court cards) and it is correct, you say, "That's right. You see how you are beginning to get insight of how to do it. Just let the impressions flow in, as you gaze into the crystal ball."

If named wrongly, say, "No honestly, as I look into the crystal, I get an impression that it is a number card [as the case may be]. Let's try now to determine what numbered card it is. Do you feel it runs from Ace to Five, or from Six to Ten?"

If such is the case, and Ace to Five is correct and is so named, say, "Great!" If wrong, say, "No, I don't feel that way at all. It seems to be in the lower sequence of cards." To transmitter in audience, "Is your card in the range of from Ace to Five?" Transmitter confirms it is. Continue right on: whatever occurs in the routine just keep it flowing smoothly, as though things are going precisely as you expect them to go. Let us assume that the card is correctly named as being from "Ace to Five" by the volunteer, say, "Alright now, now for the fine work."

To transmitter in audience, "Think of the number of your card." To receiver on stage, "What card do you feel it is from one to five? Ace, two, three, four, five." Emphasize ever so slightly on the number of the card that is correct. If volunteer gives the correct number say, "Wonderful . . . you named it correctly. The card is (name card) that has been projected to us, via telepathy, by this man in the audience.

"Is (name of card) correct, sir?" The transmitter confirms it is. On the other hand, let's say the volunteer named it wrong and said "Three" while actually it was the Five of Hearts you forced and yourself know to be correct, simply look into the "crystal ball" and state, "Let me look into the crystal and see what I can come up with. Sometimes getting the exact number of the card can be a bit difficult when you first try an experiment like this. Hmmm, here is what I get. You said it was 'three', now add to that two further numbers and what do you come up with?" The volunteer holding the crystal, says, "Five." You say "Five is correct. The Five of Heart is the card you were concentrating upon, is that correct?"

The transmitter says, "Correct!"

You turn to audience and say, "Let us give these two fine people a generous round of applause for their sincere efforts in performing this experiment in ESP. It is really mental magic you know, so please don't take it seriously."[1]

Dismiss the volunteer from stage and retrieve the card from person in audience, and the trick is complete.

This trick provides an excellent opportunity for entertaining with the psychology of magic. Win or lose by the volunteer, you always come out ahead as the magician. There will even be times when the results are surprising, and the volunteer will name all correctly. When this occurs, the audience will be flabbergasted!

Carrying Colonel rank admitted me to Officer's Clubs on all bases. These were the nicest social premises to be had. Invariably, I was asked to perform some tricks for the top brass. Card tricks were popular, but the mental magic trick I give you here proved the most popular of all, as it appears to demonstrate that the participating officer had remarkable ESP talent. People enjoy a clever

---

[1] In performing mental magic, I have found it best to refer to such demonstrations as a form of magic, rather than to convey the idea that they are genuine. I have never believed it fair to foster false beliefs on a public which is already laboring under various forms of false beliefs. You cross a thin line in performing mental magic: you don't want to depreciate from your demonstrations, while, at the same time, you do not want to directly claim to be so that which is not so. Temper this kind of magic with presentational diplomacy. Sometimes I conclude such a trick by saying, "If you believe that, you will believe anything."

trick that fools them, as it provides a challenge to figure out how it was done. That's part of the entertainment of magic, and entertainment is the heart of the art. However, they enjoy even more a clever trick that not only fools them, but makes them feel clever at the same time. That is audience identification, and audience identification is the high art of an entertainer.

This effect turns the assisting spectator into a mastermind! Throughout my "military daze", I always had it in my pocket ready to go.

Effect

I designed this trick based on an effect created by Paul Curry.

You bring forth a stack of blank business cards. Nine of these are counted off and handed over to a volunteer who is instructed to examine them and line them up in a row on the table. Then, one at a time you mark them, using a black marking pen, with a number on each – from 1 to 9. As each number is written, that card is turned face down. When number 9 is written, it is placed to one side, and spectator requested to remember what number is on the downward face of that card. The remainder of the cards are then picked up by the spectator, mixed thoroughly so that no one has the slightest idea in what sequence the numbers now are. The spectator then replaces the mixed cards number-side down on the table in a row. Now comes the mental magic of the effect, which is why I have come to call this trick "Spectator ESPing".

You ask the spectator to try his hand at ESP to see how good he is at this "wild talent". Have him point to which card he thinks is No. 1. Card touched is picked up, still face downward, and placed on stack of cards held in your left hand. Taking the marking pen, you write No. 1 on its face. Spectator is next asked to touch which card he senses is No. 2. The same procedure as with the first card is gone through with each card in turn, including card No. 7. This leaves two cards remaining on the table. You pick up what may be card No. 8 (you comment on this fact) and place it blank side up on stack you are holding, as you glance at the spectator and ask him to recall which number was written on the card that was placed to one side. Naturally, he says it is No. 9. You pick up this card and number it accordingly. Also, number No. 8 card and place on stack. Then place No. 9 card on top of it.

All is now ready for the amazing climax of the effect. You immediately deal the cards out again in a row on the table, running from No. 9 through No. 1, in front of spectator. He is requested to see how he did with his ESPing. The suspense mounts as each card is turned over. *He is 100% correct!*

Modus Operandi

Get a stack of 25 blank business cards. To prepare for the effect, in private write No. 1 on both sides of one of the cards; on both sides of the second card write No. 2, and so on up through No. 7. With the No. 7 number uppermost, drop this prenumbered group on the stack of blank cards. Then, only on one side of another card, write No. 8 and place it blank side outward on top of stack. Now turn the stack so that these prepared cards are all facing downward and unprepared blank cards upwards. Place a small pencil dot on top blank card so that you can tell at a glance when this side is uppermost. Wrap a rubber band around the stack of cards and place in your coat pocket along with a marking pen. You are now ready to present the effect.

Secure a volunteer who would like to test his ESP powers. Bring out the stack of apparently blank cards from your pocket along with marking pen. Remove the rubber band, and hold the stack so that prenumbered cards are at bottom and unprepared (blank) cards on top (a glance at pencil dot on top card assures you of this). Deal off nine blank cards and hand over to volunteer to be examined, and have him place them in a row on the table. Put the rest of the cards aside for the moment. Then, one at a time you mark a number (from 1 to 9) on each of the row of cards. As each number is written, that card is turned face downward. When No. 9 is written, it is placed to one side, and spectator asked to remember what number is on that card. The remainder of cards are then picked up by volunteer, mixed, and returned number-side down in a row on the table. Obviously, no one has the slightest idea which number is where now in the row of cards.

All is ready to test the volunteer's ESP talent. Tell him to let his intuition guide him. Ask him to point to which card he thinks is

No. 1 and touch it. You pick up the touched card and place on top of stack of remainder of cards which you have meanwhile picked up and are holding in your left hand. You write No. 1 on its face.

The volunteer is then ask to ESP again which card he thinks is No. 2 card. The same procedure is gone through, and so on with all the cards including No. 7. This leaves two cards remaining on the table. You pick up "what may be No. 8 card", and place it blank side up on stack held in left hand, as you glance at spectator and ask him to recall what number was on that card you placed aside and requested him to remember. This is your *misdirection* that subtlely accomplishes the trick:

As you ask the question, you will naturally catch the eye of the person, while, at the same time, your left hand casually drops to your side and you turn the stack of cards over in your hand (prenumbered cards are thus turned uppermost and the other cards downward in your hand, simple as that). As bottom card is blank side of No. 8 card, the stack looks exactly the same. The maneuver is indetectable. Proceed right on and mark No. 9 on card on table moving it towards stack in your left hand; then note blank card on face of stack, as you comment, "And this one you ESP'd as number eight." Mark it No. 8, and then place No. 9 card on top of it.

All is set for the climax of the effect. Simply deal out the cards in a row on table from No. 9 through No. 1. One by one, have the volunteer, himself, turn each card over and show that the numbers match 100% on each side. The volunteer has been 100% successful in his ESPing.

I left the military in a daze.

Chapter Seventeen

Natural Science

This chapter is dedicated to my entomologist friend, David Parkinson, who has contributed so much to making my collection outstanding from faraway places.

There is a portion of my life which is away from magic and hypnosis. It is my interest in natural science. I have been interested in the wonders of nature for as long as I can remember. As a boy, I recall taking long bicycle trips out in the country collecting butterflies.

In those years of the "Roaring '20s", butterflies were all about. Even home gardens had their share. Little lycaenidae (blues, copper, hairstreaks) were to be found about patches of clover flowers. Hesperiidae (skippers), in many varieties, skipped merrily from bush to bush. And showy Papilionidae (Swallowtails) soared through the air. Out in the country, butterflies were even more prevalent.

Today these beautiful insects are scarce. Inroads of subdivisions and gardening insecticides have killed off much in the way of caterpillars. Except for hardy survivors, many have vanished.

As my interest in collecting insects progressed, I answered an ad of George MacBean in the Natural Science Magazine. I purchased from him a papered assortment of 50 South American species for $5.00. I relaxed and mounted them, and my father helped me place them in cases, which he designed.

I lost touch with George, until years later, when I was clearing out my attic, I ran across a postcard advertisement of his giving a Vancouver, B.C., Canada address. On a hunch, I dropped a line. He was still there and still in business. When we played Vancouver with my show, I met him personally and obtained many fine specimens from the gentleman, who, by then, was well advanced in years. Delight was an entomologist too. She, like me, had a spot in her heart for the wonders of nature.

Our interest in natural science never subsided, and the 1960s found us presenting hundreds of school assembly shows, booked under the direction of entrepreneur, James L. Gray. On this program, we exhibited half a hundred cases of exotic butterflies, moths, and insects which we had obtained from all parts of the world. These we placed on long tables in the schools, as lines of students marched by and enjoyed the spectacular natural science treasures. Delight patiently answered all the questions the children asked. Invariably a child would ask, when pointing to a specimen that especially caught attention, "Is it rare or is it poisonous?" Some of the butterflies and moths we showed were very rare, but, of course, they were not poisonous. Some of the other insect relatives (spiders and centipedes) were.

Class after class would pass by viewing the cases up close, and then would take their seats for the assembly. We had our natural science program arranged on slides, which Delight projected upon a screen on stage, while I explained what was shown. It was a trip around the world collecting insects in many lands. We called our program, "Insect Oddities Of The World". Schools liked it, as it was educational. However, in time, we wearied of doing it, as a job repeated over and over becomes monotonous, so we let the program go. Nonetheless, it was assuredly worthwhile, and we were proud of the nice testimonials we received. These are a few examples:

> "'Insect Oddities of the World' is the most outstanding education program that has ever been presented in our school. It was highly informative, colorfully illustrated, and aroused in our pupils an enthusiastic interest in natural science."
>
> — JOHN W. EMRICH, Principal
> Washington Elementary School
> Richmond, California

> "The Natural Science Program held the students spellbound. The Ormond McGills have made a vast contribution to this area of science."
>
> — ROBERT L. MCKEE, Dist. Supt.
> Galt Joint Union School Dist.
> Galt, California

> "Any school which has the opportunity of displaying these beautiful butterflies, moths, etc., would do well to avail itself of the opportunity."
>
> — ROBERT M. MARTIN, Principal
> University High School
> Honolulu, Hawaii

"One of the finest programs that we have ever had at our school in ten years of programming, was the 'Insect Oddities of the World' presented by Mr. and Mrs. Ormond McGill."

— JOHN F. HUGHES, Principal
Jarvis E. Bishop School
Sunnyvale, California.

From butterflies our natural science interests developed into conchology (sea shells). Our friend in Canada, George MacBean gave us a letter of introduction to Bob Wind of Monterey, California. Bob was a dealer in lepidoptera. We became well acquainted. By coincidence, he had purchased a collection of sea shells and found that specimens of fine shells sold very well. As we were leaving on a trip to the Orient, he asked us to see what we might uncover in the way of such material.

In Hong Kong, we met a Chinese merchant who had a shop on the main street of Kowloon. His name was Thomas Tam, and we became close friends. To this day I correspond with him.[2] Delight and I asked him if he could get some Hong Kong sea shells for us. He said, "Come back tomorrow."

Next day, Thomas had a large box of sea shells waiting for us, at his store. They had been brought in by the "Junkers" (boat dwellers). That was the start of my sea shell business.

On returning to the States, I had Thomas Tam send over box-load after box-load of sea shells from Hong Kong waters. I sold these to shops and collectors. And then I began ordering from areas worldwide.

While at the public library in Palo Alto, I saw a large globe of the world standing in one corner. Revolving the globe the idea occurred, "Why not import shells from other exotic places?" I got to work and contacted U.S. Consulates in many countries that had borders along oceans. The co-operation was wonderful, as the United States encourages the development of private enterprises in foreign lands provided such does not interfere in American business. Soon I was corresponding with shell collectors around the world, and my business dealing in sea shells became an international project.

---

[2]More recently I even wrote a book with him on the art of bamboo painting.

For 17 years (1959–1976) I was a professional sea shell dealer, and made many friends in that field. Like magicians, conchologists are a special breed very much devoted to their hobby. Few in magic knew of my work in conchology just as those in shells did not know of my work in magic. I kept the two professions largely apart; and, for a time, dealing in sea shells became even more important to my livelihood than did performing magic.

Delight very much liked the sea shell business, and she loved to form her own collection. As each package would arrive from foreign lands, she would sort it out and personally collect those she wanted to retain. She would say to me, "That one we cannot sell; that one we must keep forever." And how well I recall her saying, "Now we have a business that we really like." While she liked magic, hitting the road with a show is hard for a woman, so shells made it possible to live happily at home. However, shells or magic, she was ever at my side, and in her quiet voice would say, "Every thing is fun with Sweetheart." Delight was an angel. I continued in shells until her death in 1976. Shells had meant so much to her; I could not bear to deal in them longer, so I let the business slide and drift away. The collection she had assembled was one of the finest in the world, many told me, and following her death I presented it to Marine World in Redwood City, as a memorial to her. Marine World/Africa USA has recently moved to Vallejo, California, and the collection is set up there for thousands to enjoy. A tribute to Delight.

Natural Science and Delight, they must almost be spoken of in the same breath. Sometimes we would pass a tree, and she would suddenly stop dead still, and, in a hushed voice, say to me, "That tree we have walked by many times, yet just today I have really come to know it. I know it now, it claims my consciousness."

If ever there was magic.

Before her death, the last time she ever walked from her room alone was when a friend came to our home with a gift for her. It was a little plaque upon which was inscribed:

THE WONDERS OF NATURE UNFOLD ENDLESSLY, AND EACH MOMENT IS A MIRACLE.

Chapter Eighteen

Once A Collector Always A Collector

I have been a collector all my life. I started collecting postage stamps when just a kid. I still do. Then onto collecting butterflies. I currently have a museum quality collection of rare specimens from tropical countries. My entomologist friend, David Parkinson has been a great help to me in obtaining specimens of butterflies and exotic moths from far away places. Then onto sea shells. For 17 years providing sea shells to collectors became a sideline business. Collecting is a hobby which I can dignify with professional names: philatelist, entomologist, conchologist.

Collecting is such fun. Just remember that the treasures one collects in the physical world must be kept in their proper perspective, that's all. Their true worth is actually directly related to the enjoyment they bring to the collector. Understand that the universe is a vast playground upon which one can play. Collecting is a form of playing. Keep it that way and enjoy the playing. That is the only secret. If your treasures also prove a joy to others, so much the better.

I rather look upon collecting in this manner:

Personal treasures and collectables which are dear to your heart are warm and rewarding.

Do not think that the passing from form to formless mars the enjoyment of collectables, for nothing that is collected, which is really fine, beautiful and worthwhile is ever lost. As it is in the physical world, so it is in the mind world which lies beyond "The Veil".

For, what is beauty but in the mind of the beholder, and what are interesting things but those which hold the attention of the mind on that which is worthwhile.

A mind filled with that which is beautiful and interesting is a good mind. Remember, all you acquire and accumulate in the physical world which is interesting and lovely goes along with you in mind and spirit, and what you found to enjoy on one side of the coin you will find equally to enjoy on the opposite side, for it remains in your consciousness forever. Appreciate the treasures you collect and know . . .

Chapter Nineteen

The Death of Delight

The reason I am still on the Planet is sponsored by Delight's love for me. She arranged things to keep me busy during this last epic of this lifetime. Ever she is close.

Delight was an angel. I am convinced she came through on a visit from the other side just to spend sometime with me. Bless her. We were together for 33 years, until she felt it was time to take a bit of leave and return to whence she came. She told me I still had things to tend to.

I recall her telling the nurse in Dr. Frank Martin's office (our physician at that time) before she died:

"I have to leave soon now. I hope Ormond can handle it okay. I will help him all I can."

Of her death what can I better say than Shakespeare's verse:

"When she shall die make her into little stars, and all the world shall fall in love with night."

Yes, it was during the decade of the 1970s that Delight died.

All through her life, Delight had never been especially comfortable in her body; however, she managed to live in it for 58 years, mostly because she wanted to be with me. Finally, she decided it was time to cast it off, and cancer took over. She kept her illness secret, and the first time I knew of it was a couple of weeks before Christmas of 1975. An examination showed it to be terminal; the cancer had cut off the functioning of one kidney and was invading the other.

The doctors gave her 6 months to live. By her will, she extended that to 8 months so that we could have a bit more time together. During that period, she told me she had been summoned three times, by guides, to make the transition. But she said, "No, I will abide with Ormond for yet a time."

Delight died on Sunday, August 23, 1976 at 3:00 p.m. She was in a coma that Sunday, and I held vigil by her bedside from 7:00 a.m. until noon. Then, her father, Ray Olmstead, came in to relieve me and take my place.

I went home and called my magician friend, Lee Grabel, asking that he come over and lend me support. At 3:00 p.m., Ray called from the hospital, saying that Delight had died, and for me to get right over and sign the death papers. As direct as that. Ray was a blunt sort of man, who in his mid-eighties had seen so many friends die that death to him was an expected event.

I left a note on the front door of my home for Lee Grabel telling him to meet me at the hospital. Just as I was getting into my car, Lee drove up. Hearing that Delight had just died, he drove me.

Lee and I entered the hospital and went into the room where Delight had died. She was seated upright in a chair; her eyes were open and a faint smile was upon her lips. To this day, I wonder what she had seen as she passed onwards; there was a look of marvelous wonder upon her face. I kissed her still lips twice, and Lee dragged me from the room. I went to sign the death certificate. I never saw the body of Delight again. She was cremated and her ashes placed in a crypt beside the ashes of her mother. Ray Olmstead died four years later, and his ashes now reside beside those of his wife and daughter.

The death of Delight was a wound so deep in me; it was literally like being cut in twain with a knife. How I ever survived the trauma of the week following her death, I will never know. I longed for death myself to join her. A time of sorrow like this really tests a man; either he can drop down into the gutter or it can be a cause of making a quantum leap upward to higher consciousness. As I am still amongst the living, I must have chosen the latter course, of which I am sure that Delight was the cause. Also, night after night, my dear friend Chuck Mignosa spent hours with me consoling with inspiration to continue on.

One week later, while lying in bed, in the early morning hours, I felt Delight's consciousness come to me. Although she was not in physical form, it was as tangible a presence of herself as ever she was while in body. Her closeness made me feel better, and I rolled over and went to sleep.

The following night, at 3:30 a.m., the same experience occurred, and I began to receive insights from her as to the nature of death and of the realm in which she now dwelt. I dismissed such as fantasizing by myself. In the morning, what she had told me about the nature of death had faded from consciousness.

Four nights in a row the same phenomena persisted, and finally I gave into the insistence and got up to write what was being given to me by her conscious presence. It occurred to me that I might have some information that would make an interesting paper relative to subjective feelings about life after death. I was wrong. I did not have a paper. I had an entire book, as for three weeks, night after night, her telling of such matters flowed into me. Page after page I wrote until the book was complete. I never called the book my own; I was but a hand that wrote what I was told. The consciousness behind it all was hers. I called the book, *The Book Of Delight* (the book's published title was *Grieve No More Beloved*). Its insights were profound, but so very personal that there is no place that I can repeat them except in an autobiography of myself; so, I will repeat here fragments of what she told me. Possibly they will be of help to others who grieve the loss of a beloved.

Says Delight to me:

"Ormond, write this book for me, for while it is a book about death, yet it will be a joyous book. Let it be a cause for celebration for all who read it, for it tells that loved ones are never lost, about life beyond death, and about immortality.

"If I am to tell you about death and what lies beyond death, we must relate with a high form of awareness. For while I use words in the telling of these matters, actually the words are but used to take you on to that which is beyond words to describe that which is transcendental. Your understanding must come from your own consciousness of these truths, even as you now experience my consciousness though I am in the formless. Only then may one come to learn about that which is eternal and immortal.

"To the peak of consciousness we apply the term "God". And the greater one advances his (her) consciousness the more God-like he (she) becomes. Consciousness is immortal and death cannot touch it at all, but death can provide a means for more awareness, and awareness is another name for consciousness.

"Death is to be looked upon as an experience in which life is increased not diminished. Death in freeing one from the physical body, which when it gets ill can be a real pain, expands consciousness which makes one more alive than ever. To be more alive removes the termination sentiments of death, which is a lie that has depressed humanity for time immemorial. If you would shatter the mystery of death, look upon it for what it actually is: *a transition to a state of being yet more alive!*

"Feel the poetry of what I have said here in your Being, and it will help you understand that death is actually the flowering of life. Life is the plant, and the plant is there for the flower. The plant should be happy, and the plant should dance when the flower comes.

"Understand that death is a door, it is not stopping. Consciousness moves but the body remains at the door. In other words, your body is left outside the temple, but your awareness enters the temple. It is a most subtle phenomenon – life is nothing before it.

"To help you understand the true nature of death, I will summarize these matters in capsuled form:

"All physical life is transitory but temporary. Be not dismayed by this fact. Rather, consider your current life and the next life as one life. How then can you lose loved ones? A bit of patience. A little waiting. That is all."

The foregoing gives only a glimpse of what Delight had me write in her book. Her book goes into detail on such matters as the experience of dying, what you really are, and the nature of your existence following death. Only the one word "Love" can come close to expressing the real meaning and purpose of the heavenly planes of Existence following death, in which is found love which casteth out all fear, blossoms in joy, and bears fruit in peace.

Truly Delight seemed more than human. She kept me alive on the Planet, and has been close ever since. She seems to state, "I can help you more from this side to do what you have to do. That is why I made the transition back to my homeland".

Chapter Twenty
Friends of Influence

Friends are among the most important treasures you collect during a lifetime. Delight was my most personal friend. She was my wife, more importantly, she was my sweetheart. A wife sounds so much like you possess the person. The truth is you can never possess another human being. Mates are a choice to be together.

Dick Waterhouse was an early friend with whom I spent many hours experimenting with psychic phenomena. We developed a human energy amplifier. Dick has long since passed onwards.

Ron Ormond was a friend with whom I travelled in the Far East making movie documentaries about Religious Mysteries of the Orient. I wrote a book so titled. Possibly the most significant of our adventures was to bring attention of "Psychic Surgery" in the Philippines to the Western World. Harold Sherman wrote further about our adventures with "Psychic Surgery" in one of his books.

We started many people on "pilgrimages" to the Philippines. Ron has long since passed onwards. Some masters have been basic to my life: Buddha, Jesus, Krishna, Lao Tzu, Patanjali, Shiva, Trilopa, Heraclitus. I revere them all.

For almost 20 years, following Delight's passing, I teamed with excellent magician, Charles Mignosa presenting magic and hypnotism shows. My interest also turned to teaching more serious things in hypnotherapy which brought in friends related to that field, i.e., Gil Boyne, Randal Churchill, Marleen Mulder, Dwight Damon, Elson Eldridge, Jr. and numerous others.

True friends are treasures, and each, somehow, plays their part in your theater of life. As Shakespeare put it . . .

"All the world's a stage, and all the men and women merely players."

And along the way, many other friends came in. All wonderful people who influenced my life in various ways, and with whom I shared many adventures. To tell of these in detail would fill a library. So, I will just list them, in alphabetical order, in this my autobiography. I look upon living life as on a playground not a battlefield. Thus, the following personal friends became my playmates:

Percy Abbott, Johnnie Alladin, Eugene Berger, Louis Berkoff, Harry Blackstone, Jr., Gil and Ann Boyne, Barry Brilliant, Lance Burton, Randal Churchill, Walt and Larraine Cunningham, Dr. Dwight Damon, Sidora Dazi, Tom and Judy Durkin, Saul Eisenstat, MD, Elson Eldridge, Jr., Diana England, Edith Fiore, Arnold Furst, Lee and Helen Grabel, Geoffrey Hansen, Dr. John and Irene Hughes, Peter Hughes, Gerald and Shirley Kein, Jorge and Grace Kesselring, Stan Kremien, Flynt (Cyote) Kussmaul, William Larsen, Sr., Art Linkletter, Serena Luminere, Jerry Manoukian, MD, Wallace Marsh, MD, Patrick and Genevieve Martin, Jeff McBride, Richard Merrill, Chuck and Eileen Mignosa, Marleen (Devi) Mulder, Geno Munari, Norman and Lupe Nielsen, Rexford North, Mr. and Mrs. Alan Olmstead, Mr. and Mrs. Douglas Olmstead, Michael and Michelle Olmstead, Ray and Anna May Olmstead, Ron and Jo Olmstead, Ron, June and Tim Ormond, David Parkinson, Channing Pollock, Cherith Powell, Wilfred Proudfoot, Peter Raveen, Martin and Glenys Roberts, Dan Russel, John Schabel, DDS, Tom Silver, Shelley and Jon Stockwell, Thomas Tam, Floyd Thayer, Jerry Valley & family, Anna Vitale, Marcel Vogel, Jack Wagner, Donn and Erna Wood, Joe and Colette Worrell.

As an entertainer, various stars of stage and screen have influenced my life, even to the extent of contributing to my own style of entertaining. I will list a few of my personal favorites (some I knew personally and some I knew by distant viewing):

Fred Astaire, Harry Blackstone, Sr., Victor Borge, Edwin Brush, John Calvert, Eddie Cantor, Cardini, Chris Carlton, Charlie Chaplin, Maurice Chevalier, Bing Crosby, Dunninger, Jimmie Durante, Gary Grant, Audrey Hepburn, Bob Hope, Al Jolson, Boris Karloff, Ted Lewis, Harold Loyd, Bela Lugosi, Joe Penner, Ralph Richards, Ginger Rogers, Red Skelton, Jimmie Stewart, Harlan Tarbell, Howard Thurston, Ed Wynn.

On and on they go, flitting upon my screen-of-mind. I could tell you of many more, but to you, the reader, many of these names have scant meaning. They will, however, have meaning to those to whom the names belong.

Friends of Influence affecting and embellishing my life as perpetual as the universe.

The Magic of Four Generations

Great Grandfather

Grandfather

Father

Ormond

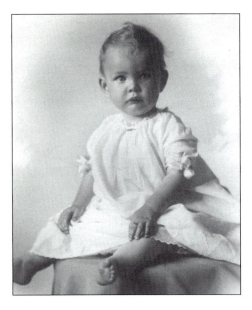

(above) At the start of a lifetime

(below) Here is my Paly High graduation photo of 1931. Some have told me it reminds them of the fiction-figure Harry Potter

(above right) Growing up

(below right) This is Delight

Frontispiece of How To Produce Miracles taken in 1940

(right) Here is how I looked in 1941, performing as Dr. Zomb. One time a kid in the audience yelled out, "You look like my Sunday School teacher."

(below) Our marriage photograph. At the time this was taken back in 1943, we thought it a nice photograph to send to family and friends

(right) Ormond McGill at mid 20th Century

(below) Bunker Hill 1943: Ormond and Delight in front of their apartment

(below right) The McGill's in the late 1950's in Palo Alto between Hawaiian shows

(left) Ormond and Delight McGill with Donn Wood

(below) Ormond and Delight McGill at the Pacific Coast Association of Magicians (PCAM) Convention banquet, sponsored by the Mystic 13, in 1959

(right) Delight and Ormond McGill in March 1960

(below right) Delight in the early 1970's

(top right) Ormond McGill in August 1998

(top left) Ormond McGill and Chuck Mignosa teaching magic in 2001

(bottom left) Faculty staff of HTI: Ormond McGill, Marleen Mulder and Randal Churchill

(bottom right) Marleen Mulder: close friend and spiritual teacher

Part Two

The Greatest Magic in the World

"When the activity of mind is under control the mind becomes like pure crystal, reflecting equally, without distortion, the perceiver, the perception and the perceived. It is through such mind that consciousness is known."

—Pantanjali
865 B.C.

Chapter Twenty-One
Magical Presentation

I have long lost count as to how many magic shows I have presented in my lifetime. It must range into the thousands, and each one has been an experience in presentation. In this Chapter, I will give you my thoughts on the presentation of magic born of my experience.

To me, it is not the tricks you do that is important but it is how you present the tricks. A baker's dozen principles make up the successful presentation of magic, viz.:

1. You as a Magician, 2. Confidence, 3. Enthusiasm, 4. Goodwill, 5. Dignity, 6. Language, 7. Patter and Pantomime, 8. Appearance, 9. Personality, 10. Identification, 11. Style, 12. Class, 13. Putting Your Consciousness into Your Magic.

Let us consider each in turn.

1. You as a Magician

Appreciate that you are the number one ingredient of your own successful performance of magic, for being a magician and PRESENTING MAGIC ARE SYNONYMOUS. If you present magic well, you are a good magician. If you present magic poorly, you are a poor magician. To be a successful magician, you must become an entertainer. Entertainment, in its own unique form, is the very heart of the art.

2. Confidence

You must have confidence in yourself to present magic properly. Learn to perform your tricks perfectly, and you will never fear that they will fail. Confidence begets confidence. Remember, you are the master; no one else in the audience (unless, perhaps, a fellow magician, and magicians enjoy magic whether they know how the tricks work or not) knows the secrets of your tricks so that they cannot help but be mystified by what you do.

3. Enthusiasm

Love performing magic, and let such shine forth as enthusiasm. Enthusiasm is contagious, and it will rub off on the spectators. Your audience will catch the spark and share your enthusiasm and love of magic with you.

4. Goodwill

When you perform magic, hold a kindly feeling for every person in your audience. Radiate goodwill and pleasantness. This is an important principle for successful performance. The great magician, Howard Thurston, used to stand in back of the front curtain before his show started, and repeated to himself, "I love my audience!" Only then did he feel he was ready to step before the footlights and begin his show. People appreciate friendliness. Radiate goodwill and pleasantness, and you'll get it in return from your audience.

5. Dignity

As a magician, always maintain your dignity. This does not mean you are to be a "stuffed shirt"; it simply means that you must *respect yourself* as the performer of the magic you perform.

6. Language

Good speaking is important for your success as a magician. To abuse language marks you as an ignorant person. Be correct in your speech; speak clearly and distinctly, and people will admire you.

7. Patter and Pantomime

Closely associated with good speech is patter. Patter is the specific contents of what you say in relation to the tricks you perform. Mainly it should be interesting, entertaining, and to the point.

In addition to patter, pantomime is sometimes used as the method of performing magic. Some performers specialize in it. The use of pantomime and patter is of superlative value to the successful presentation of magic.

8. Appearance

The audience's first impression of you is based on how you look: what you wear and how you are groomed. A neat appearance goes a long way in audience acceptance. Some performers, such as the late Liberace, for example, even went to the extremes of making appearance spectacular.

Magic places emphasis on the hands; in such regard be sure your hands are well kept. Further, hair combed, shoes shined, clothes pressed, etc., such details are important for the impression you make.

9. Personality

You must have technical skill in the performance of your magic; but above and beyond this, you must have personality. Personality is what makes a great entertainer. YOU MUST CHARM YOUR AUDIENCE. Maurice Chevalier was a fine example of this. He was never a great singer but he was a great personality. Chevalier had the ability to make each spectator feel he was performing especially for them. That's charisma!

10. Identification

Closely associated with personality is audience identification. This skill comes from performing experience. When you stand before a group of people, identification is a sense of feeling for and from them. It is a flow between audience and performer and vice versa. Allow yourself to become responsive to this feeling; become responsive to the emotions of your audience; develop a rapport with those watching you. The more spontaneous you can become in developing this empathy with your audience, the better magician you will be.

11. Style

Style is the type of magician you will be:

Will you be a clown? Will you be a comedian? Will you be a dramatic performer? Will you just be yourself? Possibly just being yourself is the best way to go, as you are the only one exactly like yourself in the entire universe.

As an example of style, I personally adopt a leisurely style of presentation. Many performers prefer a fast pace style: bang, bang, bang. Today we live in an age of speed, so this fits well. However, the opposite polarity of speed is unspeed. As long as things flow along with precision, the audience will never know whether your presentation is fast or slow; they will just, somehow, feel relaxed as they watch you perform. As I look at it, the audience has come to see you, so they are in no hurry to leave. Take your time so that what you do sinks in – just flow along. However, by all means do what works best for you – set your own style.

12. Class

This is the pinnacle of showmanship and artistry. It is an intangible quality. Some performers have it and some do not. Cultivate it, if you can. The late Fred Astair provides an example of class.

13. Putting Your Consciousness into Your Magic

The real art of magic goes beyond just entertainment, as it presents the potential of the impossible. The impossible plunges one into the unknown, and that which is unknown incites awe. To incite awe in his audience is the height of the magician's art, and to infest awe in an audience you must incite awe in yourself at the magical wonders you produce. To do this, you affirm consciousness of the effects you present. Forget their tricky modus operandi and just concentrate your mind on their magic.

Who can ever forget the Great Thurston standing at the footlights, looking up – with awe on his face – as he gazed upward to the dome of the theater where "Iasia" has just vanished from a cabinet dangling there in mid-air. And, we hear him say, "Night after night, I stand here in sheer astonishment, wondering where she has gone?"

The audience felt Thurston's awe because Thurston, himself, felt the awe. In other words, he consciously allowed himself to feel the awe. It is a projection from performer to audience.

Dozens of magicians have made a girl vanish from an illusion cabinet, but only a master showman brings a feeling of awe to the spectators who witness the apparent miracle which has occurred before their eyes. "The Magic of Consciousness" is the difference. It is the difference between a master magician and an ordinary magician; it is the quality of being able to emphasize one's inner feelings about the magic performed, and bringing that realization to the spectators – it is a transference of experiencing. This is master secret of showmanship.

To become conscious of anything within yourself means to become aware of each thing you do. So many are unaware of most of the things they do. For example, you are breathing this very moment, yet have you been conscious of your breathing? For the moment, when you think about it, you are conscious of it, but a few moments hence you will again be unconscious of it. For the most part, we are very much unconscious of what we do. Such is the case with many magicians. They perform much of what they do unconsciously; or, if they are conscious, they are most conscious of how the directions told them to perform the trick, how they should patter the trick, and how it operates to fool the spectators.

As an illustration, take the simple trick of making a handkerchief disappear using a "handkerchief pull" under the coat. The magician is conscious of secretly securing the device in his hand, of stuffing the silk into the pull, and releasing it so that it flies under his coat without being seen. Then, when it is safely stowed away, he opens his hands and shows it is gone. There is no real magic in that, as he is not surprised that it is gone. The real magic would be for you to place a handkerchief in your hand, experience it there, and suddenly when you open your hand, it is not there!

Imagine how surprised you would be if the handkerchief you put in your hand was not there when you expected it to be there. That would be magic, as it carries off impact to the spectators of the elements of a surprised consciousness. Such amazement, as a consciousness experience to yourself, is the way to use your consciousness in relation to the presentation of magic. Such awe-filled presentation of magic is the way of the great masters of magic.

Magicians everywhere believe in the magic you do. Inside yourself become as a little child who is filled with awe at the wonderment of all that occurs. And, in your inner mind visualize the magic that you caused to happen to seem as a miracle even unto yourself. Forget that you caused the magic to happen via a tricky modus operandi. Just marvel at the effect of what happened. If I can move you beyond the law of cause and effect so that you emotionally become involved only with the effect and allow that emotion to sprinkle as "fairy dust" upon your audience, then I have given you the greatest secret of all in relation to the presentation of magic in appreciating that what you experience inside yourself (your consciousness) is what your audience will experience in like manner.

And in summation:

In presenting magic think of your audience at all times and be considerate of that audience. The audience, in turn, will then be considerate of you.

Chapter Twenty-Two
Let's Pretend Magic

"Pretending is the beginning of imagination. Imagination is the beginning of believing. Believing is the beginning of reality."

– McGill 2003

Do you want to improve your performance as a magician? Do you want to be a great magician? Okay. Let's start by pretending that you are.

Everything starts with first pretending that it is. Pretending is psychology in action. Let's pretend psychology is based on the work of William James, the founding father of the psychology of kindergarten children. For who can pretend better than kindergarten children? Their world is filled with magic and things that go bump in the night. Pre-school age children can pretend so expertly because they, as yet, haven't been told that they should never pretend.

Psychology was not taught in American universities before William James began teaching the subject in 1875. James, himself, had never taken a course in psychology because none was available, as once he jested, "The first lecture in psychology that I ever heard was the first I ever gave."

William James had something to say about every topic within psychology. For years I have admired his creative genius. Like Einstein he was always open to the mysterious, and magic is mysterious. How did Einstein put it? "Out of the mysterious we discover the undiscovered." Both James and Einstein were magic fans.

Every really great magician is a magic fan. Every really great magician is a child at heart – they *believe in* magic. To believe in magic is to mean one becomes conscious of their magic, and to become conscious of their magic is what makes a great magician.

To become conscious of the magic one presents makes your audience equally conscious of what they see performed.

137

That's the secret of performing great magic: *Pretend that it is so.*

William James called "let's pretend", "acting out psychology". It is role play. The very act of role play is bringing into physical performance that which is imagined in the mind.

Here is an example of how James applied his process:

The very first thing a budding magician must get over is all vestige of stage fright. Let's say such a person came into his office, telling that he (or she) had an ambition to become a great magician but somehow he lacked confidence in addressing an audience.

James would first ask, "Think for a moment and truthfully ask yourself if you would really like to stand before a group of people and perform magic, or, do you think you would really be more comfortable remaining in the audience and enjoying the magic you are watching?" James explained that we usually behave best in ways that make us feel comfortable and contented with ourselves. If, after thinking it over carefully, the person said they were actually happier in watching magic than in performing magic, he would say, "For heaven's sake don't learn to do something that makes you uncomfortable when you are comfortable just as you are."

This was expert psychological counseling, and many a person went on their way greatly benefited by the session.

But, on the other hand, suppose – after thinking it over carefully – the person still asserts: "Yes, I definitely aspire to be a great magician, and I definitely want to get over my feelings of stage fright and feel confident in myself when I am performing magic. Then James would say, "Very good. Then let's pretend you are doing exactly that. Stand before a mirror, and let's pretend you are standing on stage and performing."

The Circle of Magic is complete. To summarise: If you want to be a great magician, start by pretending that you are. The more you can pretend, the more conscious you are that your magic is real magic, the greater the magician you will be.

Chapter Twenty-Three
Waving the Magic Wand

I have always had a special affection for "The Magic Wand". Many magicians have. "The Magic Wand" was even the title of a popular magic magazine published in England for many years. When I received the Mysto Magic Set which started me in magic (when I was 10 years old), the first prop I removed from the box was the magic wand. The directions said that the wand was traditional with magicians, and that in presenting magic it was often well to pass the wand over the trick and say "Hokus Pokus" to make the magic happen.

All the great magicians had their favorite wand. The International Brotherhood of Magicians (IBM) even calls their obituary of members who have passed onwards, "The Broken Wand". The entire history of magic is replete with wands. Have you ever wondered why wands have tips on them? It goes back to the time of Atlantis when wands were known as "Rods of Power".

The Atlanteans were very much into crystal energies, and used quartz crystals in many ways. One of the ways was to use a hollow rod, about 19 inches long and fasten a small crystal on each end, forming a wand. The crystals are said to be generators of energy, and are responsive to the thought of the person who concentrates upon them, beaming thought out with power laser fashion, the hollow tube acting as a resonator amplifying the "thought energy".

How do I know about the Atlantean use of crystals? That makes an interesting story to add to this autobiography.

I tried an experiment in "previous life regression" with a hypnotherapist friend. One memory that came out of my subconscious (fact or fantasy) was seeing myself as a stout man dressed in a brown monk-type robe. The room was hewn from rocks, and the ceiling was lined with crystals. A stone slab was in the center of the room upon which a person was lying unconscious. A crystal rested upon his forehead, on the spot known as "the third eye". There was a hole in the ceiling of the somber room, amongst the bank of crystals through which a ray of sunlight fell upon the crystal on the man's forehead. I envisioned myself bending over the prostrate figure and waving the "Rod of Power" back and forth across the beam of light. The crystals blazed! Suddenly the eyes of the "sleeper" opened, he arose, and I helped him out of the room. I saw myself as a physician in that time of long ago.

Crystals have a molecular structure which makes them unique in directing and amplifying energy. They have been used in watches, computers, and electronics in various ways. Some scientists are today studying their more subtle uses in amplifying the so-called "human energies". Such research still belongs to the realm of metaphysics, but before long it may enter the realm of physics. Directions for using crystals (activating the energies) run like this:

Quartz crystal rapidly absorbs energy from the one who wields the crystal. To use it, hold the crystal lengthwise with your right forefinger on the point (or tip) and with your right thumb on its base. Hold your left forefinger and thumb on opposite, parallel faces of the crystal barrel. The crystals should be held at the level of the heart. Now, take a deep breath, hold it while concentrating on what you want it to accomplish, and then pulse your breath out of your mouth as you gently squeeze it and hold it upon the object you wish to influence.

It is said that the wielder of the crystal establishes a direct energy connection with it by concentrating upon it while exploding the breath, programming the crystal by his concentrated thoughts. Sometimes a verbalized affirmation of this nature is given along with the process, saying:

"I program this crystal to resonate in turn with the highest forces of the universe. I program this crystal to vibrate in tune with my higher self. I program this crystal to help me accomplish what I wish to accomplish."

There are those who say that quartz crystals are nature's computers. The magician will recognize in their use the close connection to his Magic Wand, as he waves it about over a trick in pretence of its accomplishment. Back in the days of Atlantis, possibly that magic was real, as the magician waved his wand – the Rod of Power.

When you wave your Magic Wand over an effect to apparently be the cause of its happening, why not give the wand the same respect as did the original source. An audience that comes to see a magician perform wants to be enchanted. Wave your wand and produce enchantment.

I have always liked to include a trick or two using a magic wand in my show. One effect was to have the wand resting inside a vase upon a table. To everyone's surprise the wand begins moving up and down tapping inside the vase. You walk over to it, hold your hand above it, and the wand rises out of the vase to your fingers. The method is very simple as shown in the drawing, just a black thread stuck to the bottom of the wand, as it rests in the vase. A pull from backstage makes it hop up and down and rise from the vase. Simple but very effective. The thread then drops away, and the wand is clear for use.

A trick with the magic wand I have often presented is the popular one of passing a borrowed finger ring onto its center while the ends are held. I used the method described in the Sphinx Annual of 1937 (*Soc. of American Magicians*).

In this effect, a woman's ring is placed under a handkerchief. It is handed over to a spectator to hold, while he holds an empty glass in his right hand, as shown.

The spectator is told to drop the ring into the glass and  let the handkerchief drop, at the same time, to cover the glass.

You now take the magic wand and wrap another handkerchief around its center, leaving the ends of the wand exposed. Another spectator is then requested to grip the ends of the wand, one hand at each end, and at no time is he to release his grip upon the ends of the wand.

The spectator holding the glass, covered by the handkerchief in which is the borrowed ring, is then asked to shake the glass. The ring is heard to be still there.

Now comes the magic!

When the handkerchief is removed from the glass, the ring is *gone*! When the handkerchief is unwrapped from the wand, the ring is found encircling the wand, even though the ends of the wand have been held throughout.

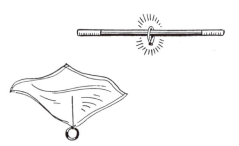

To accomplish the trick, as shown in the drawing, tie a finger ring (any ring will do, as it is never seen) to a three-inch length of thread attached to the center of the handkerchief which is held over the glass. Have this handkerchief in your pocket ready for use when performing the trick.

Explain to the audience how in this trick you will cause, through the power invested in the Magic Wand, the lady's ring to be magically transported through space from the glass to encircle the wand, even though the ends of the wand are held throughout, under close observation.

Take the handkerchief out of your pocket and conceal the ring within it, as you hold it in your left hand. Receive the borrowed ring in your right hand, and, as you place it under the handkerchief, substitute the ring there attached to the thread. Present it to be held, through the handkerchief, to a second spectator. (The borrowed ring is now actually concealed in your right hand. However, to the audience it seems you have merely placed the borrowed ring under the handkerchief, and that it is now held by a volunteer.) The volunteer is next handed an empty glass, and he holds the ring above it, as the edges of the handkerchief drop down around the glass. (Be sure handkerchief covers glass all around so that no one can see the ring inside when it is dropped.) The volunteer is now told to drop the ring he holds into the glass. He does so, and the ring is clearly heard to drop into the glass. It can also be rattled to prove it is there.

You now pick up the wand in your right hand (which has the ring palmed), and in this action secretly slip the ring over the end of the wand, and move your hand (with the ring concealed in it) along the wand to its center. Always keep your hand closed to hide the ring as you do this. Then take another handkerchief and wrap it around the center of the wand, covering the ring there. As you do this, you remove your right hand from the wand, as the ring is now concealed by the wrapped handkerchief. The second spectator is now asked to hold tight to the ends of the wand and never to release his grip even for an instant, as you are going to show some amazing Magic Wand magic.

The magic happens: with a flourish remove the handkerchief from the glass (ring attached to thread comes right along with it, and is concealed in folds of handkerchief). Glass is shown empty. Remove the other handkerchief from the center of wand, and the ring is discovered encircling its center, even though both ends of the wand have been tightly held by a bewildered person.

When you perform the trick, give the Magic Wand credit for the magic, and you'll have a "wonderful" effect.

Chapter Twenty-Four
Milkshake Magic

This is a tasty trick (no pun intended).

Ever since I was a kid, I've had a hankering for milkshakes. I have tested tasting milkshakes in many parts of the world, and to me the best milkshake is made at the Peninsula Creamery in Palo Alto, California, USA – the city in which I am a native son. I confess I may be prejudiced.

And so – just for the fun of it – I designed a milkshake-producing trick to give my audience (the lucky ones) a tasty treat.

For this purpose, I dug up the old classic, "The Kellar Vase," but in this new guise it becomes a modern novelty of magic. I came up with this effect, and it proved a hit in every show I did, and I've performed it for years.

Here's how it plays . . .

You have a box filled with colorful confetti, and a regular milk-shake shaker. You show the milkshaker empty and scoop it full to overflowing with confetti from the box. Looks pretty but hardly drinkable.

Sooo . . .

You take the shaker full of confetti and rest it on top of the box. Then showing a foot square of cloth you place it over the shaker and pleat it back and forth forming a pad atop the shaker.

Remove the pad, pick up the shaker, and to everyone's surprise the confetti has become transformed into a delicious milkshake you can pour into glasses and serve the lucky ones.

What flavor do you want? Chocolate is the one usually most preferred. However, you can take your choice.

Believe it or not, while I am at home in Palo Alto, I go to the Peninsula Creamery almost every day to get a milkshake which I enjoy. The creamery opened in 1923, and I was there on opening day. I was 10 years old at the time, and my parent took me downtown. I got a free ice cream cone.

Well let's get back to magic, and I'll tell you how the milkshake trick, I designed, works its tasty best.

You have a milkshake shaker which is a duplicate of the one filled with milkshake inside the box.

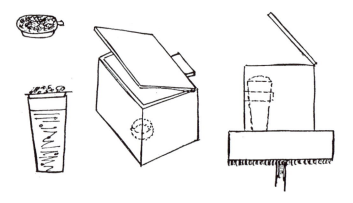

The drawing shows the apparatus, as it rests upon a table. The box is partly filled with colorful confetti. The milkshake shaker is filled with freshly made milkshake (I carry it to the show placed in a Thermos). A shallow tray covered with confetti glued to its surface just fits within the top of the shaker. With the confetti-covered shallow tray in position covering the top of the shaker, it looks like it is overflowing with confetti. There is a little tab on the tray which makes it easy to remove, when covered with a cloth, in performing the trick. Also, there is a little shelf on back of the confetti box to leave the shallow tray on when you want to get rid of it, as you will learn.

Inside the box, as shown in the drawing, is a metal band in which the milkshake-filled shaker is placed to keep it safely upright. All set. You are ready to perform Milkshake Magic.

To start the trick, open the box and scoop up some handful of confetti, and let it flutter back – just to show the box is filled with colorful confetti.

Now, take up the duplicate, empty, milkshake shaker and scoop up confetti, and dump it back, a couple of times to emphasize the idea of what you plan to do; you are going to use the shaker to scoop up confetti until it is brimful.

On the third scoop, leave the shaker in your hand in the box of confetti, and, without a pause, go right on in the movement and bring out from the box the shaker containing the milkshake. As the top of this has the little tray covered with confetti, it looks exactly the same, as did the other. As far as the audience is concerned, you have simply filled the shaker with confetti. Now, close the lid of the box and set the shaker, apparently filled with confetti on its top.

Now what are you going to do? You have to get rid of the little confetti tray on top of the shaker in a clever manner. It's easy – just follow the drawing, as they proceed along from A through G.

In A you see how you show the cloth, and holding it in front of the shaker drape over the top of the shaker. As you do this, pick up the little confetti-covered tray beneath the cloth and take it off the top of the shaker. The projecting tab makes this easy to do beneath the cloth. See C and D.

The little shelf on back of box now comes in handy. As shown in E the tray on the shelf.

Now, proceed right on and go from E to F, as you pleat the cloth back and forth ending up with a little pad of cloth atop as seen in G.

All is clear for you now . . . just pick up the shaker, with the pleated pad on top, and bring it forward. Remove the pad and glance inside the shaker with a smile. What was at first believed to have been a shaker full of confetti has magically been transformed into a shaker full of luscious milkshake.

Pour the milkshake and fill some glasses, which you serve to a receptive audience.

You have performed a clever bit of magic, but who cares. The tasty milkshake you have produced gets the lion's share of the applause.

And if you are in the mood for a shake, pour a glass for yourself.

Chapter Twenty-Five

Atomic Magic

I have always been a Sci-Fi fan. It all started with *Amazing Stories* years back, as is well known. Many other magazines of science fiction followed suit. I enjoyed them all.

I wrote my book *Atomic Magic* in 1950. It was published by Magic Inc. of Chicago. Laurie Ireland did the job. That was more than 50 years back in time, yet it still stands as solidly as entertainment, as when first written.

Back in the 1950s when I wrote *Atomic Magic* it was the Atomic Age. Today it is all Hi-Tech – it is the Computer Age. Computers rule the roost. A few presentional changes, and the same tricks of this nature fit right in to today's technology. Here are my thoughts on the presentation of "Atomic Magic".

First, in performing Atomic Magic, project your theme into the future. You are speculating on wonders of science yet to come; you are illustrating by conjuring methods things that will ultimately occur. So, in your presentation of Atomic Magic, never claim *now* for your results, rather center their happening in the future.

Second, in applying science fiction themes to your magic, remember to work from the familiar to the unfamiliar. No matter how bizarre or improbable the results you propose, if there is a note of the familiar in it, its logic will be acceptable.

Third, in relation to the magic apparatus you use in your show, you can dress it up a bit to take on a resemblance of scientific apparatus. This is effective and gives a new look to your equipment. There is no need to go overboard in this regard. Just a suggestion of the scientific will suffice: a knob here, a bit of wire there, an insulator, a coil, a meter, etc. – these when artfully applied will turn the trick.

Fourth, there may be a temptation, when thinking in terms of Atomic Magic, to want to dress the part in some futuristic Buck

Rogers type of costume, or come out in a doctor's smock. For some reason, more obvious when it is observed on stage than just written about, such garb somehow always looks amateurish. My advise would be – dress as most naturally befits you, and just be yourself. Be modern, but not ultra modern.

Here is an example of how a simple trick can be dressed up as Atomic Magic.

The Electronic Silk

The effect plays like this.

Switch on the Black Light, it glows with a violet glow. Show your hands empty, and cup them around the Black Light. Hand contact makes the bulb glow even brighter. As it brighten from your touch, a colorful silk handkerchief materializes between your fingers, as though coming directly out of the sparking electrons of the Black Light.

After exhibiting the apparently electronically produced silk, it is rolled into your left hand, formed as a fist. You place your fist on top of the Black Light, and deliberately force the tube-like bulb through it. Your hand is empty.

The silk is *gone!* – apparently back to its electronic source.

Now, pick up the seemingly empty glass and touch it to the top of the Black Light bulb, and instantly it reappears.

Besides the Black Light Bulb mounted upright on your table, you need a couple of props you can get at a magic shop: a "false finger" to produce and vanish the silk, the "Silk Flash" glass to make the silk visibly reappear, and two duplicate small silks of any color that is your pleasure.

Load the "false finger" with one of the silks, and the gimmick in the "Silk Flash" glass with the duplicate silk ready to reappear. Place the "false finger" between the second and ring finger of your right hand. As long as you keep your hand in motion, the illusion is that your hand is empty.

Ready, Set, Go!

Turn on the Black Bulb on your table. Show your hands as though empty, and cup them around the upright bulb. Then gradually, between your hand take off the false finger, and produce the silk – it appears to be materializing out of the Black Light. When silk is produced, replace the "false finger" in position and your hands appear quite ordinary, as you exhibit the silk just produced.

To make it vanish, reverse the produce, and, as you roll it, actually reload the false finger and replace it as you apparently place the rolled silk into your left hand (as a fist). To make it appear to be returned to the electrons of the Black Light, simply start at the top of the Black Light and let it pass on through your closed fist. Open your hand and the silk is *gone* . . . seemingly back to its electronic source.

Now, for the climax of the effect, pick up the "Silk Flash" glass and it seems empty. Just touch it to the top of the Black Light Bulb, as you release the gimmick catch, and instantly – and visibly – the silk *reappears*!

Such a simple trick: you produce a silk, you vanish the silk, you make the silk reappear. So what?

Try it in this electronic Sci-Fi form, and it'll cause your audience to buzz like electricity. It's "Star Trek" stuff.

Incidentally, what are you going to do with the "false finger" when you are through with it. Just ditch it in your pocket. They will never see you do it, as everyone is watching the silk seemingly electronically appear in the glass.

Chapter Twenty-Six
Some Very Tricky Tricks

From time to time, I have used these tricky tricks in my show. All are entertaining.

The Diabolical Eyes Trick

Effect

Standing center stage in the spotlight, your eyes are seen to flash. This is repeated at different times during your performance. You pretend not to notice this is occurring; however, your audience will notice that you have diabolical eyes.

Here's How You Do It

Get a couple of tiny pieces of shiny foil. Cut the foil into two crescent-shaped pieces which will fit your upper eyelids. Use a soluble glue ("spirit gum") and attach these little crescents of foil on the upper part of each eyelid. When the eyes are kept open in normal position, the bits of foil will not show. But when you blink your eyes several times quickly, they will flash in the light. They appear to be shooting out sparks. By crackie, you do have diabolical eyes.

Fun with a Cigar

Henry Gordien advertised this in the *Linking Ring* back in 1929. It is only a gag, but the best dime I ever spent. It's a sure-fire laugh when playing men's clubs.

Say that you will show the boys a trick with a cigar. Go to some fellow who is smoking up a storm with a stub of a cigar in his mouth. Ask to borrow it.

When you get the cigar, look at it quizzically, drop it on the floor, and stamp it out. Say, "This will never do. Will someone please give me an unsmoked, full-size cigar?" A nice fresh cigar is forthcoming. Take it and go over to the man who was smoking the stokie. Hand him over the fresh cigar and say, "With my compliments, Sir." *It's the best laugh in the show.*

Patter for "the Multiplying Thimbles" Trick

If you elect to become a skilful magician, you will learn how to perform "the Multiplying Thimble Trick" in which you start with manipulating one thimble with sleight of hand, and then surprise the audience by ending up with eight thimbles – one on the tip of each of your fingers.

I heard this poem patter by my friend, the late Bill Alstrand. As a magician, Bill had a nickname of "Poogies Poogie" which he frequently used in his patter as magical words to make the magic happen.

The poem goes along just right to fit the trick and ends on the production of eight thimbles on the tips of your fingers. It recites like this:

> I once knew a taylor with fingers quite nimble
> Who had a bad habit of losing his thimble.
> A jewler once sold him a thimble for cash,
> All studded with diamonds to make a great flash.
> Whether he lost it at day or at night,
> It was easy to find because it was bright.
> He would hold it like this, and squeeze it like that,
> 'Hokus Pokus' he'd murmur, and then he'd say 'Skat'.
> He would open his hand, and to his surprise,
> The thimble had flown clear up to the skies.
> He would carefully place it right down in his throat,
>   and then deliberately take it from under his coat.
> Again in his mouth the thimble would melt,
> This time he would take it from under his belt.
> One day he lost it and it couldn't be found,
> The neighbors were all looking around.

The taylor was well versed in legerdermain,
'Hokus Pokus,' he said, 'and chicken chow mein.'
He searched for his thimble, But strange to relate,
Instead of just one, he found he had eight!

Here are a couple of tricks I invented that were sold on the magic market, viz:

Hypnotizing a Rabbit

I have always liked the trick where you turn a rabbit upon its back and it is "hypnotized". Then when you turn it over, it flops back to activity. I used the stunt in many of my shows, as a demonstration following the production of a bunny. For this purpose, I wanted something that was sure acting and displayed the hypnotized rabbit to advantage. This invention did the trick.

The device consists of a trough which is sloped downwards. It is made of wood and of a convenient size to take a bunny lying on its back. A strip of cloth goes across the surface of the trough, so when the rabbit is laid on it the cloth depresses beneath its body. In the hem of the cloth is a metal rod and the other side of the cloth is tacked to the side of the sloping trough. The action is that when the rod in the hem is depressed, the cloth straightens out, flopping the rabbit over – from lying on its back to an upright position on its feet.

The "hypnotized" rabbit will remain immobile even if you were to shoot a blank gun off near it.

To awaken the rabbit, just snap your fingers above it with one hand, while your other hand presses down on the rod in the hem of the cloth. The action goes unnoticed by spectators, and it seems that the snapping of your fingers and command to "Wake up!" brings bunny back to life. All caused, of course, by the action of the device which causes the rabbit to flip over automatically from an on-back position to its feet.

This trick always got a big reaction from the audience, and this device made it practical to use at every show. Percy Abbott (*Abbott Magic Company*) sold a lot of this magical invention.

155

The Vanishing Torch

I invented this trick to open my South Sea Island Magic Show. The magician comes on stage holding a flaming torch. Suddenly, it is tossed in the air and disappears. It is a good flash opening for a show.

My friend, Fred Faltersack, in his workshop, made the first one of these for me. U.F. Grant (Mak's Magic Company) put it on the market with my permission. Here is how "The Vanishing Torch" is made and operated.

Modus Operandi

The torch is made of two metal tubes, one of which telescopes within the other. The inner tube has holes drilled in it and is stuffed with wicking. Soaked with lighter fluid, the torch when lighted will flame brightly (be careful of the flame – keep it away from stage curtains, etc.).

A cord of black elastic is attached to the inside of torch. It is arranged "pull" fashion up the right coat sleeve. In operation, the torch is brought down from the sleeve and held in the hand. When released it instantly disappears up the sleeve, and the sliding-out tube of torch immediately puts out the flame.

Operating of "the Vanishing Torch" is easy. Just bring it down from the sleeve and hold snugly in your hand. Light the torch and walk on stage. A flaming torch makes an interesting entrance. Show it to the audience, then suddenly toss it into the air (apparently – actually elastic "pull" pulls it up the sleeve). It vanishes in an instant. You've captured your audience, the "South Sea Island Magic" show goes on.

Tarbell's Enchanted Cane

The first instruction I ever had in professional magic was in taking the Tarbell Course by correspondence. Tarbell was remarkable in the way he kept in touch with his students via personal letters.

Harlan Tarbell invented this trick. I always like it and present it often in my show when conditions are right for its presentation.

Effect

After passing a hoop over a cane to show nothing is attached to it, the magician causes the cane to adhere to his fingers, balance itself at gravity defying angles, float about and remain suspended in mid-air. This puzzling magical routine is a wonderful example of apparent magnetism and levitation. The principle employed is the essence of simplicity, requiring but little preparation. It is entirely self-contained, the cane is unprepared, and the trick can be introduced at any time during the performance.

Secret Preparation

Use a fine, black silk thread and attach it to the cane, as shown in the first figure of this illustration. The length of the thread will be determined by the length of the cane and the routine the magician wishes to perform. The second and third figures show other methods of arranging the thread, should it be desired to pass cane for examination. In either case, the thread is easily attached and detached.

In describing the various moves in this routine, I will take it for granted that the first method of attaching is used. This is the one I personally use under most conditions.

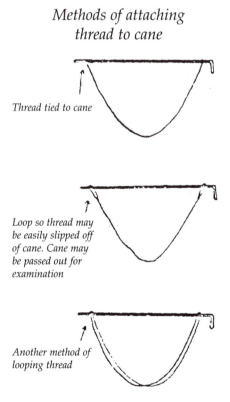

Methods of attaching thread to cane

Thread tied to cane

Loop so thread may be easily slipped off of cane. Cane may be passed out for examination

Another method of looping thread

Presentation

Pick up the cane, with thread attached, and call attention to the effect of earth's gravitation on a cane by dropping the cane from hand to hand. Explain how a cane has been used by mediums to show how it may be controlled at will. Pass a hoop over the cane to show no connections. The thread does not interfere with this.

Method of passing hoop over a threaded cane.

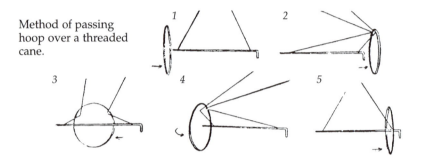

The manipulation of the cane in this routine is shown in the following illustrations.

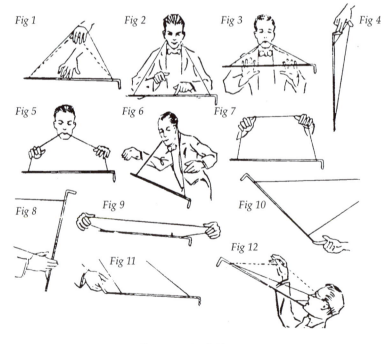

Cane manipulation

1. By allowing the thread to hang over the left hand, the cane will adhere to the fingertips of the right hand (Fig. 1). The dotted line represents a manner in which the thread may pass over the first two fingers. Move the cane up and down, shifting cane accordingly.
2. Grasp the cane with both hands, lower, then raise it high over the head, allowing the thread to fall behind the head. Lower the cane and the thread will be looped over the back of the neck (Fig. 2). In this position, the cane may be controlled very easily, care being taken to keep the thread taut. You can readily see the angle at which the cane may be manipulated, as the hands lightly push the cane away from the pivot thread which is looped around, thus enabling the taut thread to keep it suspended.
3. Figure 3 shows mouth suspension, in which the thread is held by the upper front teeth and may be placed in position very easily when the thread and cane are held as in Fig. 1. The left hand comes up and quietly loops the thread onto the teeth. The mouth is held slightly open, and the move easily blends undetectably.
4. In Fig. 4, the cane is suspended from the first and second fingers of the right hand. The thread is controlled by the thumb. Held in this manner, the cane may be moved about at different angles. Figure 5 is a method of levitation, the thread being suspended from either the mouth or the back of the neck. The hands control the thread by coming towards or away from the body, rising or lowering in accordance.
5. Figures 10, 11, and 12 show what variety of effects may be accomplished in this routine, producing the illusion of extraordinary balancing. The thread is suspended as in Figs. 1 or 2.

In Fig. 2, the cane is held in place against the chin by the thread passing over the ears and around the neck. The dotted line illustrates how the hand may also control the thread to raise or lower the cane. Stand in front of a mirror and practice: all kinds of moves will suggest themselves. Study them so that they blend into one to another in a smooth manner. For instance, when the cane is suspended, as shown in Fig. 2, you can run your fingers along it like playing a piano.

Figure 6 shows how the cane may be levitated so that the hands are free to pass over and under it. Figure 7 shows how levitation effect may be accomplished with the thread passing over both hands. Figure 8 shows the hand moving upward along the cane, causing the cane to lower itself. Figure 9 is an alternative to Fig. 7.

In performing this trick, use the finest quality black silk thread and perform under artificial light at such a distance that the thread cannot be seen. If you arrange to turn off all white and blue lights and flood yourself with red light, the thread will be absolutely invisible.

My Personal Routine for Performing "the Enchanted Cane"

I have found this trick to produce its maximum effect when handled in pantomine against a musical background. The piece "Liebestrom" is excellent for this purpose.

I will give you my routine in numbered sequence so that each step can be easily mastered. It is important that you learn the routine so exactly that it becomes second nature – each sequence blending smoothly into the next to form the whole effect. "The Enchanted Cane" should be gracefully manipulated to form a symphony of motion.

1. Pick up the cane (with the loop of thread attached) in the left hand and the hoop in the right. While casually passing it over the cane, to show it free of all connections, give this introductory patter:

"Ladies and gentlemen, this is an age of marvels, and it has been said that the next great breakthrough will be in the realm of mental science – the magic of the mind. Such forces are called PSI powers, and seem to demonstrate that the mind can control, to some extent, inanimate objects. For some reason, a cane seems to work well for such experiments. For your entertainment, I present The Enchanted Cane."

2. By now, you will have passed the hoop over the threaded cane several times and laid it aside. Drop cane from hand to hand demonstrating the normal effect of gravity upon it. At this time, have musical background commence. Now, follow this fluid

description showing how the moves blend into each other.

3. Grip the cane at its center in the left hand, get the loop of thread over the back of the right hand, and draw the hand back until the thread is taut (see Fig. 1). You can now open the fingers of the left hand wide, and cane will remain suspended (as though magnetized) flat to palm of left hand. As long as you keep the thread taut and move right hand along with left in your movements, you can swing the suspended cane in any direction desired, i.e., right or left, up or down. Finally raise the cane high over your head until the palm of the left hand is parallel to the ceiling. In this position, you can move your right hand away, clear of the thread.

4. Close the fingers of your left hand round the center of the cane. At the same time the loop of thread falls down, move cane back enough so thread drapes behind your neck. You can now perform all manner of suspensions, as explained in the Tarbell instructions (see Fig. 2).

5. Effective suspensions are to have the cane clinging to both hands; then the palm of one hand and then the other. Have the cane cling to your fingers: first four, then three, then two, then one. Finally, place cane against the tip of the thumb and it remains suspended there. All of these suspensions are easy to perform. As with the thread about your neck, all you have to do is push away from yourself; as long as the thread is kept taut, the cane will remain suspended in whatever position you place it. An interesting move is to suspend it from the tips of both your thumbs, placed one near each end of the cane, then turn your hands until the cane is suspended vertically, from the two thumbs. End this sequence by grasping the cane in one hand, close the left hand into a loose fist and push the cane down through hand, and by drawing backwards on the thread the cane will mysteriously rise up through your closed left fist.

Then turn your hands until the cane is suspended vertically, from the two thumbs. End this sequence by grasping the cane in one hand, close the left hand into a loose fist, and push the cane down through the hand, and by drawing backwards on the thread, the cane will mysteriously rise up through your closed left fist.

6. Now bend forward so that the cane is supported horizontally in front of you; the thread hanging from behind your neck (see Fig. 6).

In this position, you can "play the piano" along the cane. It seems to cling first to one finger tip and then another (see Fig. 2). Finally, place tip of cane against the tip of the left forefinger and remove your other hand entirely; the cane seems to be floating out from the tip of the finger in a horizontal position (see Fig. 11). Then remove this finger from the tip of the cane, and the cane appears floating in mid-air (see Fig. 6). Then, by placing fingers through the thread and moving hands outwards the cane rises to your hands (see Fig. 5). This levitation of the cane is startling, but for maximum effect, use it but once in the routine; used too often, it tends to expose the modus operandi. Mostly, you will find it the best deception to have one part of the cane touching some support throughout the trick. Following the levitation, this is a good time to again pass the hoop over the cane, using the moves shown in the illustrations for that purpose.

7. At this point, you can introduce some magical balancing. Place the cane against your fingertips and lean it out at an angle.

Apparently balance it carefully. Then remove your other hand, and the cane appears to be balancing out at a 45Þ angle (see Fig. 10).

You can now balance the cane out from the tip of one finger, as shown in Fig. 11. Then balance it from your chin, as shown in Fig. 12.

From this position of balancing the cane on your chin, you have a perfect opportunity to clear the thread from about your neck for the conclusion of the routine. After having balanced the cane out from your chin, grip it in your left hand, and, in removing from the chin, swing it back in a sweeping motion – back toward the top of your head and then down in front of your chest – in which action the thread is neatly cleared from your neck, and dangles down free from the cane in front of you.

8. In a pass-like motion, gather in the necessary slack in the thread in the fingers of your right hand and suspend the cane magically from your fingers, resting on the top crook of cane (see Fig. 4). The support being entirely from one hand at this point allows you freedom to swing the cane in all manner of directions, and even spin yourself around with the cane still clinging to your fingertips at its top end. If you wish, you can now reverse the cane and support it similarly from its tip end placed against only one fingertip.

9. You are now ready for the concluding move of this routine. Catch the center of the loop of thread in the fingers of your left hand, and with your right hand hold the cane at an angle on the floor. The thread passes, also, over the fingers of your right hand in doing this. Remove your hand and the cane appears to be balancing by itself at an impossible angle on the floor. Passes of the hands will cause it to move and "dance" a bit in this position. When ready to end the effect, pull back on the fingers of your left hand, and, as the thread passes over the fingers of your right hand, which functions as a fulcrum, this causes the cane to rise directly from the floor to your right hand.

This is your climax, so end the effect right there. Let the thread dangle free and twirl the cane in your fingers. The music swells and fades as you take your bow.

Remember: Perform this trick with your stage flooded with red light, and you will have an absolutely charming mystery. No wonder, Tarbell called it "The Enchanted Cane". It is almost like a dance.

The Brain Illusion

Years ago, Nelmar of Chicago called my attention to this effect. I included it in my book, *How To Produce Miracles*. It's a dandy party stunt. I have even presented it against a black curtain on stage as an eerie demonstration.

Effect

You explain that you will make it possible for an observer to see a vision of his own brain. You hand the person a lighted candle and request that he gaze earnestly through the flame at a black cloth tacked on the wall. As the operation is performed, you make mysterious passes about his head, and then he sees it! Before his eyes appears the image of his own brain, in full color.

Here's How You Do It

This weird effect is accomplished through a unique optical illusion produced as the result of the situation in which the observer is placed.

To perform the experiment, tack a yard square of black cloth on the wall, at such a height that the bottom edge of the cloth is at eye level when the subject is seated in a chair. If performing it as a demonstration on the stage, you can use the black curtain for the purpose. Just place a chair before it and line the spectators up on stage to try it, one by one.

Place the chair about a foot in front of the black cloth and have the observer take a seat. Darken the room and hand over a lighted candle to the person. Explain that you are going to give him the "power" to look within his head and see a vision of his brain.

Have the person sit in the chair slanting his head downward a bit and look upward at the black cloth, at about a 45° angle. Now, have him pass the burning candle he is holding from side to side, slower and slower, before his eyes.

Suddenly he will see the image, a startling illusion that appears as a vision of his own brain. Actually what he is seeing is an optical illusion produced by the light of the candle flame reflecting the capillaries in the retina of his eye. In appearance it looks very much like a brain. While the effect is physiological, it is the psychological build-up which makes the effect appear as a miracle.

The Brain Illusion is amazingly effective.

Chapter Twenty-Seven

A Treasure Trove of Mental Magic

As a magician, I really enjoy performing Mental magic. Magical effects of this nature make quite an impression on an audience. Mental magic has been called the most adult form of magic. Basically, conjuring can be divided into two sections: The Magic of the Hands and Magic of the Mind. Of the two, the Magic of the Mind is the greatest. Here are some clever mental magic tricks you can do.

Card Crystal Gazing

Effect

A card is selected by one spectator. A glass is filled with water and a second spectator is told to gaze into it and see if he (or she) can name the card the first person chose. He names it correctly to the surprise of both.

Here's How You Do It

Use the Eight of Hearts in this trick, which is the card you are going to "force". Place this card on the top of the deck. Get a clear flat-bottomed glass, cut a disc of thin transparent plastic to fit inside the bottom of the glass. On this paint with black paint "8H" (meaning Eight of Hearts, naturally). Place the disc inside of the glass so that it fits neatly on the bottom and rest the glass on the black cloth on your table. The glass appears to be empty. Have some water in an opaque pitcher on the table beside the glass. Have a spectator stand by the table and watch as you pour water from the pitcher into glass. Explain that the glass of water is to be used for "crystal gaz-

165

ing" in the experiment, using cards, and that by crystal gazing he is to try to name the card which another person will select.

Then "force" the Eight of Hearts on another spectator. This is easily accomplished by the heap elimination method.

The desired card to be forced is placed on top of the deck. Cut the deck into three heaps, place the top heap in the center, and ask a spectator to select one of the heaps. If he chooses the center heap (most people do), remove the top card of that heap and hand it to him, as the selected card to be used in the experiment in "crystal gazing".

If he points to the center heap, there you are. If he points to one of the other heaps, remove it and have him point to another of the remaining two heaps. If it is the center heap, remove the other heap, which leaves the center heap with the desired card on top, as the selected card. If he points to the other heap, remove it, and the center heap remains. This is called "forcing". Then hand him the top card of the center heap, and the trick proceeds. You are all set to have the second spectator reveal the card by gazing into the glass of water.

This is how. Have a spectator, standing by the table, pick up the glass and place it on his left palm. Gazing down through the water he will clearly see the "8H", and names that card as the card the other person has selected. Once the card is named, immediately take the glass from the spectator and pour the water back into the opaque pitcher – the disc goes with it unseen, and the glass is clean to be passed out for examination.

Poker Clairvoyance

Effect

A royal flush of hearts is shown (five cards: Ace, Ten, Jack, Queen, King of Hearts). The spectators are asked to commit the cards to memory, and then each card is sealed in an envelope (use little manila pay envelopes of such size that will neatly hold the card). A spectator then mixes the envelopes, and it is obvious that the performer has no possible way of knowing which card is in which envelope.

The sealed envelopes are now placed in the performer's hands and held behind his back. He asks a spectator to think strongly of one of the sealed cards in the royal flush and name it. Immediately, he brings forth a sealed envelope from behind his back and hands it over to the spectator to be opened. It proves to be the card named. This is repeated until all of the cards sealed in the envelopes have been correctly brought forth.

Here's How You Do It

You have a duplicate set of the Royal Flush of Hearts (that is duplicates of the five cards used in the trick) sealed in duplicate envelopes. You have memorized the order of these cards in envelopes and placed this duplicate set in your trouser's back pocket.

When the spectator hands you over the sealed cards in envelopes, hold them behind your back and face audience. It is but the work of an instant to exchange this set for the duplicate set in your back pocket, and having memorized the order of the envelopes, you are ready to bring them forth as rapidly as the cards are named.

With the Eyes of Dr. Reese

Bert Reese was the greatest billet reader of his day. Here is a method he used.

Effect

A person writes a question on a slip of paper, crushes it up small with writing inside, and drops into a glass. The glass is covered with a handkerchief, and a rubber band snapped around it. Standing at the opposite side of the room, the performer answers the question. Upon removing the handkerchief from the glass, the billet is removed to verify the prognostication.

Here's How You Do It

The glass used is a "bottomless tumbler" (that is the bottom of a glass has been neatly cut out; this will not be noticed and the glass appears ordinary).

Pick up the glass and hold it in your right hand. Have spectator take a small slip of paper (billet) and write his question upon it, crush it into a small ball with the writing inside, and drop it into the glass. You then take a handkerchief and drape it over the glass. Now transfer the glass from your right hand to your left hand; the right hand palming the billet goes into coat pocket for a rubber band. The rubber band is then snapped over the handkerchief around the mouth of tumbler. Then set the glass on table.

You ask the spectator to concentrate on his (or her) question while you walk to the opposite end of the room, explaining that you will have your back turned to him and to note that you stand as far away from him, as the room allows. This gives you ample opportunity to secure the billet from your pocket, and, while your back is turned, open it and read the question asked. There is no hurry about anything: just take your time as you walk to the opposite end of the room, turn your back, and perform the needful.

Having secretly read the question, crumple it up again in your right hand, and *answer the question* in your best mentalist fashion.

With the palmed slip in your right hand, walk back to the table and pick up the glass – placing it over the palmed slip. Pull off the handkerchief and dump the billet into spectator's hand. The mental magic is complete.

What makes this trick especially interesting is the fact that you answer the question from way across the room from the billet. Actually, this distance is what makes this handling possible, yet is the very factor that makes the feat outstanding to the participant.

A Prelude to Mystery Mindreading

To perform this mental magic trick, you need nine blank business cards (you can get these from any printer). Or, you can make your own – about 2 x 3.5 inches – out of stiff paper (use file card stock). In bold letters, write one of the following names on each card:

ALICE	DAISY	MOLLY
HARRY	JAMES	HENRY
PERCY	DORIS	AGNES

Start the trick by calling attention to the fact that each card has a different name on it. Ask a spectator to mix the cards and to think of one of the names. Then take back the cards and deal them out twice, face up. As you re-gather the cards, say the name the spectator is thinking of. Surprise. It seems like you must have read his mind.

Now, climax the mystery by spelling out that name as you deal one card at a time face down on the table, letter by letter. On turning over the last card you were holding when you spelled the last letter of the name, it proves to be the card with the selected name.

Here's How It Works

Show your audience the nine name cards. Then have the cards shuffled and ask a spectator to think of one of the names. Only he (or she) knows what name they are thinking. Take the cards back and deal the first three cards face up in one pile, the next three in a second pile, and the last three in a third pile. Now, ask the spectator to touch the pile where the thought of the name is. Place this pile between the other two piles when you pick them up.

Next, deal the cards out face up. This time, start a new pile with each of the first three cards dealt. Continue dealing by placing the fourth card on top of the first card (pile number one), the fifth card on top of the second card (pile number two), and the sixth card on top of the third card (pile number three). The seventh card goes on pile one, the eighth on pile two, and the ninth on pile three.

Ask the spectator to again tell which pile their chosen name is in. When they do this, pick up this pile, and, with the names on the cards facing you, note the middle card of the pile. This reveals the name they mentally selected. Remember this name and place the pile between the other two, as you did before. Turn over the entire stack of name cards so that they are all face down.

Now, tell the spectator to concentrate on the name thought of and state you will read their mind. Dramatically call out the name that you remembered from the middle pile, and you will be correct. A mindreading surprise!

Note the subtle psychology of your handling of mental magic. You do not tell the person to think of the name on the cards, you just tell them to think of the name. The audience forgets about the cards, and when you call out the very name the person is thinking of it seems like mindreading.

You are standing holding the stack of cards face down. For the climax of the trick, deal the cards out face down from the top of the stack, one card for each letter of the chosen name. When you reach the last letter, turn over. The name stares them in the face!

Your audience is almost certain to ask you to repeat the trick. Don't do it. Use it as an interest-gathering prologue to the Mysterious Mindreading Act you are now going to mystify them with.

The Mysterious Mindreading Act

You pass out business size cards, with a little envelope into which the card fits, to persons in the audience who have a personal question they would like to have a psychic opinion on. Questions are briefly written on the cards, and each sealed in their respective envelope. Then, you, or your assistant, gathers up the envelopes and brings them to the stage. It is convenient to collect the sealed envelopes in a bowl, which is placed on your table center stage.

You open the act with the comment that you always pretest yourself to see if you are in sync before you attempt to get a mental impression for the audience. To privately test yourself, mix the envelopes in the bowl and bring one out at random. Hold the sealed envelope to your forehead and make up any imaginary question you please, for example, "I get an impression that the question asked in this envelope involves something about moving to the East Coast. Let me check for myself and see how my 'psychic impressions' are operating tonight."

Cut open the envelope and remove the card. Read it silently to yourself, apparently to check – to yourself – how accurate your "psychic perception" was. Make no comment, just smile and nod your head, as though pleased at your perception. "Okay, I seem to be in sync, so let's get busy and see what psychic perception I can do for you." What you have actually done is to memorize the question written on the card taken from the envelope just opened.

The act now proceeds right on target.

Reach in the bowl and bring out another envelope. Hold it to your forehead, as though seeking an impression, and call out the question you have memorized. Look into the audience and ask the person who wrote that question to please stand so that you can work directly with them. Then proceed to answer the question using the clairvoyant method you have learned.

After answering this question, open the envelope and remove the card. Look it over and under the pretex of checking the question to see if you answered it correctly; you memorize the question on the card while calling out the question you have just answered. Have the person in the audience acknowledge you are correct. Then place the envelope and card aside.

Reach into the bowl again and take out another envelope. Hold it to your head, as though receiving a psychic impression, and call out the question. Answer this question by answering the second question which you have just memorized. After answering, cut open the envelope and remove the card, and call out the question you have just answered, as though reading it from the card, just as you did before. At the same time, memorize the actual question on the card. In other words, pretend that you are reading the second question out loud as you memorize the third. You will then be ready to answer the third question from what is apparently the third card, as you remove it from the envelope.

Continue answering all the questions in the bowl, keeping one question ahead each time. Proceed on until you wish to conclude the act. Leave a few unanswered questions in the bowl.

You will amaze your audience when you perform this Mysterious Mindreading Act. Give perceptive answers to the questions, but remember you are an entertainer not a psychiatrist, so keep your answers somewhat lighthearted. Some people take clairvoyant insight very seriously. Always emphasize you are giving *psychic opinions*.

Mindreading in Reverse

I sometime close my Mindreading Act by using this tricky bit of mental magic. It is a demonstration of mindreading in reverse. It appears that the spectator can read your mind.

For this effect, cut five discs from stiff paper and write the following words on these discs, as shown.

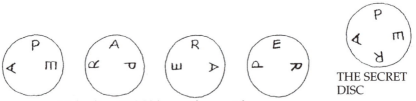

THE SECRET DISC

Make these DISCS larger if you wish

Each of the four discs has a three-letter word on it: APE, RAP, ERA, PER. The fifth disc has four letters on it. This is your "secret disc." Have a hat handy for the demonstration, so you can hide this "secret disc" inside its inner band. You are now, ready, set, GO!

Presentation

Commence with this patter:

"Ladies and gentlemen! people often ask me how they can develop their own psychic talents to receive psychic impressions. Everyone has a natural talent for it. I started practising with this little experiment, using these four discs from the ESP laboratory. [Show the four discs.] Each disc has a simple word on it. On this disc is the word, APE. On this disc is the word RAP. On this the word, ERA. And on this last disc, the word PER. I will show you how to use them in practising psychic perception. Who would like to practise this experiment with me. Someone please volunteer who feels they have talent in the ESP direction."

A volunteer comes forward and stands beside you.

"Thank you! I will show you how you use these discs in practising psychic perception. Remember these four words which are on the discs, as I place them on the table: Remember the word APE. Remember the word RAP. Remember the word ERA. Remember the word PER. Okay, have you got these words memorized?"

Spectator affirms.

"I will place these four discs in this hat, so you can no longer see them visually."

Casually show that the hat is empty (secret disc hidden under inside hat band will not be noticed).

"Now, I will show you how to practise psychic perception. Some call it ESP, which means 'Extra Sensory Perception'. Move now and stand about six feet away from me; turn and face me, and look at the space between my eyebrows, in the center of my forehead."

Spectator does as directed.

"Without looking, I will reach inside the hat and remove one of the discs. What word will be upon it, as yet we do not know."

Keep your gaze upon the spectator, while you reach inside the hat. Fumble around a bit, as though mixing the discs, and bring one out (actually you bring out your "secret disc" from the inside hatband). Hold this four-letter disc towards yourself, so letters do not show.

"Alright, let's try an experiment now to see how well you can do with ESP. Keep gazing at my forehead and make your mind as blank as you can. I will now look at the disc I drew at random and concentrate upon the word selected. As you have remembered, it will be one of these four words: APE, RAP, ERA, PER. Notice these words have a sort of mental ring about them, which is why they are used in the first practice of ESP."

You and spectator keep gazing at each other. Hold up the disc (back outward – letters towards yourself) and comment:

"I am concentrating upon one of these words, selected here now. As you keep looking at the center of my forehead, which of these four words come most strongly into your mind? Don't guess. Allow an impression to come in, as though seeing one of these four words appear inside your head. See it now, while I concentrate on the word on this disc I hold before me. When you get that visualized impression of the word inside your head, call out what impression you get. Take your time."

After a few moments, ask the spectator to call out which word he mentally perceives. When he names the word, you are ready to present the climax of this bit of mental magic. Because your "secret disc" has all four letters used in each of the three-letter words used in the test, when a word is named, all you have to do is grip the disc and cover the extra letter with your thumb when you show the disc, as indicated in the sketch. And there you are – the spectator succeeded in the psychic perception test.

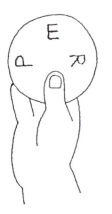

Turn the disc to face the audience and show the word upon it that the spectator has named. Obviously you can thus show the disc with any of the four remembered words. Display the disc showing the correctness of the spectator's Psychic Perception. Handled in this pseudo-scientific manner, this mental trick plays very strong, indeed strong enough to close your mindreading act upon. Audiences like this kind of feat, in which the spectator (who is actually one of them) is successful in accomplishing the demonstration.

I call this mental magic trick, "Mindreading In Reverse".

Zanzig's Blackboard Mystery

This is a feature mindreading act as used by the world's renowned Zanzigs. A blackboard is placed center stage, and a volunteer is invited on stage to assist in the demonstration.

Effect

The performer is blindfolded by his personal assistant. (Use a stiff cloth blindfolded which makes it possible for you to peep down the sides of your nose unknown to the audience.)

The volunteer is handed over a piece of chalk and an eraser. He is instructed to write any word on the blackboard he wishes. He then erases it. He is then told to write any number he wishes from 1 to 5000 and erase it. Finally, he is to draw a geometric design of his choice and erase it. The blackboard is left blank.

You are now led to the blackboard and are handed over a piece of chalk. You ask the person to think of the word he first wrote. Letter by letter you reproduce it on the blackboard. Proven to be correct it is then erased, and you proceed in the same manner to reproduce from the thoughts of the spectator the number he wrote and the geometric design. In every case, you are correct.

You can increase the scope of the trick if you wish to invite three volunteers to the stage and use each in an individual test. Also, it is good showmanship to get the word wrong in the first test, then erase it, and try again – getting it right this time. Get the second test right immediately. Then, on the third test in drawing the design, do a little experimenting and stalling, finally making it perfect.

Here's How You Do It

The blackboard used has no tray on its bottom, so the performer has to be handed over a piece of chalk to draw with by his assistant. The secret is that the chalk has two of its sides smoothed down so that they can be written upon. The assistant standing in the wings sees what has been drawn upon the blackboard in each instance. Using a sharp-pointed lead pencil he writes the word, number, and geometric design on the chalk. When the time comes, the chalk is then handed over to the performer to draw with on the blackboard. As you face the blackboard, hold the chalk at your waist, and looking down the sides of your nose at the chalk, you can easily discern the word, number, and design your assistant has secretly written on the chalk. Thus, you can perform all tests successfully.

When you complete the experiments, casually place the chalk in the coat pocket and exchange it for an unprepared chalk of similar size. The switch will never be noticed, and chalk may be placed on table for examination should anyone care to look at it.

The Electronic Thought Catcher

This is a Mental Magic trick presented with a Sci-Fi theme. It lends itself to same interesting patter:

"Ladies and gentlemen! Among the wonders of the future are bound to be scientific developments in using the wonderful powers of the mind, paramount among such will be telepathy. Indeed, in time you will never think of sending a telegram. It will be a 'telepathgram'. The process will very likely be something like what I will show you tonight.

"You will enter the telepathgram office, place your head within some sort of a head helmet, think your message, and a few seconds later the message will have been received by the person for whom the thought was thought.

"That future is almost here. Let me show you an experimental model – I call it The Electronic Thought Catcher."

You exhibit a wire-cage head helmet, as shown in the sketch. You give it to your assistant to take into the audience for examination. A deck of cards is then thoroughly shuffled, and five or so persons – right in the audience – select a card, with absolute freedom of choice.

Each person is asked to look directly at the card and concentrate on it. Then, the assistant places the Thought Catcher cage helmet over the head of one of those concentrating on their card. You place a duplicate cage helmet on your own head on the stage. You are well away from each other, yet via The Electronic Thought Catcher, as it were, you name each selected card, in turn, as it is concentrated upon.

For the climax of this Sci-Fi Mental Magic effect, you ask a person in the audience to think of one of the popular ESP symbols, i.e. circle, square, triangle, wavy lines or star . . . and draw the image of which he (or she) is thinking upon a slate. His head enclosed in the cage helmet, he concentrates on his drawing. Simultaneously, on your slate you draw the mental impression you receive. On turning both slates over, they are a perfect match.

You have demonstrated: *The future is here!*

Here's How You Do It

To accomplish this sci-fi feat in catching thoughts, construct two wire helmet cages of such size as to loosely fit over a person's head. These can easily be made of copper door screen, fitted up with insulators and mysterious-looking wires, and a ball-like knob on top of the cage helmet. You can make these as simple or as elaborate as you please. The drawing shows the general appearance of the device.

The trick is accomplished by the employment of a simple code used in conjunction with the "thought-catching helmets". When your assistant approaches a spectator to have a card selected, he places the helmet on the floor beside him and requests the spectator to hold his card in front of his eyes and concentrate upon it. At this time, he glimpses the selected card.

The suit of the card is transmitted to the performer on stage in a manner by which the assistant lifts the helmet off the floor to place it over the head of the spectator/participant. If he raises it with his left hand, the suit of the card is Hearts. If he lifts it with his right hand, the suit of the card is Diamonds. If he lifts it with both hands, the suit of the card is Clubs. If he lifts it by the knob on top, the suit of the card is Spades.

The number of the card is conveyed by the position his hand takes on the helmet, as he adjusts it over the spectator's head. The helmet is mentally divided into five divisions on its front and five down its back, as shown.

Thus, your assistant secretly cues you the number of the card the spectator is concentrating upon, by the position of his hand upon the helmet, as he places it over the spectator's head.

These divisions take care of the cards numbered from one to ten. The Jack is signalled by touching the wires on the side of the helmet, the Queen by touching the wires on the right side of the helmet, and the King by touching the knob on top of the helmet after it is over spectator's head.

Thus, in the simple act of picking up the helmet and adjusting it over the spectator's head, the name of the selected card the volunteer is concentrating upon becomes known to you.

The last test, with the ESP symbols, is even simpler . . . but the duplicating of the drawing of the symbols on the slates builds it up to a climax.

In this case, you and your assistant have memorized the ESP in the following order:

1. Circle
2. Square
3. Triangle

4. Wavy lines
5. Star.

The assistant touching signals on the helmet, as it is adjusted to the head of the volunteer, instantly informs you what symbol is being drawn, and you duplicate the same upon your slate.

Perform the effect with showmanship. Take your time. Even adjust your own helmet in various ways to appear to be getting it in sync with the helmet worn by the spectator in the audience so that you can get a telepathgram across.

Simple as the effect and its modus operandi is, when presented with the scientific "Thought-Catching Helmets", and the suggestion you are demonstrating how telegrams in the future will be sent as telepathgrams lifts this mental magic trick into Big Time Theater.

Chapter Twenty-Eight

The Greatest Magic in the World

Delight and I lived always close to nature, and were perfectly content just to be ordinary as is the nature of nature just to be as it is. It is in the ordinary that is found the extraordinary. No ego is involved in this. It is just the case and it makes great magic!

Webster defines magic as the art which purports to produce effect (or is believed to produce them) by the assistance of supernatural beings or by a master of secret forces in nature, hence any seemingly occult power.

The dictionary defines a conjuror as one who pretends to create magic: an entertainer with "legerdemain" (sleight of hand).

In the combining of these two definitions, we have the true art of magic.

As I have mentioned in this autobiography, I have been a professional magician for far more than half a century; in which space and time I have presented many a clever and deceptive tricks. And ever the realization has been that that which is imitated must have a reality from which it is imitated. What and where is this reality to be found? What is the secret modus operandi of that magic? Throughout the world, for a lifetime, I have sought that modus operandi.

The trick of creating in the universe is the ultimate performance of magic. This should be of interest to all magicians, so I will, as best I can, explain the modus operandi to you so that you can perform the trick of *direct creation* and bring what you want into your life.

Modus Operandi for Direct Creation

The basic secret of what will be explained is how to operate the universe as you wish to operate it for the benefit of your life. To do this, first appreciate that since you live in the physical world, in this space and time, you have the personal power to create whatever it is you wish in physical reality. Sounds like magic? Yes, it is magic, yet there is nothing mystical about it; it is a scientific fact.

If it is true that you can directly create what you desire, it is obvious that you create wisely. Indeed, the ability to use your mind wisely is as important as is the ability to mentally create.

Some call this power to directly create in the universe "the magic of believing". Others call it "the power of creative visualization". Those of a more religious nature very likely would call it "the power of God". This last conjecture is not too bad, as the very base of the universe is its divine nature; and, as man is a part of that universe, man is a divinity. And Divinity is God.

To understand this creative power of mind in the universe, we should, perhaps, commence at the beginning. This is nonsense, of course, for the reality is that the universe has neither beginning nor ending. However, most people have habits of organizing their thoughts in a way which likes to start on a beginning, so we may as well concur.

The story on which *The Bible* begins is as good a start as any:

> In the beginning there was void, and the hand of God moved across the void, and therefrom created the heavens and the earth, and man was given dominion over the earth.

"Void" to Buddha meant "nothingness". "Void" to Plato meant "logos". "Void" to Einstein meant "space". All are synonyms. "Void" means that which has no form, that which is just pure energy and energy is the basis of all matter. It would seem therefore (if we must be logical), that the formless is more basic than is form.

To create form out of the formless requires "the hand of God", and "the hand of God" is consciousness, as the entire universe is sentient. Consciousness is the correct term rather than mind, for mind does not exist as fact – mind is only a process for producing thoughts, and thoughts are things which manifest in the physical universe, and behind it all is consciousness.

What is consciousness?

The only way you can understand consciousness is in relation to yourself; it is your awareness of your being (that you are). In other words, it is your *self* within yourself. Please try to understand: it is not your outside self which you see reflected in a mirror; rather, it is your inside *self* which you cannot see at all, yet which you instinctively know is there. And that *self* can manifest as "the hand of God" in the universe.

Consciousness creates and interrelates to consciousness; thus, the accumulation of consciousness of all can be regarded as "ultimate consciousness" and/or "God consciousness". Some call it "Cosmic Consciousness". As previously mentioned, the entire universe appears to have a sentence about it in which can be recognized that the Creator and the Creation are one. Thus, all is God (if you can relate to that term), and man, as part of that creation, can even so create – and he does it best when he is aware (conscious of) that he can.

When you look out into the cosmos and appreciate the vast reaches of space in which there are countless galaxies millions of light years distant; and when you realize that infinity extends to such an extent that there are as many galaxies in the universe as there are grains of sand upon all the beaches of the earth, one can assuredly come to feel very tiny and insignificant before such vastness.

There is no need to when you appreciate that size is relative to what it is being compared to; then you will appreciate that "bigness" has no meaning in connection with the universe, and that it is not impossible but that which you see as a vast universe could be but the inside of an atom in a yet larger universe, and on it goes in a continuum, in an ever expanding universe. As the Hermeticists express it, "As above so below." Or, you can say, "The macro and the micro are but polar opposites of each other." And, as for infinity, it can be looked upon as a point located everywhere at all times, and that we are in infinity where we stand, just as it is infinity in the farthest reaches of space.

If you can come to look at the universe in this way, you will come to recognize that you are as large and significant to this vastness as you are tiny and insignificant to this vastness, and you will become conscious of the fact that you stand – in relation to yourself – at the very center of the universe. It is, thus, that you have the personal power to create (even as God) in that universe.

How do you create in the universe and turn what you wish into physical reality? Before giving you a precise modus operandi, let's consider the various processes involved.

First, to create anything, energy is required. And, since the entire universe operates on energy, you obviously have an infinite supply to use for whatever purpose you please. There is no need for you to create energy. All you have to do is become open to the energy which is there and allow it to flow in and through you. No effort is needed for obtaining the energy for creation, as it is as natural as breathing. In fact, the energy comes into you along with your breath. The process of creation can best be understood if you will but look upon the universe as a great dynamo of energy while you are the one who throws the switch and directs its operation.

To close that switch do this.

Just close your eyes and note what you see before your closed eyes. You see space. That space in physical reality is only a microfraction of an inch between your eyeballs and your inner eyelids, but to your consciousness that space goes on to infinity. That space you are conscious of before your closed eyes is your "screen of mind" – it is your inner space, which is directly linked to the infinity of outer space. Thus, it is upon your "screen of mind" that you can create what you wish to have become reality in the universe – for yourself.

How?

Allow your "self" to use the process of mind to create the thoughts of what it is you wish to create. Let your thoughts *imagine* what is your wish, for imagination is the creative power of the mind. All that *is* starts in imagination, and the more vividly you can imagine your wish, the more potently do you create it, as a fact in the universe.

Now, form these thoughts into mental pictures. Mental picturing is visualization. For example, if it is wealth you wish, visualize stacks of money and prosperity coming to you. If it is health you seek, visualize yourself strong and well – with your body functioning perfectly in every way. If it is youth, visualize yourself becoming more youthful and vital with each passing year; in this you are literally reversing the aging process within yourself. *Nothing is denied you*. Whatever you wish, you can create such as a physical reality in the universe directly through the process of "creative mind", activated by your "self" (your consciousness). It is the greatest magic in the world.

There is a tremendous power being revealed to you here, but it must be remembered that the power is impersonal in its operation.

Accordingly, it can be used for either good or evil, so make certain your spirit is cleansed so that you use it only for good. This is extremely important, for creativity used for good elevates the quality of the universe just that much more, while, conversely, evil lowers it in equal measure.

What you are really doing through the process of visualization is creating a matrix in the basic substance of the universe (from which all matter evolves) which is moldable by thought. In this process, you have commenced the turning of creative thought into physical reality, *and the more vividly the matrix is made and energized, the more rapid and effective is the creation*. Frankly, the universe does not care. But it is of concern to yourself.

The modus operandi of the creative process is as follows:

Decide what it is you wish to create in the universe to become your reality. Make your wish clear in your mind, and then let your wish drop into your heart so that it becomes charged with emotion. From your heart let it drop down deep within you (to your consciousness, which will seem to be located in your body behind your navel center) until your wish is centered in your Being.

Thus, powerfully knowing your wish, you are ready to turn it into reality. For this purpose, lie down on your back and relax. Allow your hands to rest by your sides, palms upwards. Now begin breathing deeply and freely in a regular rhythm, and, as you do this, think of energy from the universe entering your body along with the breath. *Think it and you will feel it*. Become sensitive to the energy as it enters you, and you will experience it as a flow of force mounting within you. The sensation is not unlike that of a flow of electrical current.

Now, close your eyes and witness your "screen of mind" before you as infinite space, and recognize that your inner space is linked with infinite outer space. Use your imagination and visualize that which you desire – then project that mental picture upon your "screen of mind". The more clearly and distinctly you can see that which you have visualized, the better.

With your eyes still closed, turn your attention to the space which is located within your head, between your eyebrows. This has been called the location of what is known as "the third eye". Visualize this so-called "third eye" becoming like a bright star right in the center of your forehead, and direct the energy you have developed in your body into this star, and from that center let the energy beam as a searchlight upon the visualized image you have projected upon your "screen of mind". Beneath this beam of mental light (energy), see your image light up . . . and you will know its creation is underway.

There is a factor which must be recognized in relation to direct creation of a thought form into physical reality, which is that there is action and counter-energy action in the universe.

The universe responds much like a delicately balanced scale: if the positive force of creation is more weighty, the scale will dip in that direction. On the other hand, if the negative force of creation is more weighty, the scale will dip in the direction opposing the creation. *And the degree of influence, for or against creation, is in direct ratio to the positive or negative energy directed towards the matrix.*

This positive or negative influence can be either self-produced or from an outside source. That is to say, if there is no thought in opposition to what you desire to create for yourself as reality in the physical universe, its realization will be readily produced. Conversely, if there is opposition to what you desire to create, its reality will be negated and/or retarded in accordance to the degree of negative energy directed against it.

To counter negativity towards what you wish to create in transforming the formless into form, it is well to develop a matrix of protection against negative influences affecting the original matrix. Usually this is done by visualizing a white light surrounding the original matrix, while holding the thought that this white light is a protective influence warding off all negative influences which could interfere with your creation. This precaution is, of course, unnecessary when what you wish to create is of such a positive nature that there is no cause for negative influences to be directed against it. However, if there is the possibility of counter-negative influences affecting the creation, then it is well to use this method of protection in connection with the creative process.

In addition to visualizing the creation, some like to reinforce the process by verbalizing at the same time, saying in effect, "Mastermind of the universe, I send that which I wish to have created as fact in my life, as it is visualized and energized before me upon my 'screen of mind'. Let this image form as a matrix in space forming the formless into form so that this creation becomes a physical reality in my existence."

Having expressed this affirmation, always add a benediction to the process (which is really a gift of the universe to man) by expressing, "Thank you, Mastermind, for making it so!" This is a form of prayer, and prayer is the way you speak to God, as it were.

Some even like to intensify this affirmation by, in addition to verbalizing it, writing it down on a sheet of paper (which is a way of starting to place in physical form that which is thought of mentally). Some write their wish in the form of a letter to God, to their Guarding Angel, or whatever they feel closest to, as a guiding force in their life. The "letter" is then burned and the affirmation relegated to the universe, as seen in the rising smoke as it disperses into space.

Having sent your affirmation, in whatever manner you prefer, and having said, "Thank you, Mastermind for making it so", (which is the same as saying "Amen" to a prayer) . . . let it go upon its way and visualize what you have asked for to be created as drifting out into space while *knowing* deep within your "self" that that for which you wished is now on its way to become factualized in physical reality – for you!

Such is the way of using this creative process, which is known as "The Secret of the Mastermind" when you work alone. But, when you apply the process in combination with two or more persons who are in harmony with the same creative wish and lend their energy to augment yours, *the power is compounded.*

The use of the Mastermind Principle to create reality in the universe has been used from time immemorial throughout the world. Every primitive tribe has its group of elders. Royalty has its body of peers. Jesus had his group of 12 disciples. In modern times, every corporation has its board of executives energizing the successful handling of the business. Most are unaware of the process they are employing, but it operates regardless of whether or not the users consciously know of the Mastermind Principle, as such is the way the creative force in the universe operates – automatically once it is commenced. However, when one is aware of what is being done, the effectiveness of this method of using "creative mind" is augmented, as it is placed under your direct control.

Such is the secret of The Greatest Magic In The World. As a master magician, use it. It stands as its own proof.

Those who are worthy of being called "great magician" are subtle, spiritual, profound and wise. They are cautious, like men wading a river in winter. They are reserved, like guests in the presence of their host. They are elusive, like ice at the point of melting. They are obscure, like muddied waters.

When magic is really great, men know little of its greatness. It is so mundane in its greatness that its greatness is most often overlooked.

Magic that is very good, but not truly great, wins praise from the audience. An ordinary magician is tolerated by the spectators, while a bad one is despised. When a magician lacks faith in his magic, he seeks in vain to find it in his audience. The really great magician chooses his words, performs his magic and accumulates merit, and his audience comes to feel his magic is their own.

As a magician, if you would truly be a master, never allow the situation to become the master of you. Remember, Master of Magic, you have consciousness while the situation has none.

Chapter Twenty-Nine
Magical Wisdom

There are many secrets revealed in this book. The tricks are magical. Darn good conjuring. However, the greatest secrets I can give you in my autobiography are the two dozen and one of *real magic* presented in this chapter. And they cannot even be exhibited; in fact, they can scarcely be spoken of. Remember, the wise say little . . . it is the ignorant who jabber. I give you these as gifts. They have added to my life; perchance they will to yours.

1. The Nature of God

Unless one is asked about God, it is wisdom to say nothing. For the truth is what can you say about that which is the mystery of mysteries?

About all one can say is that God is the infinite idea, and that the Creator and the Creation are one.

Appreciating this is quite sufficient to put one on the spiritual path. No temple is needed, no church is needed, no cathedral is needed. If one feels a need for a cathedral, go alone into a forest and stand among the stately trees.

2. Recognition of Opposites

For anything to exist it must have its opposites, just as a river must have opposite banks to exist as a river. In the Orient, it is called "The Yin and Yang of Existence".

Opposites are everywhere: beauty must be compared with ugliness to be recognized as beauty. The same with goodness. It is the same with the difficult and easy; the long with the short; the high and the low; the loud and soft; the before and after – all are opposites and each reveals the other. Even existence and nonexistence must exist together to be.

In this understanding, the wise ones are not conspicuous in their affairs; though troubled, they are not irritated; they produce but do not claim; they perform acts but expect no merit. They build but do not dwell therein, and because they do not dwell therein such a one never has to leave.

3. Promoting Peacefulness

Helping others to be happy with themselves is an aim of a wise one. When one does not overly praise anyone, then others do not fill with envy, just as not praising a rare treasure deters a man from becoming a thief.

Therefore, the wise one does not suggest unnecessary things to prove any special worth, but simply seeks to satisfy others by promoting harmony. Such a one tries to keep those who are ignorant content and those who have knowledge to restrain from using it unwisely. When such a one practices restraint, then things become more at peace.

4. Impartiality

The universe is not like most humans, as it is impartial. All things are regarded without judgment and are accepted as they are.

The wise man is also impartial. To such a one all men are similar and none particularly favored. Because of this, all seek him as their friend. The gossip soon has no friends, as it is doubtful that he can be impartial.

5. The Value of Humility

Heaven is eternal and earth is lasting. The reason why heaven and earth are eternal and lasting is because they do not exist for themselves.

From this the wise man learns his lesson and keeps his ego out of sight. By doing so he becomes notable. He subordinates his personality, and therefore he is praised.

6. *The Nature of Goodness*

True goodness is like water. Like water it ever seeks the lowest place – the place that most avoid. In that gentle spot is found contentment.

For a dwelling he chooses the quiet meadow; for a heart the circling eddy. In generosity he is kind; in speech he is sincere; in authority he is order; in affairs he is ability; in movement he is rhythm.

7. *Keeping Things in Moderation*

If one continues to fill a pail with water after it is full - the water is wasted. Continuing to grind an axe after it is sharp will soon wear away the axe.

In like manner, it is difficult to protect a building in which are gold and jewels. The price of wealth, position, and possessions bring about their own misfortunes. To win true merit, to perceive just fame, the personality must be kept in moderation.

8. *What the Wise One Finds Possible*

By being patient the restless mind can be disciplined. By self-control one can unify his character. By close attention to the will, compelling gentleness, all wrath subsides. By purifying desires one can lessen faults.

In measuring out rewards, the wise man will act like a mother bird. While sharply penetrating into every corner, he appears to be unsuspecting. While directing people he takes no pride in commanding. He benefits everyone but without claim of payment. He will persuade, but does not compel by force. By self-control one can unify his character. By close attention to the will, compelling gentleness, all wrath subsides. By purifying desires one can lessen faults. By loving people must distrust can be avoided.

9. *Where Real Value Lies*

Although the wheel may have 30 spokes, its utility lies in the emptiness of the hub. The outside of a jar may attract attention, but its usefulness consists in its capacity. A room is made by cutting out windows and doors through the walls, but the space the walls contain measure the room's real value.

In the same way, the outside of a man may glitter, but it is what is inside of him that is of true importance.

10. *The Inner Significance of Things*

An excess of light blinds the eyes; an excess of noise harms the ear; an excess of food deadens the taste; the lure of treasure tempts one to steal.

Therefore the wise one attends to the inner significance of things *and* does not be overly concerned with outward appearance. This is another way or saying, the wise one ignores matter and seeks the spirit.

11. *On Avoiding Stress*

Favor and disgrace are alike to be feared just as too great care or anxiety are bad for bodily health. Why are favor and disgrace alike to be feared?

To be favored is very taxing; to obtain it is as much to be dreaded as to lose it. And, of course, to lose it is so much like disgrace.

Why are excessive care and anxiety bad for one's body? The very reason you have anxiety is because you have a body. If you had no body then how could you be anxious.

Therefore let him or her who has business in the world esteem the business as their own body, then such a one is worthy to be trusted with the business.

12. *Appreciating that which is Profound*

It is unseen because it is colorless; it is unheared because it makes no sound, when seeking to grasp something, if it eludes the grasp it is because it is immaterial.

Because of these qualities it cannot be examined, yet such form an essential unity. Superficially it appears obscure, but in its depths it is not obscure.

It appears and then disappears, as a magician makes things happen on the stage. It is what is known as the form of the formless, the image of the imageless. Its face cannot be seen in front or its back behind.

And so the wise man may understand the present because he knows the origin of the past.

13. *The Code of the Great Magician*

Ones who are worthy to be called great magicians are subtle, spiritual, profound, and wise. They are cautious like men wading a river in winter. They are reserved like guests in the presence of their host. They are elusive like ice at the point of melting. They are obscure like muddied waters.

The great magician can clarify muddied waters by slowly quieting them. He can make conscious unconscious men by slowly moving them. He does not desire more. Being content, he is able to mature without wishing to be newly fashioned.

14. *The Simplicity of Great Magic*

When magic is really great, men know little of its greatness. It is so common placed in its greatness that its greatness is overlooked.

Magic that is very good, but not truly great, wins praise from the audience. An ordinary magician is tolerated by the spectators, while a bad one is despised.

When a magician lacks faith in his magic, he may seek in vain to find it in his audience.

How carefully the really great magician chooses his words. He performs his illusions and accumulates merit, and his audience comes to feel his magic as their own.

15. The Way of Greatness

To become great do not seek greatness. The wise man, embracing unity as he does, will become the world's model, and that is greatness. For then he serves a purpose for others and not for himself alone. Not pushing himself forward he will become a leader; not asserting himself he will become distinguished; not boasting of himself he will acquire merit; not approving himself he will endure. For as much as he will not quarrel, the world will not quarrel with him.

16. More on Greatness

It is not natural to stand on tiptoe or when riding to try to walk. One who displays himself is not bright, or one who overly asserts himself cannot shine. A self-approving man has little merit nor does one who praises himself grow.

The relation of these things to true greatness is as offal is to food. They are excrescences from the system. A great man does not dwell in them.

17. Returning to Simplicity

When one abandons the show of greatness and relinquishes excessive prudence, then people will benefit a hundredfold. Abandoning ostentations and conspicuous righteousness, then people will appreciate real affection. Abandon cleverness and relinquish gains, then thieves and robbers will disappear.

Here are three fundamentals on which you can depend: let all hold to that which is reliable, namely recognize simplicity, cherish purity, and diminish desires for what one does not really need.

That is the simple life, and a simple life is free of complications.

18. *The Development of Skill*

Good walkers leave no tracks, good speakers do not stutter, good mathematicians need no calculator, and good wardens have no need for jails, as no one can get by them. Good binders can dispense with rope and cord, yet none can unloose their hold.

Therefore, the wise man trusting in goodness appreciates all men and there are no outcasts to him. Trusting in goodness such a one appreciates all things, for there is nothing valueless.

Therefore, the good man is the instructor of the evil man, and the evil man is the good man's wealth. And the evil man who becomes a good man does not esteem his instructor or value his wealth lest he become confused. Herein lies the significance of spirituality.

19. *Recognizing the Value of Self*

He who knows his manhood and understands womanhood becomes useful like a spring which brings forth water. Being like a spring he will be filled with the vitality which is the nature of things. And with the increasing of his vitality evermore is the increasing of the value of himself.

He who knows his innocence and recognizes his faults becomes a model for other men. He who knows the glory of his nature and also recognizes his limitations becomes useful. Being useful he will revert to simplicity. Radiating simplicity he will make of men vessels of usefulness.

20. On Being Willing to Let Things be as They Are

One who desires to remake the world will fail. The world is a divine thing that cannot be remade. He who attempts it will mar it.

He who seeks to grasp it will lose it. People differ: some lead, others follow, some are ardent, others are formal, some are strong, others weak, some succeed, others fail.

Therefore, he who is content lets thing be and practices moderation; he abandons excessive pleasure, extravagance, and indulgence.

21. Obtaining a Tranquil Mind

Obtaining a peaceful mind is the greatest of gifts. Obtaining an open mind brings in composure, remembering . . .

All things are in process, rising and returning. Plants come to blossom, but only to return to the root. Returning to the root is like seeking tranquility; it is moving towards its destiny. To move toward destiny is like eternity. To know eternity is enlightenment, and not to recognize eternity brings disorder to the mind.

Knowing eternity makes one comprehensive; comprehension makes one broadminded; broadmindedness bring nobility, and nobility is like heaven. And heaven is to have a tranquil mind.

22. The Virtue of Discrimination

He who knows others is intelligent; he who understands himself is enlightened; he who is able to conquer others has force, but he who is able to control himself is mighty. He who appreciates contentment is wealthy. He who dares to act has nerve; if he can maintain his position he will endure; but, he who, dying, does not perish is immortal.

23. The Tenderest is the Strongest

The more tender things of creation race over the hardest. A non-material existence enters into the most impenetrable. Therefore, recognize the advantage of a doctrine that just goes with the flow and accepts all life offers as a miracle. How few there are alert enough to accept this assertion.

24. The Position of Great Magic

Great Magic is all pervading. It can be on both the right hand and the left. Everything relies upon it for its existence and it does not fail it. It lovingly nourishes everything, but does not claim ownership. It has no special desires, so it can be classed with the small as well as with the large. It can be classed with the great.

Therefore, the wise man to this end will not pose as a great magician, and by doing so will express his greatness.

25. Returning to the Mysteries of Mysteries

The universe is sentient; there is within its nature BEING that is all-inclusive which existed before heaven and earth.

That BEING is calm and incorporeal. It is alone and changeless.

Everywhere it functions unhindered. It therefore becomes the Creator of all Creation. No man fully knows its nature, as it is distant and evasive. Yet the distant is ever coming near.

If I were to give it name, I would call it THE MYSTERY OF MYSTERIES. What better magic can I give you.

Chapter Thirty

Some Famous Magicians I Have Seen

As you grow in magic, the performances of famous magicians you have come to see contribute to your growth, and some even give you a favorite feat of magic along the way.

The first magician who impressed me was Herman Hanson. My folks took me to see a vaudeville show at the Pantages Theater in San Francisco. That was back in 1925. Hanson and the Burton Sisters were on the bill. I remember it well.

Hanson

Herman Hanson was a tall, slender man with a great sense of theater. He was known as "the Magic Man". For years he was stage manager and illusion builder for "the Great Thurston Show". His full stage vaudeville magic act, combined with the talents of the musical comedy stars, the Burton Sisters, was an unforgettable event.

The act opened with the Sisters singing a song and producing ribbons from their hats. Hanson entered and produced a number of doves from the ribbons.

Hanson removed his gloves and changed them into an egg; the egg multiplied to four. One egg enlarged. The giant egg was cracked open, and a hen produced.

One of the Burton Sisters came out with a kewpie doll and took center stage. She sang, "My kewpie baby". Hanson took the doll and placed it in an empty small cabinet. The cabinet grew to twice its size, and opened to reveal a full-size person dressed as the kewpie; the girl who brought the doll walked the kewpie off stage. His show continued right on music cue.

Hanson borrowed a watch and changed it into a canary. The canary was placed in a paper bag and hung over the bulls' eye of a target. A shot was fired and the target changed into a cage with the canary inside. The watch was finally recovered tied about the neck of a teddy bear in a nest of boxes.

Hanson closed his act with a flag tableau, in which a cabinet was shown empty and the curtain closed. Flags of many nations sprung up from the top and sides of the cabinet; the curtains opened and the Burton Sisters stepped forth dressed to represent the Army and Navy of the U.S.A.

Hanson was a mechanical genius at creating illusions. The illusion which impressed me the most was the enlarging kewpie doll. Here is the effect and construction details:

Effect

A large ABC block is seen on the stage with a toy balloon floating above and tied to the block with a silk ribbon. The ribbon runs through the top of the block and is fastened on the bottom with a thumb tack to keep it in position. The front doors of the block are opened, and it is wheeled around and shown empty (see below).

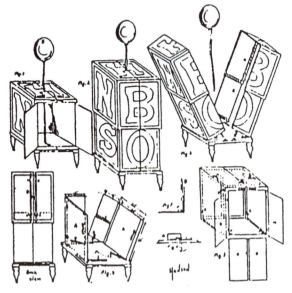

Hanson's Kewpie Doll Illusion

A small kewpie doll is placed inside the ABC block, and the doors closed. On Hanson's command, the block slowly slides upward to twice its height. It then splits in half revealing one of the Burton Sisters dressed as the kewpie doll. She is holding the ribbon attached to the balloon, as the girls walk off stage together.

Modus Operandi

The girl representing a kewpie doll, with a papier-mache head, is concealed behind mirrors. The ribbon holding the balloon conceals the front edges of the mirrors. When the front doors of the ABC block are closed, the girl inside opens the mirrors which lay flat against the inside of block, then places the small kewpie doll back of the elastic band and holds the position while performer turns the cabinet halfway around with the back facing the audience. The girl then gets in position and takes handles, one in each hand, and on cue slowly pushes the outside shell (of block) upwards, until the hinges are automatically closed. Girl now opens hooks and at cue from performer pushes the two halves apart, revealing herself as the large kewpie doll. In the action, she frees the ribbon and holds it attached to the balloon. To the audience, it appears that the little doll has grown into a full-size person.

Richards

The first full evening magic show I saw when a boy was Ralph Richards. As many magicians have, he billed himself as "the World's Greatest Magician", and his show was one of the best. I saw it twice at the Liberty Theater in San Jose, just before I started high school in 1927. He impressed me tremendously. His show, lasting two and a half hours, was in three acts. Richards was a tall, bald-headed man of rapid speech. He had dash! In Acts One and Two, he presented magic and illusions. Act Three featured mentalism. He called it "Psychomlency."

Using a crystal ball, standing in the midst of an oriental setting, he answered questions for spectators in the audience. It was an Alexander style of presentation. Richards must have considered mentalism his forté, for he later dropped magic and did a psychic question-answering radio program from a station in Mexico across the border from Texas.

Carter

In 1928, I saw the show of Carter the Great. My folks took me to see Carter at the Curran Theater in San Francisco. He had booked the engagement to rehearse his show *live* before an audience prior to taking it on tour in the Orient. He died in India during that tour.

Charles Carter was a stocky man with gray hair. He presented his magic in a business-like way, carefully explaining each effect to the audience. His show ran like this:

Carter opened by placing a red silk handkerchief in a decanter. The silk instantly vanished and reappeared in a second decanter on a table. Feigning surprise, Carter removed the silk and filled the decanter with water. He then covered it with a cloth, which he promptly removed to show the water had turned to ink. The ink then visibly changed back to water.

A series of card flourishes was then performed, after which three cards were selected by members of the audience. The cards were returned to the deck, and the deck placed in a glass on stage. In answer to Carter's command the cards rose, one by one, from the deck. A fourth card was selected, torn to bits, and the pieces placed in a pistol along with a thumb tack. Carter aimed the pistol at a derby hat on stage, fired it, and the card appeared, restored and tacked to the crown of the hat.

Three cups were shown empty. The first was filled with bits of white paper, the second with colored confetti, and the third with bran. Magically the paper bits changed to milk, the confetti to sugar, and the bran to coffee. Carter's assistants served some to the audience.

A spiritualistic effect was next performed in which a carved-wood lady's hand was placed in the center of a transparent pane of glass resting across the backs of two chairs. The hand rapped in spirit code (one rap for "No", two raps for "Yes", and three raps for

"Maybe") the answers to questions asked by the audience.

Carter borrowed four rings from four ladies, and loaded them into a pistol. The pistol was fired at a box which had been hanging in front of the curtain all evening. On opening the box another was revealed, inside of which was yet another, and finally one more. Opening this last box, three of the rings were found and returned to their owners. The fourth ring was missing. Carter apologized and offered the party a consoling drink poured from a wine bottle. The bottle was broken and inside was found a white rat with the fourth ring tied about its neck. The ring was removed and returned to its owner. Wrapping the rat in a newspaper and unwrapping it, the rat had transformed into a rose which was given to the lady by the gracious magician.

The first act of the show was concluded by Carter performing the popular "Sawing a Woman in Half" Illusion.

The second act of the show began following the "Ben Bolt Overture". The curtain opened on an Oriental Temple scene. Carter presented the "Levitation Illusion," in which a girl floated in mid-air.

An open frame cabinet was then displayed with a chair attached to rope in its center. A girl sat in the chair, and was raised in the air. Carter fired a pistol; the chair dropped to the stage; the girl was GONE!

A Spirit Seance was next presented, in which a cabinet was shown empty and the doors closed. There were little windows in the doors, and hands appeared out of the openings. When the cabinet opened, nothing was inside. It was a spooky effect.

Carter then introduced Evelyn Maxwell, billed as a "Psychic Marvel." Blindfolded she answered questions which members of the audience had deposited in a bowl in the theater lobby.

Following Miss Maxwell, Carter presented a series of illusions, climaxing with hoisting a platform bearing six persons. A pistol shot, the platform crashed to the stage, and all six had vanished.

I learned a lot about how to put together a full evening show from watching Carter the Great.

Some years later, at a theater in Oakland, California, following Carter's death, I saw his brother perform the show. The magic and illusions were the same, but the magician lacked the precise showmanship of the original Carter. It takes experience.

There is an interesting "tag" to Carter's life. For years no one knew what had become of his massive equipment until workmen, demolishing a condemned house in San Francisco, discovered the cache in a secret room. Many of the pieces are on display at Earthquake McGoons in the City by the Golden Gate.

Brush

I was a sophomore in high school when Brush the Great came to Paly Hi to present an assembly show.

In his heyday, Edwin Brush had been a top performer in Chautauqua. His presentation of magic was in the style of that era. Brush insisted on including a moral lesson in his show.

I recall him inviting a dozen boys upon the stage to stand in a row while he squeezed a rubber bulb beneath the nose of each, and asked what they smelt. They said, "cigarettes". Brush then delivered a brief lecture on the hazards of smoking and how detrimental it was to health. He was ahead of his time. Today the Surgeon General of the United States gives the same warning.

After the show, Principal Nichols took me backstage to meet Brush. He was kind to me, and sponsored my joining the International Brotherhood of Magicians (I.B.M.). W.W. Durbin was president of the I.B.M. at that time. Each month members received the organization's magazine "The Linking Ring". It contained lots of tricks and dealer's ads of magical things you could buy. Joining the I.B.M. gave my career in magic a big boost.

Edwin Brush and I became good friends over the years. I visited him a numbers of times at his home in Stockton, California, prior to his death in 1967. Ed and I would discuss magic into the wee morning hours. He gave me his "Traveling Croquet Ball" trick. It went like this:

Effect

A boy is invited on stage to assist the performer. The magician shows a large cloth bag. The boy reaches inside and removes a full-size croquet ball made of solid wood. The cloth bag is shown empty, and the boy holds it tightly.

The magician takes the croquet ball, drops it on the floor to prove it solid, then places it inside a paper bag. The bag's top is tied with string, and the bag suspended from a stand on table top. A pistol (blank gun) is fired at the paper bag, blowing it to bits. THE CROQUET BALL IS GONE! The boy reaches inside the cloth bag he is holding and discovers that the ball has traveled back to it.

Modus Operandi

Two duplicate croquet balls are used (both wood balls with a stripe of color painted around them as customary). The cloth bag used in

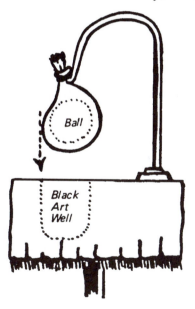

"Traveling Croquet Ball" trick

the trick is an oversized "Egg Bag", with the secret pocket inside so that it may be shown empty, and then allow the concealed ball inside to drop down into the bottom of the bag ready to be produced when desired.

One of the croquet balls is concealed in the secret pocket, and the other is in the bag proper. The boy reaches in and removes the ball from the bottom of the bag. The bag is apparently shown empty by turning it inside out, and back again, in which process the concealed ball drops into the bottom of the bag and the boy holds it tightly at the top. If the bag is made of heavy cloth (velour is best), all works fine for this part of the effect.

The magician then takes the visible ball and drops it on the floor with a THUD to show it is solid. It is then placed in a paper bag, the top being tied with string. Bag with ball in it is then hung from a stand mounted on table top. Unknown to the spectators, a "black art well" is in the table top, directly under the suspended ball, as shown in the illustration.

To make the croquet ball vanish, all you have to do is blow the paper bag to pieces with the blank pistol. Shoot it right up close. Due to the concussion of the gun, the blinking of the audience's eyes as it discharges, the bits of paper bag flying about, and the weight of the ball falling directly downward into the "black art well", the vanishing of the ball is a complete mystery. It happens so quickly you could say it happens in the "blinking of an eye!"

All you have to do now is have the boy reach in the bag he is holding and remove the duplicate ball. The trick is complete.

Cardini and Charlton

The Golden Gate Theater in San Francisco was a mecca of vaudeville shows. It was on that stage that I saw some top performers during my early years in magic. It was there that I saw Cardini and Charlton perform. Cardini inspired my cigarette production act, and Charlton inspired my favorite "Cut and Restored Rope" routine.

Cardini was a feature act in the Burns and Allen Revue when I first saw him perform. He was a wonderful sleight-of-hand magician.

Absolute perfection. His act ran only twelve minutes, but it stopped the show. Performing immaculately dressed in tails, with just a trace of being tipsy, he produced myriads of playing cards in his gloved hands, manipulated billiard balls, and caught lighted cigarettes from the air, closing with a surprise production of a lighted cigar and then a pipe, as he sauntered off the stage.

Chris Charlton was an English magician. He was a friendly man whom audiences liked immediately. I later met him and his daughter at a party given in his honor by the Oakland Magic Circle. Among the tricks he performed in his act was the classic "Mixed Up Handkerchief", in which a borrowed pocket handkerchief turns into pieces, then becomes a long strip, and is finally restored. I worked up a simplified method for doing it.

Effect

The loan of a white pocket handkerchief is requested, and a boy is asked to bring the handkerchief on stage and help with the trick. You explain to the boy that you will teach him how to make the handkerchief disappear by magic.

You carefully fold the borrowed handkerchief and place it in a cloth bag. The boy is told to say "the magic words" (something difficult so that he'll stumble over it). The handkerchief fails to vanish, and is removed from the bag. The folded handkerchief is placed in the boy's hands, and he is instructed to try again. Again the handkerchief fails to vanish, and is discovered to have gone to pieces (into 16 small squares of cloth).

The 16 pieces of handkerchief are gathered up in your hands and the boy told to again say "the magic word" to restore the handkerchief. He tries. When you pull out the pieces, they are seen to have formed into a long strip. Exasperated, you place the strip back in the cloth bag. The boy tries again to make it vanish, but fails. On reaching inside the bag, the handkerchief is still there. He brings it out, and it is seen to be in its original form – RESTORED! You comment, "We'd better get the handkerchief back to its owner while all's well that ends well!"

Modus Operandi

To make this trick, take a large white pocket handkerchief and cut it into 16 squares approximately 3" x 3" in size. See Fig. 1 of drawing. Two of these squares are now sewn around their three sides forming a bag-like square. See Fig. 2. Next get a strip of white cloth approximately 1½" wide by 4" in length. One end of this strip is sewn to the edge of the mouth of the "bag square". See Fig. 3. So prepared, fold this strip up carefully – keeping it flat by zigzagging back and forth – and place it neatly folded within the "bag square". Stack the other 14 small squares of handkerchief on top of the loaded "bag square", and press them down tightly so that they make as flat a bundle as possible and look like a folded pocket handkerchief. The cloth bag used in the effect is called by magicians

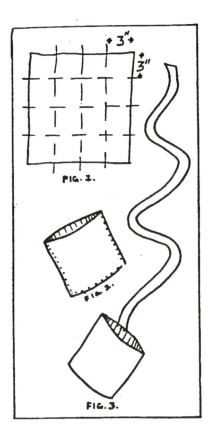

"Mixed Up Handerchief" Trick

a "Changing Bag" (this consists of a cloth bag with a partition down its center so that what is placed in one side of the bag can be exchanged for what is in the other side, and the bag turned inside out to show empty. Any magic shop can supply you with a "Changing Bag" professionally made. Place the bundle of pieces in the "Changing Bag" so that they are hidden behind the partition in it. The bag may now be shown empty as desired. All is now ready for your performance.

As outlined in the effect, borrow a plain white pocket handkerchief and request a boy to bring it up on stage. Accepting the handkerchief, you explain to the boy that you will show him how to make it disappear by magic. You fold the handkerchief neatly into a small parcel (so that it resembles the bundle of pieces you have within the "Changing Bag") and hand it over to the boy while you show the bag empty. The boy is then requested to place the folded handkerchief inside of the bag. Immediately, make the secret exchange within the bag, as you tell the boy to pronounce the magic words needed to make the handkerchief vanish. The boy tries and fails, as on reaching into the bag the handkerchief is removed. (Actually, what is removed are the prepared pieces which you have secretly exchanged for the handkerchief.) The boy is given the bundle of pieces (apparently the folded handkerchief) and told to hold them tightly. At this point, you can casually show that the bag is empty by turning it inside out.

The boy is then requested to try again to make the handkerchief vanish. He holds it tightly. On opening his hands, it is still there; so, you pick it up and discover that it has gone to pieces. As you show the small squares of handkerchief, one by one, drop them on the boy's outspread hand until you come to the last three (of which the very last is the "bag square" with the folded strip inside). These latter pieces you fan in your hand as you look quizzically over the strange turn of events.

You attempt to remedy the situation by gathering up the pieces and bunching them together in your right hand. As you do this, keep track of the position of the "hag square" and its opening, so you can grasp the end of the long strip and pull it out when desired.

Having bunched up the cloth squares, you ask the boy to try again repeating the magic words. He fails again, but, now, instead of small squares, they are seen to have formed into a long strip. This humorous result is easily accomplished simply by reaching into your right fist with the left fingertips and gripping the end of the long strip which you pull out to its full length. The small squares remain bunched up in your right hand; the presence of the long strip covers them perfectly.

Seemingly further exasperated at this new turn of affairs, you gather in the long strip and place it back into the "Changing Bag" (the whole bundle – little squares and all – goes in at the same time), and you make the switch inside of the bag. Again boy tries to vanish the handkerchief in its now mutilated condition. You ask him to reach inside the bag and see if it's gone, and he pulls out the original handkerchief now back in its original form. During this surprise, you turn the bag inside out showing it empty and, while all is well that ends well, request the boy to return the borrowed handkerchief to its owner.

Thurston

Seeing the Great Thurston Show has always been one of the highlights of my life in magic. I saw Howard Thurston perform on the stage of the Orpheum Theater in San Francisco in 1932. I was attending San Jose State College at the time. During that period, Thurston had condensed his full evening show and was playing vaudeville houses in conjunction with a motion picture.

The Thurston Show was tremendous, carrying 30 people and tons of equipment. The man himself was even more tremendous. He was a master of theater. He had an incredible control of his audience, as he knew the magic of consciousness. His audience responded as he felt within himself. He produced laughter when he wanted it; he produced awe when he wanted it. Thurston would have the audience laughing, and with a mere raising of his hand for silence, the audience would hush on the instant – children as well as adults. In some ways, Thurston loved children the most and they knew it; we are all children at heart especially when it comes to magic. Thurston's show was a love affair with his audience. I have only seen one other performer with such remarkable audience control: Maurice Chevalier.

I wrote Howard Thurston a letter asking if I might meet him back-stage. He sent me an invitation. I met him in his dressing room. He was eating oranges. I remember it well.

Calvert

John Calvert is another big-time magician I saw perform. I caught his show both in San Francisco and in Hollywood. Calvert had an air about him of an Errol Flynn. He worked in a jaunty style, dressed in sport coat and white flannel trousers, amidst a stageful of gorgeous girls. I remember him coming on stage singing, "There's a 'Bluebird On My Shoulder". and producing a blue bird which he placed upon his shoulder.

Calvert was always the actor, and later did a number of starring roles in motion pictures, as "the Falcon". He became a world traveller on his own yatch and performed in leading capitals of the world. He is still going strong as a top name in magic. A biography of his life has just been published.

Calvert was a personal friend of my partner, Ron Ormond, so I got to know him well. I worked in a motion picture with him produced by Ron Ormond's son, Tim. Later, I saw Calvert perform as fea-tured artist for the National Guild of Hypnotists Convention in Nashua, New Hampshire. Calvert is quite a man, and his lovely wife, Tammy is ever there.

Raymond

Close on to seeing "the Great Thurston Show", while attending San Jose State College, in 1932, I had the opportunity to see" the Great Raymond" perform. After class one evening, I walked over to the Fox California Theater to see what stage show was play-ing. It turned out to be a Fanchon & Marco Revue starring Raymond. I was delighted. I was treated to the performance of a truly great magician. Maurice Raymond was a smiling gray-haired gentleman – elegant and charming. The show Fanchon & Marco had built around him was splendid. I especially recall his opening.

Following the overture, the curtain parted to full stage in the center of which was a frame cabinet at the top of a flight of stairs. The Fanchon & Marco girls entered and did a chorus line number, then parted to form two rows facing the stairs. There was a flash of fire, and Raymond magically appeared in the cabinet. He walked down the stairs and the show started. His show was smoothly paced interspersed with chorus girl production routines. The first trick Raymond did was to cover a bowl with a foulard and fill it with oranges, which were tossed to the audience. I have used the routine since in my own shows. It goes like this:

Effect

A bowl covered with a foulard rest on a draped table. Foulard is removed and shown. It is then replaced over bowl, and bowl is removed from under and exhibited empty. Magician picks up foulard from table and deposits inside bowl. Table drape is whipped aside and discarded. Bowl with foulard inside is placed on the now bare table. Magician picks up foulard and oranges tumble out and fill the bowl to overflowing.

Magician advances to front of stage and tosses the oranges as gifts to audience.

Raymond had two such outfits on opposite sides of stage, and produced two bowlful of oranges.

Modus Operandi

The trick is accomplished by having a special bag loaded with oranges hanging behind table. As table is covered with a drape, it is concealed from audience view. Empty bowl with foulard over it rests on table top.

In performing, the action of the trick is as described: first the foulard is picked up from the bowl and displayed. It is then redraped over bowl, in which action bowl is removed from under foulard, which falls to surface of table with its center directly over the support hook of load bag, at rear of table. Bowl is then shown empty, and foulard is again picked up from table (this time secretly carrying load bag, filled with oranges, beneath its folds. The foulard (load and all) is then crumpled into bowl. Table drape is whipped off and tossed into air. Bowl (with crumpled foulard inside) is then placed on bare table top. All is brought forward to footlights, and the magic is ready to occur.

Gripping the "load bag" through the cloth of foulard, a mere tap on the bottom of the bag on inside of bowl, and the oranges tumble out filling the bowl. It is a surprising production which is climaxed by tossing the oranges to the spectators.

Fig 1   *Fig 2*

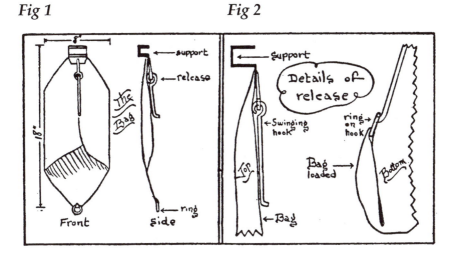

The drawings show the construction of the apparatus. Fig. 1 is the load bag showing how release of the oranges is accomplished, in tapping it inside the bowl. Fig. 2 details the hook arrangement for hanging load bag behind table and release of oranges which tumble out to fill the bowl, in the presentation. Fig. 3 is a side view showing how the load bag with the oranges hangs at rear of table hidden by table drape. Fig. 4 shows a front view of how the apparatus appears to the audience.

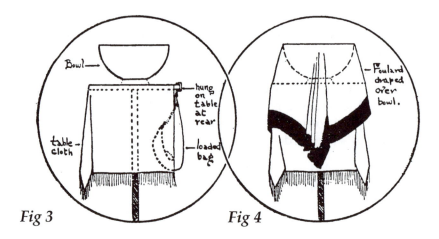

Fig 3   Fig 4

It is a fast, showy production effect that got Raymond off to a good start with his audience, who were pleased to get the pleasant gift of oranges.

The late Loyd Enoch, of Modesto, California, manufactured an apparatus called "Assisto" that worked perfectly for this trick. The Enoch's apparatus has become a collector's item.

Lee Grabel

Lee Grabel, assisted by his lovely wife Helene, is one of the best magicians I know. A real artist. Some say we even look somewhat alike, as though we might be brothers. Even our performing styles have a similarity – relaxed and leisurely.

I first met Lee in an elevator of the Golden Gate Theater Building in San Francisco. He was on his way to the office of his theatrical agent, Ken Daily, and I was on my way to the office of mine, Lou Emmel. We paused to chat.

Lee told of his plans to eventually build "The Floating and Revolving Piano Illusion". It was only a dream at the time, but it became a reality, and was featured in his big show. It proved a box office winner for Lee Grabel.

As the years passed, Lee advanced to become America's leading magician of the 1950s. His was a unique time in the history of magic. Vaudeville was a thing of the past. Television was in its infancy. Las Vegas was not the entertainment capital of the world, as it is today. During that era, Grabel developed a route in Middle America with one of the most extravagant illusion shows ever produced. He inspired a generation and joined the Royal Dynasty of Magic: Kellar, Thurston, Blackstone, Dante. Just prior to his death, Dante elected to place his mantle upon the shoulders of Grabel, and call him Danton.

In 1986, I wrote *The Magic and Illusions of Lee Gravel*. The book was illustrated by Patrick Martin. Both Lee Grabel and Patrick Martin are expert magicians and close friends who have been of value to my life.

The really outstanding books of magic have been those which have documented the magic developed by master magicians such as "The Magic of Malini", "The Magic of Leipzig", "The Magic of Paul Rosini", "The Magic of Robert Harbin", etc. Such books represent a lifetime of creative efforts by men devoted to the art of magic – not only as outstanding performers but as originators of magic. I am proud to say I wrote such a book as *The Magic and Illusions of Lee Grabel*.

As mentioned, Grabel's was a unique time in the History of Magic. World War II was over, vaudeville was a thing of the past. Las Vegas was not the glitter capitol of entertainment that it is today; television was in its infancy and did not consider the magician a headline attraction, such as Henning, Copperfield, and Siegfried & Roy later made it. Broadway was still into wartime musicals. During this period, Grabel travelled America with one of the most elaborate travelling illusion shows ever presented. He stayed out of metropolitan areas and union control, playing the same cities every two years, and made a fortune enabling him to retire in 1959.

A Gift For You

Here is a favorite card trick from Lee Grabel's repertoire.

Lee Grabel didn't invent the trick given here which is one of the most remarkable card trick ever devised, but he did perform it often. The trick was actually invented by Kolar. Kolar tricks were very popular with magicians during the 1930s. Like most tricks in magic, things change with the times and tricks fade away. This trick is too good to let fade away.

Effect

A card is selected, remembered by spectator, and placed on top of the deck. It is then deliberately cut to the center, being lost in the pack. The magician says he will attempt to locate the card while the deck is held behind his back. He tries and fails, as the card he brings forth is the wrong card. The magician affixes a label, to which a length of ribbon is attached, to the back of the "wrong card". The label is initialled by the spectator. The "wrong card" is then buried in the deck, with the ribbon extending from the center of the pack. On the ribbon being pulled upon, the card fastened to it by the sticker is withdrawn, and it is seen to have changed into the selected card. Remarkably, the initialled label is still affixed to its back.

Here's How You Do It

Use a deck of cards with an overall back pattern for this trick (such as a Bee Deck). A gimmick card is used. The gimmick card is made by cutting a half-moon circle in the end of any card in the pack, as shown in the illustration. The gimmick card rests on top of the deck and, thanks to the overall pattern, is not noticed.

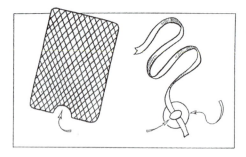

In performing the trick, a card is selected and then placed on top of deck (over the gimmick card). Deck is then cut burying the selected card in center of deck. You can cut the deck several times, losing the card completely. It seems there is no way you could possibly be able to find the card. You then announce that you will attempt to locate the selected card while the deck is held behind your back. This you can readily do, as when you riffle cards with your thumb against bottom edge of deck; it will automatically break at the card with the half-moon cutout. At break, cut deck which brings gimmick card on top of deck and chosen card to bottom. While still holding deck behind your back, place bottom card under gimmick car on top of deck; then, bring out pack from behind your back. Show gimmick card as though you believe you have found the selected card (as you do this, conceal half-moon cutout with fingers. Spectator will deny that it is his card. Replace this card on top of deck (half-moon cutout blends with overall pattern of deck and is invisible).

Now, take sticker, which is fastened to end of ribbon, moisten it with tongue, and stick it directly on lower edge of back of card. This label is constructed as shown in the illustration so that it looks like it is being stuck to back of top card; it is actually – thanks to the half-moon cutout–being stuck to the card beneath (which is the chosen card). Label is initialled by spectator, and cards cut burying "wrong card" in the center of the deck, from which ribbon now extends.

For the climax of this unusual card trick, the ribbon is withdrawn from the deck and attached to its end; by the initialled label, it is discovered that the "wrong card" has turned into the "right card", under seemingly impossible conditions.

Doug Henning

Doug Henning was a young magician who rose like a meteor in the sky of magic. He hailed from Canada, was starred in an off Broadway Show in New York that earned critical acclaim. His magic was playful with just a touch of the hippie years. Combining smaller magic with large illusions gave him a show of wonderful variety.

Doug Henning was a pioneer in steering a Magic Show into becoming a major special on National Television. He was the first to do this. For a number of years, Doug Henning presenting a full hour-length special. Fast paced yet respectful of the magic he presented. Many magical classics were shown in his excellent program.

Doug Henning was an excellent showman with a distinct style all his own. Audience liked Doug Henning. The man was more important than his magic. That is the art of presence.

Doug Henning rose to be one of the most famous magicians in the world during his short but spectacular career. At the height of his career, Henning suddenly left show business and moved to India. Learning real magic with the Yogi claimed his interest.

Doug Henning died at a rather young age in India. Undoubtedly, he goes onward to study yet higher magic.

Lance Burton

The last famous magician I have seen perform is Lance Burton to whom Lee Grabel introduced me. One personal friend to another personal friend adds up to yet another personal friend.

Lance Burton is a modern magical giant who performs continuously at his own theater in Las Vegas, Nevada.

Most of the famous magicians I have seen were of 20th century vintage. Burton is definitely 21st century.

Lance Burton's show is right up to date, yet still reserves a flair for the Thurston/Dante regime. Indeed, another personal friend (Grabel) bestowed upon him the Royal Dynasty Mantle of Magic: Kellar, Thurston, Dante, Grabel, and now Lance Burton.

Lance Burton has the talent of performing magic artistry making magic intelligent without challenging the audience's intelligence.

The high art of magic is to present illusion for the sake of appreciating the illusion, which brings one closer to the Masterful Illusion which is the Universe. The Yogi refer to it as "Maya". The Magic of Lance Burton approaches Maya.

Other great names in magic I had had the pleasure of seeing perform were Blackstone Sr. and Jr., Dante, Virgil, Gwyne, Duval, Frankson, Long Tack Sam, Keith Clark, Mullholland, Tommy Martin, Patrick Martin, the Pendragons, Seigfried & Roy, David Copperfield. All are outstanding. Daily, more arrive to claim their share of fame.

Part Three

Hypnotism

"Hypnotism is the process for producing the state-of-mind of hypnosis. Hypnosis is an altered state of consciousness capable of causing changes in perception and behaviour of the individual even to the extent of the bizarre."

—McGill

Chapter Thirty-One

"Magic of the Mind" Contemplation

Hypnosis I consider as "the magic of the mind". I enjoy contemplation on the magic of the mind. Here are some "magics" to contemplate upon. I always like to pause a bit between each before going on to the next.

Current scientific studies confirm that our thoughts will not only affect the world around us, but confirm that our thoughts are not only interpreted but actually created in our physical reality.

PAUSE AND CONTEMPLATE

A good computer on our desk has 800 million neuron-like connections. Our biocomputer brain has over one hundred billion neurons – if we could line them up, they would extend from New York to Boston.

PAUSE AND CONTEMPLATE

This vital neural network our biocomputer brain possesses has been reverently referred to as "beating wings of the mysterious butterfly world of the soul".

PAUSE AND CONTEMPLATE

Recent research affirms that we can increase the neurons in our brain in quantity throughout our life if we continually learn and use our mind vigorously.

PAUSE AND CONTEMPLATE

The more we understand about the brain, the more it appears to function like a physical transmitter and receiver, decoding and encoding information between our bodies and the outer world.

PAUSE AND CONTEMPLATE

Your SELF is your individual CONSCIOUSNESS of which there is no duplicate in the entire universe. It is immortal . . . It is deathless . . . it is perpetual. As mind belongs to its functioning, mind, too, is immortal.

PAUSE AND CONTEMPLATE

Recognize that you are a trinity of *Body, Mind, Consciousness,* and you will comprehend yourself.

PAUSE AND CONTEMPLATE

No computer is self-operating. Heaven help us if it learns how to program itself. No such worry yet.

Observe the relationship:

Consciousness is the programmer.

Mind is the keyboard to program the brain as consciousness directs.

Brain is the computer, and it performs as it is programmed to perform.

How does it work? Need you need to know? Just use it. Most who operate a computer are content just to use it, without being concerned with its inner operation. Be equally content with using your biocomputer brain.

Goodness, gracious, golly! So much to do. So much to understand. Not really. Just let it take care of itself. Buddha said, "Nothing need be done." Lao Tzu said, "Just go with the flow." Delight said, "Just be like a log drifting down the stream, and among the things you will bump into will be found the real treasures of your life."

PAUSE AND CONTEMPLATE

The brain is an intricate system of electrical activity. Energy jumps between neurons producing a spark which forms a wave called frequency . . . thus, brain activity has a wave rate pattern for mental states.

PAUSE AND CONTEMPLATE

The brain functions as a biocomputer. It is a far greater computer than any electronically constructed. Learning to use it to full capacity is a great purpose, many of which will be revealed in the yet-to-come future.

PAUSE AND CONTEMPLATE

The MIND is nothing tangible. It is a process for producing THOUGHTS. Thoughts can elevate to genius or descent to insanity depending upon the thoughts produced.

PAUSE AND CONTEMPLATE

The universe does not care how MIND is used. Up or down, both provide practice in using. Most are in the middle.

PAUSE AND CONTEMPLATE

The biocomputer brain is not immortal, as it is a mechanism. A mechanism can wear out and be discarded – which is to say it can *die*. The MIND cannot die for it is not a mechanism. It cannot wear out, for the more it is used, the better it works.

PAUSE AND CONTEMPLATE

Mind is a process to produce thoughts used by SELF. Your SELF is your CONSCIOUSNESS that you are. It is the individual YOU that you recognize existing behind your eyes when you look closely at your reflection. By that careful looking, you can SEE THAT SELF THAT IS YOU LOOKING BACK AT YOURSELF.

PAUSE AND CONTEMPLATE

The more I pause and contemplate the more I sense that the entire universe is a vast consciousness.

Such a paradox! Of course. The entire UNIVERSE is a paradox. A paradox is much like a puzzle. Do you have fun trying to solve puzzles. If you do, HAVE FUN.

Just, remember, as Shiva told Devi, as she sat on his lap, "Don't take what I say about it seriously, gal, or you'll miss the truth."

What wisdom Shiva told Devi here. "Don't take it seriously." Life is like a game played upon a giant board that stretches out to infinity. You sit beside the game board and play the game. The people that come into your life are pieces upon the game board. They take different positions and do many things; some you let remain and some your remove from the game board, for it is a game you play, and you can play it as you wish. *For you have free will.* Remember that and you will stop worrying, for basically a game is not to be taken seriously. You play it for the enjoyment of the playing. If it seems serious, it is because you make it so. Basically, life is an adventure to learn through and be enjoyed. We learn best that which we enjoy. If you have the wisdom to play your life (as I repeatedly comment) as though upon a playground rather than upon a battlefield, you are a very wise person indeed. Mind thinks best when things are not taken too seriously.

Seriousness is a judgment, and judgment can miss truth. The truth is that things are just as they are. The universe is neither for nor against, and everything that happens is a miracle that it can happen. Talk about magic!

By taking an attitude of *play* towards all that happens in life, you come closer to truth.

And possibly I should add . . .

The entire universe is a vast consciousness, and the more you can connect with that vast consciousness, the more you will understand. But try to understand too much and then you get overloaded. Leave some room for the mysterious to enter.

Have fun, pause and contemplate, and appreciate the miracle that you are . . .

Chapter Thirty-Two

Some Thoughts on Stage Hypnotism

I have presented stage hypnotism shows since 1927 and still present them. That's a lot of years of presenting.

To me, demonstrating hypnotic phenomena on stage provides a wonderful opportunity to acquaint people with the great power of their mind, which resides inside themselves.

Since stage hypnotism is presented as entertainment it offers a most pleasant way of learning. When what you learn is entertaining, it becomes the very best of learning.

After 20 years of presenting my first epoch of hypnotism shows, I wrote the *Encyclopedia of Genuine Stage Hypnotism*. That was back in 1947. At that time, I dedicated the book to magicians. Since then other books on stage hypnotism have followed. Gil Boyne in the foreword to my latest book on this field tells of this:

> "No man in the history of hypnotism has had more impact on stage hypnotism than has Ormond McGill. Hundreds of professionals have profited by his works.
>
> "In 1947, Ormond McGill wrote his original *Encyclopedia of Genuine Stage Hypnotism*, which was published by Abbott's Magic Company of Colon, Michigan. 'The book' has gone through five editions and has become known as The Bible of stage hypnotists. Still in print, it presents his work in the field from 1927 to 1947.
>
> "In 1970, he wrote *The Art of Stage Hypnotism*, which presented his work from 1947 to 1970. The first edition was published by Lloyd Jones Magic Limited of Oakland, California. The book is now out of print, and is a collector's treasure.
>
> "A check with the Library of Congress in Washington, D.C., reveals that no copyright was ever obtained on the original book, and in 1977, a revised, copyrighted version of the first book was published by my firm – Westwood Publishing Company – entitled, *Professional Stage Hypnotism*.

"Ormond McGill has now written his latest and masterwork on stage hypnotism which is all-inclusive of his previous works combined with much new, up-to-the-minute material added for today's mastery. Its coverage is encyclopedic in scope: Part One dealing with mastering hypnotizing and Part Two dealing with stage hypnotism providing a book that is paramount in its field.

"Ormond McGill was a pioneer in presenting hypnotism on television, and his contemporary work in hypnosis has earned him the reputation of 'The Dean of American Hypnotists', through an international reputation gained by his many performances and his excellent books on magic, hypnotism, meditation, and mysticism, East and West. During the last decades, Ormond McGill, in addition to his stage performances, has turned his attention to innovative work in the field of hypnotherapy.

"I am pleased to write the foreword to his latest book on stage hypnotism: *The New Encyclopedia of Stage Hypnotism* to join the ranks of classical literary achievements in the domain of hypnotism."

— GIL BOYNE, President
American Council of Hypnotists Examiners (A.C.H.E.)

The New Encyclopedia of Stage Hypnotism was published in the UK by Crown House Publishing Limited. First published 1996. Reprinted 1997, 1998, 1999, 2000, 2001, and 2003.

Personal Observations on Stage Hypnotism

Recent years have taken my work more into the hypnotherapy and instructional fields in relation to hypnotism. However, as a good portion of my professional life has been devoted to presenting both magic and hypnotism shows, I have found it of value to include, in my seminars, instructions of how to present stage hypnotism properly. The secret is to make the demonstrations educational and entertaining to the audience. In such regard, *performing attitude* holds a prominent place.

My shows have combined magic and hypnotism, which means I have played the dual role of both magician and hypnotist. Both of these forms of entertaining are closely allied in relation to the matter of ego, and on stage both the magician and hypnotist have to be cautious of ego showing, as no one likes ego except their own. The artist (performer) without ego is the true artist, as it is not what one does that is important, but it is how well one does what one does that counts. Skill is always appreciated.

There is a tendency for the hypnotic show (to an extent even in magic shows) to grandize the performer and belittle the volunteers, that is to say, the operator becomes "The Great Hypnotist", while the subjects appear submissive and often ridiculous. The performer must be on guard not to allow this attitude to engulf his show. To do so is "entertainment suicide", as the onstage volunteers are actually representative of the audience itself.

If you will always remember to place the "crown of success" on the heads of the volunteers, you will be on your way to success as a stage hypnotist. For this purpose follow these six directives:

1. Whenever an applause response is indicated, direct it towards the volunteers.
2. Explain that all hypnotic efforts are the result of the excellent concentration on the part of the subjects. (This is not entirely true; however, it is appreciated presentation by the audience.)
3. Explain in any demonstration that might seem ridiculous the underlying psychological significance of the demonstration.
4. Emphasize the dynamics of the hypnotic situation as being one of cooperation and trust between hypnotist and subject in which each has their respective role to achieve the unique state of mind of hypnosis.
5. Never "upstage" your subjects. This means, in a literal sense, do not stand in front of the volunteer while performing a demonstration. Allow the subject to be clearly visible to the audience at all times.
6. The volunteers from the audience are temporarily placing themselves in the hands of the hypnotist, on good faith. In all ways, both psychologically and physiologically, the hypnotist must honor that faith.

Extremely important in making the hypnotism show entertaining is the phenomenon of *presence*, on the part of the performer. Presence is that "certain something" that makes a performer great, not because of what you do but because you are YOU. *Presence* produces a "love affair" between the performer and the audience.

Presence can be looked upon as personality, charisma, magnetic charm, call it what you will. Really, it is a matter of consciousness.

It is being there, on stage, with a flame in your heart. How does one develop a flame in their heart?

Try this: WAKING, DREAMING, DEEPLY SLEEPING KNOW YOURSELF AS LIGHT.

First, start with waking. Your state of mind can be said to be mainly in three divisions: waking, dreaming, and sleeping – as being like clouds in the sky of consciousness in which they move. That consciousness is your authentic self. Being authentic is the very heart of the master performer whatever his (or her) entertainer role may be. And so . . .

While awake . . . moving, eating, working, whatever . . . *come to know yourself as light*. Visualize the image of yourself as if your heart has become a flaming torch and is burning brightly, and your body is an aura around the flame. Allow this image to go deep within your mind and saturate your consciousness. Imbibe it! Let the image become an integral part of your consciousness of yourself. It then becomes your personality.

Go on imagining this flame in your heart and feel it! While awake see yourself as a flame moving. It will not be long before those you come in contact with will sense a subtle light around you. Something is beginning to happen to you that is beautiful; something that makes you stand out as distinctive from others. This is the beginning of the developing of *presence*.

Now, take this imagining of your flaming heart and your surrounding body as an aura of light into dreaming. As you move the flame in your heart into your dreams, you advance your *presence*. It is no longer imagining; it has become a reality. Through this process you uncover reality. It is reality, for basically you are light.

When falling asleep go on thinking of the flame, go on visualizing it burning in your heart. Feel it, and so remembering, fall asleep. In the beginning, you will start having dreams in which you will move with this sensing. And once this feeling enters your dreams, your dreams will start disappearing; there will be less and less dreaming and more and more deep sleep. When the dreams disappear, then you can carry this feeling of the flame in your heart into sleep. You will become aware of it even while you sleep.

You now enter the fourth stage and that is the state of conscious-ness. All the three stages you have passed through are divisions of the mind: waking, dreaming, and deeply sleeping. You have become a "traveller", and these stages become "stations" along the way, so you can move from here to there, and come back again. These "stations" are parts of the mind, and you have become the fourth . . . one who goes through them all and yet is none of them. YOU are the fourth, and that fourth makes people aware of your *presence* – on stage and off.

Try this technique and see how it works for you. YOU will become an entertaining presence to your audience when you perform; whatever it is you perform: be it hypnotism, magic or anything.

Burke Spotlight Stage Induction Method

While presenting a seminar at the Regent College in London, under sponsorship of the Atkinson-Ball College of Advanced Hypnotherapy, I met a stage hypnotist who was touring English theaters with his hypnotism stage show. He kindly gave me his method of hypnotizing groups of persons who came on stage. As it is a personal gift, I include it in my autobiography.

Persons who want to be in the show are invited to volunteer to be hypnotized. Those who come up stand in a row, in front of their respective chair.

Each person is requested to place their fingertips to their temples and gaze into the spotlight.

Hypnotist suggests:

> "Look into the spotlight and concentrate upon the light. Bright as spotlight is, it is far distant in the theater so is unharmful to the eyes, yet powerfully captures and holds your attention.
>
> "That's it. You are doing fine. Keep looking and concentrating upon the light. Keep staring into the light, and do not blink your eyes."

Hypnotist now goes and stands before each person, in turn, and gazes into their eyes. Instructing . . .

"Look into my eyes. Now close your eyes, and beneath your closed eyelids roll your eyes upwards as though looking inside your head; at the spot, I will tap upon the top of your head. (Tap in center of top of head.) You are becoming hypnotized, and you will find you cannot now open your eyes, no matter how hard you try. (Subject tries in vain to open eyes.) Now, let your eyes roll downward, drop your hands from your temples, and go to SLEEP, as you listen to the music."

Soft dreamy music comes into the background (use meditative music, such as "Golden Voyage", "Ancient Echoes" or some such).

Hypnotist stands before each person while giving these instructions. Volunteers do as instructed.

Hypnotist goes to the next person standing in the row, and repeats the process described. Move quickly. A row of fifteen or so subjects can be covered within five minutes. The speed of working is what makes this striking as a method of hypnotizing for stage show.

When all eyes are closed and have failed to open, go back to the first subject and say, *"Relax and go limp!"*, simultaneously pulling down their hands from temples to their sides. Then, push them on the forehead causing them to fall backwards into their chair, with the suggestion, *"You are falling back, back, backward into your chair, and go deep to sleep in profound hypnosis. Drop down into your chair now, and go fast asleep in profound hypnosis."*

In response to the gentle backward pushing and suggestions, the subject will drop down backwards to his (or her) chair, relaxed and fast asleep in hypnosis.

BE SURE TO HAVE YOUR ASSISTANT STAND BEHIND EACH CHAIR AND GENTLY LOWER SUBJECT INTO CHAIR, SO THE FALLING BACKWARDS IS HANDLED SAFELY.

Hypnotist performs the same action with each subject standing in the row in turn, until all are hypnotically sleeping in their chairs. Then suggest:

"You are safely seated in your chair now, so go on down deeper and deeper to sleep in profound hypnosis, and you will have a wonderful time following every suggestion given to you, as you participate in the show."

The volunteer subjects have been quickly hypnotized by this method, and the show is ready to roll.

You will find this SPOTLIGHT METHOD very effective for stage show use. It works remarkably as the blinding light dazzles the eyes and seems to leave the persons in darkness about themselves, as nothing can be seen beyond the light. Yet, as was mentioned, the light is at sufficient distance so as not to harm the eyes by staring into it. Further, being in the spotlight has the psychological effect of putting the subject, "on the spot", as it were. It calls for obedience of response. In other words, the blinding light confuses the mind and produces a mental state extremely responsive to suggestions.

Additional Thoughts

Stage Hypnotism has developed into a very popular form of entertainment, and I am glad to have been able to contribute to the field.

Hypnosis is such an interesting paradox. It looks like sleep, and is even produced by suggesting "GO TO SLEEP!" — yet the mental state produced is more like an intensive wakefulness than it is like sleep, i.e. this intensification of attention is productive of an entirely divergent state of mind than that characteristic of sleep, as in normal sleep the element of attention is disfused while in hypnosis it is concentrated.

In sleep, the body relaxes and the element of conscious attention dissolves, while in hypnosis the body relaxes and the element of concentrated (centered) attention increases.

I have experimented with various types of hypnotism shows. I tried using "The Force" as a theme when "The Force" was made popular in the exciting George Lukas STAR WAR movies. Another theme I tried was "The Guardian Angel Hypnotism Show".

Now that I have completed my regular touring, I enjoy performing for my students attending my Hypnotherapy seminars. And recently I have started co-teaching in unique instructional seminars in Stage Hypnotism arranged and presented with the popular hypnotist, Jerry Valley (known as THE CHARMING HYPNOTIST).

Chapter Thirty-Three
My Conscious Self-Hypnosis Method

I always like to have a good self-hypnosis process at my command. I can use it for myself, and also adapt it for hetero-hypnosis for my clients. I wrote this method for Dr. Rexford L. North, who was director for the Hypnotism Center in Boston. Dr. North was the originator of what eventually enlarged, under the excellent direction of Dr. Dwight F. Damon and Elson Elridge, Jr., to become the National Guild of Hypnotists, Inc.

As to what happened to Dr. North – no one knows. He vanished into space. I give you here my original technique of Conscious Self-Hypnosis, as I wrote it back in 1953 for Dr. North's original Journal of Hypnotism.

The technique of Conscious Self-Hypnosis has within itself all the factors for successful induction and use, i.e. the laws of suggestion and hypnosis being artfully combined. The first thing in applying self-hypnosis is to familiarize oneself with the purpose of the session, i.e. having in mind the general formula of suggestions that are to be given to the mind while in the hypnotic receptive state. By this advance preparation it is easy to keep the flow of mood suggestions going, without having to stop and think about the exact words being self-suggested.

Having decided on your objective, write down the suggestions you desire to implant in your mind while in the hypnotic state. As the hypnotic state of mind is passive, it is best to do this in advance of the session.

In this regard, make your suggestions brief and to the point; stating them POSITIVELY. The exactly wording of the suggestions is not important as long as the "suggested idea" of desired objective is conveyed in a positive and direct manner.

You are now ready to prepare conditions for the induction of hypnosis in yourself. For your "fixation object" to concentrate on use a burning candle. Place this on a table in front of your easy chair. Next, darken the room, seat yourself comfortably, and you are ready to begin the session.

Fasten your eyes on the candle flame. Don't concentrate on anything in particular for the moment. Just relax back pleasantly in your chair, and let your mind drift, allowing whatever thoughts that come in to just pass through it. Make no effort; just relax and let yourself GO!

Now, breathe in deeply through your nose, hold the breath for about five seconds, then exhale *very slowly* through the mouth. Repeat this ten times. You will find your mind becoming surprisingly quiescent.

Now, *think to yourself*: "The muscles of the top of my scalp are relaxing. I can feel a pleasant tingling in my scalp." Think it and you will feel it. Then let your thoughts pass down over your face, thinking of relaxing all the facial muscles.

From your face, let your thoughts go to the muscles of your shoulders and chest. As you sit back deep in the comfort of your chair, hunch up your shoulders, hold them that way a few moments, then suddenly let them relax and droop.

Now, follow your thoughts on down through your stomach muscles; draw in tightly your abdominal muscles, hold it, then LET GO!

Next think of your arms and hands relaxing. Think of how heavy they are becoming, as they rest in your lap. Let your thoughts go on down through your legs to your feet – thinking how very heavy your feet are, as they rest upon the floor.

Now, center your thoughts on your whole body relaxing. Suddenly – all together – LET GO! LET GO! LET GO! – Your whole body LET GO! Relax all over.

During this entire progressive relaxation process, you have continued to stare at the burning candle. By this time your eyes will have become fatigued. Think now that your eyes are so tired you must close them. Close your eyes. Think how good it feels to have closed your eyes, and now you are commencing to feel sleepy. You are becoming sleepy, so very, very sleepy.

Continue right on, thinking of how very sleepy you are becoming. How very sleepy you are. Think of how deep and full your breaths are becoming – breathing in deep and full in the slow rhythm of the breathing you have in sleep. How relaxed and pleasant your entire body feels . . . just as though you didn't have a body.

You will begin to experience a sort of numbness stealing over your body. Your fingertips are beginning to tingle. You can even feel a little pulse begin to beat in your fingers, as they tingle more and more. You are sinking down, down into the realm of sleep.

Continue thinking these "mood suggestions" repeating them over and over until you reach a point when all of your bodily sensations will almost have ceased to be. And, you feel drowsy all over, so very, very drowsy. You can tell when this point is reached, as it will become just too much effort to think of suggestions of sleep – all your want to do is GO TO SLEEP.

This is the time in your voluntarily induced self-hypnosis in which the *outcropping of the subconscious occurs*. This is the psychological moment to implant your desired suggestion into subconsciousness.

Now, slowly lift up your hands and place the palms gently over your ears, pressing the hands flat against the head. Then repeat SPEAKING OUT LOUD the suggestions you have written in advance . . . they will be partially memorized.

Your mind is not consciously alert in its present state, so don't try to reason about what you have to say; just repeat the suggestions over and over in a sort of sing-song fashion, almost as though it were a meaningless rhyme you were chanting. The subconscious phase of mind does not have to react to intelligent discourses . . . *it responds to suggestions of a completed premise, and, accepting same, carries on from there to make the premise a reality.*

Repeat whatever are the suggestions you desire to give your sub-conscious at least seven times. You will probably feel so weary by

235

the end of that repetition it will seem like too much effort to do further.

Now, let your hands drop from your ears onto your lap. Now, doze (sleep) off if you wish. Whether you go to sleep or merely rest is of no consequence. Gradually, the drowsiness will disappear. And, you will arouse yourself feeling refreshed and rested.

That ends the session . . . the ending of a self-hypnosis session is completely undramatic. It is over that is all, and you continue right on with your regular activities. Don't try to think about the success or nonsuccess of your session; such thinking belongs to critical mind and interests the subconscious not one iota. Never fear, *it will automatically carry out the suggestions thus presented to it into action in direct ratio to the degree to which the suggestions have been implanted in noncritical mind (subconscious).*

How will you know you have achieved your goal? Very simply, as you will find yourself easily accomplishing the very things you desired to accomplish.

Chapter Thirty-Four

"Effort Without Effort" Self-Hypnosis

This is a favorite of mine, and a gift to you. Making the effort to achieve something without effort to achieve is the high goal of real achievement. Making effort without effort affirms that the goal (whatsoever) has been reached, and it no longer requires effort to perform (achieve) the goal. In other words, mastery has been attained.

To understand:

Can you imagine a virtuoso pianist making effort to play his concert? Being a virtuoso means that his/her effort to be a virtuoso is behind him, and he presents his concert free of effort. His artistry just flows on its own. It has become so firmly established in his subconscious that conscious thought is no longer required for the performance. Performing is an effort, but if it takes effort to perform (do) it is not true artistry (mastery). The virtuoso has moved beyond trying to do, and just does. It is the same with all forms of great artistic achievement and creative endeavor.

Take "Effort Without Effort" into the realm of the inventor. Many an inventor has striven for years to create his invention without success. Then, one night in a dream the solution is reached, in a flash of intuition. There is no effort in having a dream; a dream is a subconscious phenomenon. The inventor has solved his problem by an effortless process. Conscious striving is effort to achieve something. Subconscious mastery is always without effort. There is great hypnotherapy here which makes it possible to achieve (overcome and improve) an objective spontaneously. "Effort Without Effort" means the achievement has become spontaneous. Only in spontaneous performance is true mastery shown. Masters have told of this down through the ages, each in their own way:

Buddha puts it, "Become empty inside."

Jesus puts it, "Trust your Heavenly Father."

Shiva puts it, "Make life a playground not a battlefield."

Krishna puts it, "Enjoy the miracle that you are."

Lao Tzu puts it, "Go with the flow."

Patanjali puts it, "Make the effort without effort."

To these I would like to add my own, "Less and less try to make things happen and more and more just let things happen."

Using hypnosis to instill in the subconscious "Make the Effort Without Effort" is not difficult, as your subconscious wants you to move beyond conscious effort and achieve without effort.

Modus Operandi of "Effort Without Effort" Self Hypnosis

To initiate an achievement, make all the effort one pleases to achieve the achievement. Then, when one has gone as far as one can in learning and performing on the conscious level; take it into the realm of the subconscious for effortless mastery.

How?

Induce the subjective state of hypnosis, and directly suggest:

> "You have consciously learned and practiced what you wish to achieve. Your effort will now be rewarded as you now achieve and perform that effort without effort. It becomes a flow. Effort is now behind you, and you perform and do what you have learned how to do, henceforth without effort. It becomes an art you perform just for the joy of the performance.
>
> "Subconscious mind, when you make this 'effort without effort' become reality, arouse the person from the hypnosis. They have become master of their achievement."

There it is. Direct and right on target. It presents a beautiful hypnotherapeutic experience.

Chapter Thirty-Five

Rainbow Self-Hypnosis

I consider this a glorious method of self-hypnosis which I developed recently. I enjoy it like a rainbow.

Modus Operandi

Sit quietly, alone, with a straight spine. Close your eyes and become silent inside. Let your mind chatter until it quiets on its own. When it becomes quiet, proceed on.

Visualize a shaft of white light – like a searchlight beam – coming down from outer space to illuminate the crown of your head and infuse your brain.

Allow the light to penetrate and flow on down your spine until it reaches the center of your body behind your navel: YOUR CENTER OF BEING.

You will instinctively know when you are there. Now, within your CENTER OF BEING mentally construct (visualize) a prismatic crystal – a prism. As the "White Light of Creation" falls upon the prism, it refracts into multicolored spectrum and refracts the light into rainbow hues. Like a rainbow of colored snowflakes they flood your BEING.

Visualize this creation strongly.

Allow the snowflakes of colors to flow throughout your entire body and encompass your mind. Allow the colors to flow beyond your body's surface to infuse your aura, and on to radiate out to all that IS.

You touch all life – all CREATION – with the prismatic color of your creation.

YOU HAVE BECOME A RAINBOW.

Chapter Thirty-Six

Hypnotherapy

I started this lifetime in 1913. It is now 2003, which places me at 90 years. These later years have been productive, not only in stage shows and writing, but also in the field of hypnotherapy which is revolutionizing the counseling professions. To go back in time a scant 25 years, the number of persons practicing hypnotherapy was relatively small. As is obvious from scanning the Yellow Pages of current telephone directories, today there are many listings. Every city of any size has many of professional hypnotherapists. Hypnotherapy schools abound. I would venture a prediction that by the mid 21st century, hypnotherapy will be along side of the medical profession, as a healing modality.

In 1981, I joined the staff of HTI (Hypnotherapy Training Institute). I have been teaching students and professionals there for 23 years as the "Dean of American Hypnotists". My dear friends Randal Churchill and Marleen Mulder are Directors of the hypnotherapy institute which has grown to be one of the largest and most highly regarded schools of hypnotherapy in America. It is licensed by the State of California Bureau of Postsecondary and Vocational Education.

HTI has been leading the way for 25 years with innovative therapy methods using hypnosis, and has trained thousands of graduates from over 30 countries in this excellent profession.

What is Hypnotherapy?

Hypnotherapy is precisely what the name implies. Therapy means healing of some kind and hypno by means of hypnosis. Hypnotherapy does not invade the medical profession, but complements it. It does not diagnose or treat physical ailments. It is concentrated in making you master of your mind rather than being mastered by your mind. For example, hypnotherapy can dramatically help with improving performance of things you want to do: improving confidence, relationships, recall, concentration, fears and phobias, stress reduction, self-expression, and mastering unwanted habits.

I enjoy teaching hypnotherapy and presenting weekend seminars at HTI. Also teaching annually for organizations such as Gil Boynes' A.C.H.E. (American Counsel of Hypnotist Examiners) in Southern California and the National Guild of Hypnotists, Inc. (NGH) in New Hampshire. Some of my hypnotherapy seminars have even taken me overseas to New Zealand, Australia and England. Marleen has accompanied me on many of these. I enjoy teaching seminars with her. Many of the esoteric insights presented in this Autobiography are among the teachings of the hypnotherapy seminars. While preparing for these classes at the school over the years, I was also inspired to record most of my audio tapes.

This page tells of HTI instructors Randal and Marleen including myself.

"RANDAL CHURCHILL, President of the American Council of Hypnotist Examiners, the original and primary Hypnotherapy Certification organization in the United States, is celebrating 35 years in the field. He received his degree in Psychology with Honors from Sonoma State University and has completed over 30,000 hours of hypnotherapy in a practice that began in 1968. He is founder of HTI, one of the first licensed schools of hypnotherapy in the world, and began training professionals full-time in 1978.

Randal has received international acclaim for his skill, creativity, and comprehensive approach to a wide range of challenging issues, including by the assimilation of various modalities with hypnotherapy. An intuitive, supportive therapist, he is originator of Hypnotic Dreamwork™ and has been a pioneering leader for over 30 years presenting Gestalt therapy, regression, and advanced ideomotor methods.

Randal Churchill's award-winning text, *Become the Dream*, is the first book about the integration of dreamwork and hypnotherapy. Experts have called his new 427-page text, *Regression Hypnotherapy*, the most important book about regression ever published. He has been a featured teacher at many International Hypnotherapy Conferences, and has instructed at numerous institutions, including teaching psychiatrists at Napa State Hospital.

MARLEEN MULDER is a State Approved Hypnotherapy Instructor and A.C.H.E. Designated Examiner. Celebrating 30 years as a teacher and therapist, she brought with her a vast background when she became Co-director of the Hypnotherapy Training Institute in 1980. She was educated in the Netherlands at the University of Groningen Medical School and at a newly developed teachers college, Ubbo Emmius, Groningen, where she played an important role in the school administration. In the 1970s, she taught various forms of meditation and holistic healing in Europe and Japan. She has taught hypnotherapy at various training centers and symposiums on this continent and in Australia and New Zealand.

A veteran of over 25,000 hours of hypnotherapy sessions, Marleen has made a highly creative art of therapy for crisis situations, major transitions, and spiritual growth. She is well known for her sensitive hypnotherapy work with children, as well as her comprehensive, revolutionary therapy for addictions and habit control. Inspiring and charismatic, she is one of the world's premier hypnotherapy instructors.

The legendary ORMOND McGILL, *The Dean of American Hypnotists*, is on the Board of Advisors of the A.C.H.E. In the field since 1927, he received international recognition beginning in the 1940s for his excellent books integrating hypnotism and meditation and exploring creative hypnotic strategies. Having celebrated his 75th Anniversary in the field, he has written more than 20 books, including several classics.

Ormond McGill, "one of the true giants in the history of hypnotism", has made many of his greatest insights in recent years. He has combined his profound mastery of many hypnotic techniques; his deep personal understanding of Eastern systems of meditation, mysticism, wisdom and healing; and his creativity, vision, compassion, humor and life experience. Ormond McGill has been teaching hypnotherapy at HTI on a continual basis since 1981. It is at our Institute that he began to train hypnotherapists, and it is only at HTI that he has taught on an ongoing basis. He has led hypnotherapy seminars periodically at conferences in the United States, Great Britain, Australia and New Zealand."

My method of teaching hypnotherapy is to first ascertain the students' particular interest in the learning. Most seem interested in developing skill in hypnotherapy, as a career.

Following, an opportunity is provided for the groups to experience hypnosis for themselves. One learns best what one personally experiences.

Various induction methods are instructed with student cooperative participation. An understanding of conscious and subconscious mind is studied. As the class advances, actual hypnotherapy sessions are conducted under careful supervision.

To get powerful, lasting and rapid results in hypnotherapy it is essential that the methods employed reach and affect the subconscious phase of mind. The subconscious houses the emotions, imagination, memory, habits, and is the pathway to inspired intuition. It also regulates automatic bodily functions.

Through hypnosis, we have access to the subconscious. Hypnosis can be regarded as an altered state beyond ordinary consciousness, but it can also be regarded as a natural state that can occur spontaneously, such as various forms of absent mindedness we continuously experience. Hypnotherapy offers a vast array of means to harness subconscious mental states. Dave Elman gives a concise definition of what hypnosis is, in stating, "Hypnosis bypasses critical mind and establishes selective thinking".

Generally, the most well-known characteristic of hypnosis is an increased suggestibility. Though there are varying degrees of this heightened responsiveness to suggestions, the potential power of this direct access to the subconscious should not be underestimated.

An important aspect of hypnotherapy is to increase the ability to concentrate. Concentration typically increases dramatically during hypnosis. Poor students have become "A" students.

The recall of lost memories can be recalled through hypnosis. Often it has been used to access buried memories to find missing objects of value.

The pain threshold changes greatly during hypnosis. Hypnosis can provide relief from chronic pains such as arthritis, headaches or recovery from injury.

In deeper levels of hypnosis, major surgical operations have been performed with no other anesthetic agent. Hypnosis can be used to promote happy states of mind, such as overcoming stress, which is a serious problem in our society.

Compared with traditional therapeutic modalities, the results of a relatively brief series of hypnotherapy sessions are often faster and more effective than other methods.

For those intending to pursue a career in hypnotherapy, this exciting profession is recognized by the United States Department of Labor, including listing in the Dictionary of Occupational Titles, and diplomas are approved by the California State Bureau for Private Postsecondary and Vocational Education.

Hypnotherapy can be a very effective adjunct to any therapeutic specialty. Many professionals in the health and counseling fields have successfully integrated hypnotism into their work. Examples include physicians, dentists, chiropractors, psychologists, social workers, marriage counselors, nurses, massage practitioners, and physical therapists.

I could go on naming various benefits the use of hypnotherapy can be to individuals. Little wonder that I devote a goodly portion of my latter years to giving scientific instructions in hypnotherapy.

And on a personal level is the opportunity hypnotherapy provides to help many people through difficult times in their lives. It is wonderful to help others who are in need of help. I enjoy working with private sessions at the school.

As mentioned, I started instructing in hypnotherapy in 1981, and it is still going strong. I find that I enjoy teaching hypnotherapy as much as I do performing stage shows. That's a blazing truth.

Chapter Thirty-Seven
Cosmic Love Connection Hypnosis

This method of hypnosis is priceless to me. I trust it will be priceless to you.

To achieve the maximum of effectiveness with each client session, present it filled with a Cosmic Love Connection.

How can you obtain a Cosmic Love Connection, when a Cosmic Love Connection is like the wind when it's no longer windy?

Simply, you cannot make a Cosmic Love Connection when you try. The only way is to KNOW you have a Cosmic Love Connection already. You must feel it in your heart with all the hypnotherapy you do.

If you wish, you can make a little symbolic reminder of this fact.

Take two uncancelled adhesive postage stamps with a love design. Place the adhesive backs together and squeeze tight. They will bind so closely you can't get them apart. A good reminder of the "Power of Suggestion" combined with "Cosmic Love".

Cosmic Love Hypnotherapy (Love from the Void)

This is a great form of hypnotherapy of benefit to your clients.

First, you must learn about the Void. The void from which all creation springs. The void which is the great Mystery of Mysteries. Out of the void comes love. As it has been told in the long corridors of time, "God Is Love". And God is known to all mankind as the great Mystery of Mysteries. God and the void are ONE.

From out of the void, all manifestations of love comes forth: Love of God; Love between husband and wife; Love between sweethearts, etc. Love for the Planet upon which we live. Love is even found amongst the atoms; scientists call it "charm".

The void has been within the consciousness of mankind since time immemorial. It has been known via a variety of names: Buddha called it "emptiness" – the emptiness that is infinitely full. Jesus knew it in a very personal way as "My Father In Heaven". The lofty philosophy of Plato called it "Lagos". Einstein called it "Space". The void is ever flowing with the energy of love. You are part of the void.

All matter is composed of atoms, so minute as to be beyond microscopic viewing. Each atom has a nucleus in its center, around which swirl electrons like a miniature solar system. So rapid is the electron movement, as to appear like a misty cloud of force. Out of atoms, what is created in the universe appears as solid form, but actually it is mostly void. Indeed, if an atom were enlarged to the size of the head of a pin, the orbit of the nearest electron would be 46 inches distant from the nucleus.

Each atom is 99% void, and outer space is like that too. All size is relative and outer space is 99% void. That which seems so solid is mostly void. And come to know, you stand at the very center of the universe, in relation to yourself. Christ told it so well: "God is Within You." And it is to be understood that the Creation and the Creator are ONE. As it is written, "The hand of God moved across the void, and creation started." As God is Love, so love flows through all creation. In knowing this, one makes a quantum leap in consciousness.

Entering "The Void" Hypnotherapy (with soft music background)

"Wherever you are or however you are, lie down or sit down, it makes no difference. Just relax all over. Become quiet inside and just let your mind drift. Now think of a yawn. Actually yawn. Yawn. Yawn. Yawn. It makes you feel more relaxed all over, the more you yawn.

"Now, breathe deeply through your nose . . . hold the breath and exhale slowly. Do it two more times.

"How quiet and peaceful you feel. How peaceful and serene you feel. You are drifting down into the realm of sleep and dreams. The flow of relaxation covers your entire body, and your mind also has become relaxed. Deep into the realm of sleep you go. Every breath you take sends you down deeper and deeper into the realm of sleep . . . and your conscious mind moves to one side and your subconscious mind takes center stage.

Continue to client:

"Cosmic love enters you. Love flows into you from out of the void, of which you are a part. Allow these suggestions to enter now and become your reality. See yourself as pure and good, and immersed in the energy of love. Now, see within your mind's eyes a white glowing ball of light. See this ball of light as being the center of your being from which you radiate out in all directions. It is the energy of the void entering into you; it is the energy of cosmic love. And you can use this energy for anything you please, by using your creative mind. You can use it to bring love of all kinds into your life. You can use it to bring success and abundance into your life. You can radiate out the energy for the benefit of all.

"Now, rest in silence for some moments. Silence. Silence.

"How wonderful and full of life you feel. Prepare to come back from hypnosis now. You know now the meaning of cosmic love, for it has become your reality. Your subconscious will arouse you, when you feel your heart overflowing with cosmic love. The session is complete."

You have made the Cosmic Love Connection. . . . I use it continuously with my hypnotherapy.

Chapter Thirty-Eight
Hypnotherapy of Zen

Enlightenment = The Brilliance of Instinctive Knowing

I have a personal affinity for Eastern sentiments. This method of hypnotherapy is Eastern. The Zen insights are transcendental. They develop a "peace with the world" state of mind. Good mental therapy.

Zen hypnotherapy for clients that lean in that direction can provide great benefits. When what Zen suggested is subconsciously accepted, all stress in the world vanishes, for it is above the world.

Zen is a "mind game". Hypnotherapy is a "mind game". When played together – in combination – the results are remarkable.

The "mind game" of Zen is filled with koans, paradoxes, and contradictions. As an example this koan: "What is the sound of one hand clapping?" You can concentrate on it for hours and come up with nothing. Clearing the mind with "nothing" is great hypnotherapy. Many troubles people have are based in a mind filled with ceaseless chattering about how miserable they are.

A client comes into your office having spent many years in training their mind to be wonderfully miserable, and asks you – as a hypnotherapist – to take away the misery so carefully produced so they can have some peace within themself. Finding that inner peace is the purpose of Zen hypnotherapy.

Zen gives you opinions and then tells you not to have opinions. Zen is the most stupid thing you will ever study that is positively brilliant. Brilliant produces light (lightness). Lightness as a mental activity is called "enlightenment".

Modus Operandi for Zen Hypnotherapy

Hypnotize client into a relaxed state of hypnotic reverie . . . Then suggest:

> "In this pleasant, serene, and relaxed state of mind you are now in, your subconscious OPENS WIDE to understand and accept these suggestions of ZEN which I will now read to you. Just relax and listen, and let what is given to you here become your very own. It will flood your mind with the brilliance of ENLIGHTENMENT."

THE "SUGGESTION FORMULA" of ZEN (to be softly read to client while in hypnosis, against a background of soft meditative music or serenity resonance sound).

Enlightenment comes most readily for those who have few preferences. When wishing for and wishing against are both absent, everything becomes clear and undisguised. Make distinctions, however, and heaven and earth are set far apart. If you wish to see the truth, then hold no opinions for or against anything. To set up what you like against what you dislike is the disease of the mind. When the deep meaning of things is not understood, the mind's essential peace is disturbed.

The universe is perfect like vast space, where nothing is lacking and nothing is in excess. Indeed, it is due to our choosing to accept or reject that we do not see the true nature of things. Live neither in the entanglements of outer things, nor in one's inner feelings. Just be serene in the oneness of things and such erroneous views will disappear by themselves. When you try to stop activity to achieve passivity, your very efforts fill you with activity. As long as you remain in one extreme or the other, you will never know oneness.

Those who do not live in the single way fail in both activity and passivity. To deny the reality of things is to miss their reality, just as to assert the purposelessness of things is likewise to miss their reality. The more you talk and think about it, the further astray you can wander from the truth. It has been said by many masters that if one stops talking and thinking, there is nothing you will not be able to know. At the moment of inner enlightenment, there is a going beyond that which appears to be and that which appears not to be. Thus, do not search for the truth; only cease to cherish opinions.

Do not exist in a dualistic state, for if there is even a trace of this and that, of right and wrong, the mind will be lost in confusion. At their roots, all dualities come from a single source, which we can call the One . . . but do not become attached even to this One. When the mind is undisturbed as to which way it should choose, but just allows what IS to be, there is nothing in the world which can offend. And when a thing can no longer offend, it ceases to exist with the strength it had.

To live in the way of enlightenment is neither easy nor difficult, but those with limited views are fearful and irresolute, and the faster they hurry the slower they go, and clinging (attachment) cannot be limited; even to be attached to the idea of enlightenment is to go astray. Just let things be in their own way, and there will be neither coming nor going.

Obey your natural nature and you will walk freely and undisturbed. When thought is in bondage, the truth is hidden, for everything is murky and unclear, and the burdensome practice of judging brings annoyance and weariness as no benefits can be derived from distinctions and separations.

If you wish to move in the way of enlightenment, do not dislike the world of senses and ideas. Indeed, to accept them fully is identical with true enlightenment. The wise strive for no goals; only the foolish fetter themselves. Distinctions arise from the clinging needs of the ignorant. To seek enlightenment with a discriminating mind is the greatest of all mistakes.

For the unified mind in accord with that which IS, all self – centered striving ceases. Doubts and irresolutions vanish, and the real fullness of living is possible. When all is empty, clear, and illuminated with no exertion of the mind's power, we are freed from bondage. For in this world of suchness there is neither self nor other than self.

To come directly into harmony with existence, simply say that nothing is separate and nothing is excluded. No matter when or where or how, enlightenment means entering this truth. And this thought is beyond extension or diminution in time or space, as it is a single thought in eternity.

To the enlightened one, the universe always stands before your eyes as infinitely large and infinitely small: no difference, for definitions have vanished and no boundaries are seen. So too is it with your Being and non-Being. Don't waste time in doubts and arguments, but move along and intermingle with all things without distinction. To live in this realization is to be without anxiety about non-perfection. To live in this faith is the way to non-quality because the non-dual is one with the trusting mind. Truly, the way of enlightenment is beyond language, for in it is found the great truth that in reality there is only the eternal KNOWINGNESS OF ISNESS.

The Arousal from Zen Hypnotherapy

At the end of the reading of this dissertation about the nature of Zen, which is another way for saying the nature and way to enlightenment, which many in the world constantly seek. And here it is all wrapped up for you in ZEN HYPNOTHERAPY. Ready for the arousal, suggest:

"Relax now and go ever deeper and deeper into the subjective state of hypnosis. There is no need to hold all you have here in conscious recollection as it is perpetually retained in the memory banks of your mental computer (your subconscious mind). What you have been given in this session will stay with you, and bring you serenity and peace. It causes you to stop fighting yourself. Get ready to arouse from hypnosis now, filled with serenity and peace, with the brilliance of enlightenment your very own.

"I count from one to five . . . with each count you will come up from the depth of hypnosis and return most enjoyably to the here and now:

"One . . . two . . . three . . . four . . . FIVE!

"You are fully aroused, fully alert, feeling wonderful and fine with a peacefulness within yourself which passeth understanding."

Chapter Thirty-Nine

Vitality Hypnosis

After you practice Self-Hypnosis for awhile, you will find you can enter the state very quickly. I just sit in a comfortable chair and drift away. I do that often, as I deeply relax and use this Vitality Hypnosis method.

When you are in the receptive subjective mood of hypnosis, start by imagining a mass of energy about the size of a glowing light bulb forming in the base of your spine. Feel a warmth gathering there and you are ready to move it throughout your body moving from organ to organ.

Visualize the energy from the base of your spine moving up your spine to the top of your head.

REST A MOMENT AND EXPERIENCE IT

Then, visualize the energy moving on down from the top of your head on down between your eyes, clear down to the tip of your nose.

REST A MOMENT AND EXPERIENCE IT

Now, take a deep breath, and draw the energy (see it as a "Light", if you wish) into your nose, and down your throat into your lungs.

REST A MOMENT AND EXPERIENCE IT

Now, imagine the energy permeating your lungs – filling all the inside space of your body between the armpits. Visualize your lungs lighting up with light.

REST A MOMENT AND EXPERIENCE IT

Now, move the energy down the front of your arms to the thumbs. Feel the thumbs become warm and tingle. Then let the energy spark across to your forefingers . . . and allow the energy to spark on to other fingers, until your hands are alive with energy.

REST A MOMENT AND EXPERIENCE IT

Now, move the energy up your arms to your shoulders . . . then move the energy across your shoulders to your neck to the point where you jaws meet your cheeks.

REST A MOMENT AND EXPERIENCE IT

Now, move the energy from your face down to your navel . . . to a point in the area of your appendix just right of the navel.

REST A MOMENT AND EXPERIENCE IT

Now, move the energy up the right side of your abdomen moving into the colon . . . bathing any obstruction there in the light and healing energy.

REST A MOMENT AND EXPERIENCE IT

Now, let the energy move out of the rectum.

REST A MOMENT AND EXPERIENCE IT

Imagine warm tingling energy flowing over your sex organs, and straight up the front of your body . . . up to and over your chin . . . now let it divide and move over each cheek just below the bottom of each eye.

REST A MOMENT AND EXPERIENCE IT

Now, let the energy flow down your cheeks over the sides of your jaw . . . and move it clear down to your stomach. Bathe your stomach in the energy. Feel your stomach glow, filling the entire center of your being with warmth.

REST A MOMENT AND EXPERIENCE IT

Now, move the energy down either side of your abdomen and on across your groin . . . move it on down the front of your legs letting it find the way to your feet, and move on across to the second toe.

(above) Ormond performing 'The Great London Hypnotic Seance' as Dr. Zomb

(left) Ormond McGill with Art Linkletter demonstrating hypnotism on the original NBC Art Linkletter People Are Funny radio show, 1944

(below) Hypnotism on television with Art Linkletter (Life With Linkletter) ABCTV, 1945

Presenting hypnotism on television (American Broadcasting Company) way back in 1946

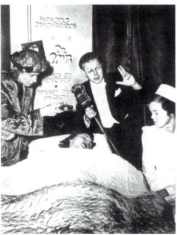

(above) Ormond McGill presenting "The Blindfold Drive" as a publicity feature for his Dr. Zomb's "Séance of Wonders" midnight show, Tower Theatre, Santa Rosa, California, 1948

(left) "The Window Sleep" via "Hypnotism Over Radio" 1950. This demonstration was conducted in the main display window of the gigantic Hudson Bay Store, Vancouver, B.C., Canada by Ormond McGill as Dr. Zomb.

(below) The Ormond McGill "East Indian Miracles" Show in 1952 presenting a demonstration of Hindu Magic with a hypnotized girl sleeping on a bed of nails

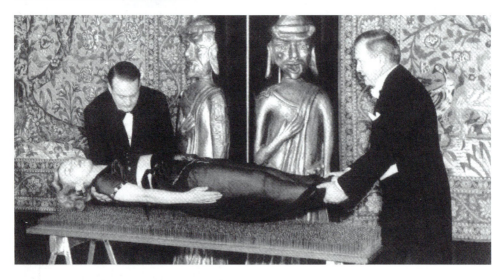

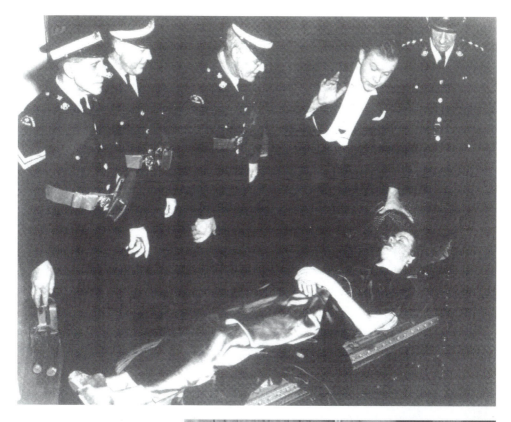

(above) Ormond McGill
and "The Window Sleeper"
under guard in the lobby
of the Orpheum Theatre in
Vancouver, B.C., Canada. An
Ivan Thackery promotion for
a 1952 stage show.

(right) Ormond McGill
on stage presenting his
"Sacrificial Cremation"
with Donn Wood (Merlin)
assisting

(above) Delight and Ormond McGill Tahiti tour, January 1, 1970

(right) Ormond McGill portrays the role of hypnotherapist in the Ron Ormond motion picture production, Please Don't Touch Me, with Lash LaRue and Billie Lee Hart.

Touring "South Sea Island Magic" in the 1960's. Ormond McGill performing his original "Coconut and Pineapple Mystery".

REST A MOMENT AND EXPERIENCE IT

Let the energy leap from toe to toe until your toes are tingling with the energy. Finally, let the energy leap to the tip of your big toe on each foot.

REST A MOMENT AND EXPERIENCE IT

Now, move the energy up the inside of your feet to your ankles, and up the inside of each leg.

REST A MOMENT AND EXPERIENCE IT

Let the energy move into the inside of your thighs.

REST A MOMENT AND EXPERIENCE IT

Move the energy across your groins and then divide it, so it passes up each side of the center of your body moving up to reach under each armpit.

REST A MOMENT AND EXPERIENCE IT

Now, let the energy move to the area of your pancreas which is located on the left side of your abdomen just below the bottom of the rib cage. Feel this entire area becoming warm. Feel a freedom from all tension from this area of your body.

REST A MOMENT AND EXPERIENCE IT

Now let the life force – energy – move to the center of your body to your heart.

REST A MOMENT AND EXPERIENCE IT

Feel your heart become filled with the energy . . . healing your heart in every way, and opening it up to loving emotion and every-thing. Let the energy bathe your heart.

REST A MOMENT AND EXPERIENCE IT

Now, move the energy back into your armpits . . . then move it down the inside of each arm, and across the palms of your hands to the fingers. Feel your fingers tingle.

REST A MOMENT AND EXPERIENCE IT

Now, move the energy up the back of your arms to the outside of your elbows . . . and on up the armpits . . . on across your shoulders.

REST A MOMENT AND EXPERIENCE IT

Now, move the energy across your jawbone and bury itself in either cheek. Now imagine the energy manifesting itself deep in the center of each ear.

REST A MOMENT AND EXPERIENCE IT

Now, move the energy to the point between your eyebrows . . . and imagine a glowing light in that center.

REST A MOMENT AND EXPERIENCE IT

Let the glow move from between your eyes and move up to the top of your head. Feel the top of your head become hot with the energy . . . then see it in your mind's eyes as sending a searchlight of energy as a beam from the top of your head into space.

REST A MOMENT AND EXPERIENCE IT

Your entire head is aglow with energy. Your brain is filled with energy . . . the energy brings in KNOWING of truth to you, and activates your powers of ESP and intuition.

REST A MOMENT AND EXPERIENCE IT

You have benefited your body in every way . . . you are filled with energy . . . you are aglow with vitality.

REST A MOMENT AND EXPERIENCE IT

Now rest, rest, rest. Feel your entire body filled with vitality. You are aglow with energy. You are filled with vitality. Breathe deeply and fully and just relax as the energy surges through you.

Gradually allow it to now subside . . . sink into rest . . . and gradually return to your place in life.

THE PROCESS IS COMPLETE.

Chapter Forty

Whirling Dervish Hypnosis

The Sufi-order, founded by Rumi, practices a kind of dance. They use rapid rotation of the body (in a whirling-like dance) to entrance themselves.

In Persia it was regarded as a spiritual experience. It is spiritual because the intent of use is spiritual, not because the trance induced is spiritual.

The Dervish technique of body revolving (whirling) can be used as an effective method of hypnotic induction by contemporary hypnotherapists, in working with clients. It is presented here in a developed western form.

The Whirling Dervish Hypnotic Induction Method

Place a lighted candle in each corner of the session room. Blacken the room. Client stands in center of room, while induced hypnosis occurs. Hypnotherapist stands beside client in the blackout room.

In the blackout room, only the four lighted candles (one in each corner of the room) stand out. Hypnotherapist tells client they can use this effective whirling Dervish method to quickly enter hypnosis, by following performance instructions, revolving their body slowly at first, doubling their breathing and suggestions while gazing at each candle in turn, and then proceeding in a rapid series of whirls as each candle is blown out. By the time the last candle is blown out, they will be in profound hypnosis.

Start by staring at candle #1. Client takes one deep breath, holds the breath, exhales and relaxes . . . then repeats to self, "*I am going into hypnosis. I am going to sleep in profound hypnosis.*" Client revolves his body around one time while repeating these suggestions out loud to self. The circling of body ends positioned to stare at candle #2.

While staring at candle #2, client takes two deep breaths in succession: inhale, hold, exhale. Inhale, hold, exhale. Relax. Then, client repeats out loud to self these suggestions, "*I am going into hypnosis. I am going into hypnosis. I am going to sleep in profound hypnosis. I am going to sleep in profound hypnosis.*"

Client revolves their body slowly around twice while thus doubling their breathing and hypnotic suggestions. The twice circling of body ends positioned to stare at candle #3.

While staring at candle #3, client takes three deep breaths: inhale, hold, exhale; inhale, hold, exhale; inhale, hold exhale. Relax. "*I am going into hypnosis. I am going into hypnosis. I am going into hypnosis. I am going to sleep in profound hypnosis. I am going to sleep in profound hypnosis. I am going to sleep in profound hypnosis.*"

Client revolves their body slowly around three times while repeating these suggestions. The thrice circling of body ends positioned to stare at candle #4.

While staring at candle #4, client takes four deep breaths: inhale, hold, exhale; inhale, hold, exhale; inhale, hold, exhale; inhale, hold, exhale. RELAX!

Then, client repeats out loud to self, "*I am going into hypnosis. I am going into hypnosis. I am going into hypnosis. I am going into hypnosis. I am going to sleep in profound hypnosis. I am going to sleep in profound hypnosis. I am going to sleep in profound hypnosis. I am going to sleep in profound hypnosis. As I stare at candle #4, I drop down in profound hypnosis and go deeply asleep in profound hypnosis. Yet, my feet are steady, and I will not fall. My eyes close and roll upward beneath my eyelids. I am in hypnosis now, and I am ready to be led to a pleasant seat by my hypnotherapist ready to proceed with a beneficial session in hypnosis.*"

While repeating these hypnotic suggestions *out loud* to self, client revolves body around four times, ending with eyes closed and rolled upwards beneath closed eyelids.

Hypnotherapist now instructs client, "*With your eyes thus closed start whirling around and around as rapidly as you can. It will send you into a deep hypnotic trance. Continue whirling around and around while I blow out the four candles each in turn. Keep whirling while I blow out* the candles. As each candle is blown out, you will go deeper and deeper into hypnosis, and by the time the fourth candle is blown out, you will be in profound hypnosis, and you can stop whirling.

"While in the whirling Dervish trance I will lead you to a chair; you will be wonderfully comfortable and go deeper and deeper into hypnosis. Our therapy session will then begin, and all the beneficial suggestions will become realized in your life."

Hypnotherapist then proceeds to blow out the four candles, and comments: "I have blown out candle number one and you go deep into hypnosis. I have blown out candle number two and you go even more deeply into hypnosis. I have blown out candle number three and you go even more deeply into hypnosis. I have blown out out candle number four and you go deeply into profound hypnosis. You can stop whirling now, and I will lead you to a chair. You are ready to benefit wonderfully by your session Whirling Dervish Hypnosis makes it so."

Session proceeds. This will be found an effective method of inducing hypnosis.

Chapter Forty-One

Acupressure Hypnotherapy

I have found this method to be effective as a hypnotherapy technique.

Pressure upon the meridian centers of the body (these centers are nerve sensitive) automatically commands attention, and compounds in influence with the suggestions of the hypnotist, as a form of hypnotherapy.

These meridian centers can be felt as little depressions in the body into which the fingertips can be inserted in maintaining pressure (some prefer an insistent tapping upon these centers to a steady pressure, both methods work). Some areas are quite sensitive, so be gentle in using *Acupressure Hypnotic Induction.*

The method can be applied to the subject (client or patient) in either a seated position or reclining.

Begin by energizing your hands.

The latter is recommended.

Shake your hands vigorously and clap them together several times. Get the blood circulating in the hands. Feel them tingle. Then, place them palm to palm and slowly separate. Note the "force" that flows between them.

Your "charged" hands are now ready to be applied to the meridian centers via a pressure technique.

STEP ONE:

Have subject remove any excess clothing and shoes. Then recline in a comfortable position with hands resting at sides and feet slightly apart. Explain that in this method of hypnotizing you are going to apply pressure to various meridian centers of the body, using scientific Acupressure; that the process will cause him to automatically relax, and that he will very likely doze off to sleep. Tell him to just let himself GO!

STEP TWO:

Have subject close eyes and take three deep breaths. Then touch center top of his head and instruct him to roll his eyes back under his closed lids as though looking at the point being touched. Tell him to keep looking at this point, as you suggest "Eyelid Fixation". In this position, the subject will find it physically impossible to open his eyes. This successful, tell him to relax his eyes downward now and drift off to sleep as you stimulate the meridian enters of his body, starting at his feet and advancing to his head—each pressure point sending him down deeper and deeper into hypnosis.

STEP THREE:

Locate point on left foot just behind ball of foot in line with middle toe. Press in deep. Hold for 5 seconds, while suggesting to subject he will notice how relaxed the pressure on this center causes his foot to become. It feels numb.

Do same on right foot.

STEP FOUR:

Locate point on left foot just below the bulge of inner ankle. Press in deep. Hold for 5 seconds. Continue suggestions of how relaxed the pressure is making foot become.

Do same on right foot.

STEP FIVE:

Move fingers up left leg about 3 inches above ankle, and press in on the inner rear edge of shin bone. Hold for 5 seconds. Suggest that the numbness and relaxation in feet is now beginning to rise on up his legs.

Do same on right leg.

STEP SIX:

Locate point on left leg just below level of knee cap. Press in at top of calf muscle. This is a tender spot. Suggest leg becoming relaxed and numb.

Do same on right leg.

STEP SEVEN:

Locate point on front of body midway between pubic hair and naval. Press in firmly. Present suggestions, "Just let yourself GO now and drift away to pleasant sleep, as the pressures on the meridians centers continue on up your body."

Relax between.

STEP EIGHT:

Locate point on front of body just below end of breastbone. Press in firmly. Suggest, "Let yourself go completely now, and drift away into sleep."

Relax between.

STEP NINE:

Locate point on body 3 inches up from last point depressed, and press in thus upon center of breastbone. Press firmly. Suggest, "Sleep, go deeply to sleep now."

Relax between.

STEP TEN:

Perform pressure together using both thumbs at points in depression end of shoulder bones–where arms and shoulders meet. Continue suggestions of "Sleep. Deep sleep. Drift away into sleep, as you feel the pressure. The pressure will melt away as you drift into sleep. Breathe deep and sleep."

Relax between.

STEP ELEVEN:

Locate point (called "Joy of Living" point) at the inner crease of left elbow. Bend elbow and place tip of thumb in crease. Then unbend arm and press in. Press on relaxed tissue always. Suggest, "Sleep. Sleep. Deep sleep."

Perform same on right elbow.

STEP TWELVE:

Move hand down left arm from point 11, to point located 2 inches down arm on outside of left arm. Press in. "Your arms are becoming numb and you are going to sleep. Deep sleep."

Suggest, sleep.

Perform same on right arm.

STEP THIRTEEN:

Move on down left arm further on outside to point 2 inches up from wrist, in line with little finger. Press in. Suggest, "Sleep. Deep sleep."

Perform same on right arm.

STEP FOURTEEN:

Locate point on back of left hand between thumb and index finger. Press in. Suggest, "Sleep, pressure, and repeat the suggestions, Deep sleep."

Then relax the Perform this pressure and relaxation, while repeating the suggestions for five consecutive times.

Perform same on right hand.

STEP FIFTEEN:

Locate point on crease inside of left wrist, in line with little finger.

Press in. Suggest, "Sleep. Deep sleep. Breathe deeply and go deep to sleep."

Watch subject's breathing in response to these suggestions. It deepens, hypnosis is ensuing.

Perform same on right wrist.

STEP SIXTEEN:

Move both hands upward now, and locate point top of each shoulder, midway between neck and tip of shoulder. Press deeply with both hands together. Suggest, "Sound asleep now. Deep sound sleep now. Deep into hypnotic sleep now."

Relax between allowing time for suggestions to sink home.

STEP SEVENTEEN:

Locate point on subject's face, and press in on crevass between upper lip and tip of nose. Suggest, "You are deep in hypnosis now. Sleep deep in hypnosis now."

Relax between.

STEP EIGHTEEN:

Press in on area between the eyes (between the eyebrows). Skull bone structure does not allow depressing, but on this point surface pressure will suffice. Maintain a steady pressure, as you suggest, "You are in deep hypnosis now, and as you sleep your subconscious mind opens wide to receive the beneficial suggestions which will now be given it. Present this "suggestion formula" of general well-being.

"Every bit of stress is leaving you. You are absolutely relaxed in both mind and body. Both your mind and body are becoming completely refreshed. Day by day, in every way, you are becoming better and better."

STEP NINETEEN:

Press on top of head in small depression located there. Continue steady pressure on top of head, as you suggest, "Sleep on deeply now completely undisturbed, but your subconscious mind is fully alert and is receptive to the beneficial suggestions you are giving it. Repeat the foregoing "suggestions formula" three times. Then suggest:

"These suggestions go deep into your subconscious and become your habitual way of healthful behavior for yourself, when they have become thus established as reality in your subconscious, you will automatically arouse yourself from the hypnosis feeling wonderful and fine, with a KNOWING that you have successfully accomplished your desire of perfection of your BEING."

Allow subject to "sleep on" in hypnosis until awakening from the trance of their own subconscious deciding. Acupressure hypnosis will benefit the subject in every way.

This will be found a superlative method of hypnotizing, as the acupressure upon the meridian centers automatically produces relaxation and produces a sleep response. The method embodies both a physical causation combined with the psychological aspects of suggestions producing a state of hypnosis which is virtually irresistible.

Chapter Forty-Two

"I Can't be Hypnotized" Hypnosis

This is the "Acting Out Hypnosis" method. It is an associate of "The Let's Pretend Magic" method (see Chapter Twenty-Two). I use it often.

Session Room Accessories

Conventional recliner. Big-cushion earphones connected with microphone – to be worn by client so that when hypnotherapist speaks in microphone words are conveyed directly into ears of client.

Session Handling

This method will be found effective in hypnotizing clients who come for hypnotherapeutic help and then affirm THEY RESIST HYPNOSIS. THEY CANNOT BE HYPNOTIZED. In consultation with such clients, get their message clearly of what they want, and then agree that they can't be hypnotized.

Hypnotherapist/Client Agreement

"Since you can't be hypnotized, there is little point in using hypnosis to solve your problem. To use hypnosis the person has to allow himself to enter a passive-reverie somnamistic state of mind which is highly subjective. Since you find you cannot be hypnotized, you obviously are just the opposite type of person who desires to remain alert and conscious at all times . . . however, it will be possible for you to *act out being hypnotized*, as acting out something successfully is based on being fully alert and conscious of what acting role the person is playing. Understand?"

Get client's agreement of understanding.

"So, while you cannot be hypnotized, you can play an acting role of pretending to be hypnotized. Doing that will cause you to become more alert and conscious than ever. It is just the opposite to being hypnotized. Will it be agreeable for you to just deliberately act out the role of being hypnotized? If it is, then without your being hypnotized I can help you with what you seek help on. Is such agreeable?"

Get client's agreement that it will be okay to act out consciously and play the role of being hypnotized.

"Okay, let's begin. Station yourself upon this recliner, so you are comfortable. There is no need to relax or anything; just be alert and fully conscious of everything. Above all do not go to sleep. Place these earphones on, which will give you a feeling of privacy, and I will tell you what acting role I want you to consciously play during this session. You will be alert and conscious all the time which is just the opposite of being hypnotized."

Client dons earphones and reclines on recliner. Hypnotherapist gives these instructions of how to consciously play the role of being hypnotized. Present these instructions in a WHISPERING to client via the microphone-to-earphones.

"Okay, just rest comfortably without trying to especially relax. Remain fully alert and conscious at all times. Remember, you are not to go to sleep. Let's now start acting out the role of being hypnotized. Be alert and conscious, at all times, of the role of being hypnotized you are playing.

"Recline back and close your eyes. Now become conscious of your breathing. Take a deep breath . . . hold the breath . . . then exhale the breath. As you do this, become fully conscious of the breath going into your nostrils, into your lungs, and on down deep inside yourself. Continue this deep breathing, and, as you do so, become fully conscious of your breathing."

Allow clients some moments to themselves to act out this role of being conscious of their deep breathing.

"You may find this being conscious of your deep breathing may make you kind of sleepy, in this role you are playing, but do not go to sleep.

"Now, continue on playing the role of being hypnotized. You are doing a great job of acting out the role. THINK of how every breath you are conscious of is causing you to become more and more relaxed and is sending you down into hypnosis. Continue right on acting out the role of being hypnotized. It is lots of fun playing that acting role. Enjoy it every moment.

"Now, comes the real test of your acting in playing the role of being hypnotized. The part you are playing calls for you to take 69 rapid breaths – in and out – as the consecutive numbers are called. I will call the numbers, so all you have to do with each number called is to breathe rapidly in and out. I will allow you a moment between each number called, during which time *think* to yourself the word, *sleep*. THINK sleep in anyway you please. Just enjoy the experience. All ready to start this acting role. Ready, set, GO!

"*One* . . . take a rapid breath in and out. Relax a moment. Think "sleep" to yourself. *Two*. Do the same again. *Three*. Do the same again. Do the same with each number I count thus from 1 to 69. *Four*. I will keep right on counting on to 69. Somewhere along the line of counting, it may be that you will lose track of the counting, and will act out the role of being hypnotized."

Continue the counting in same rhythm – number by number one to 69, allowing a pause between each number while client thinks of sleep.

Having reached the sixty-ninth breath, very likely you will find your client has dozed away into hypnosis, but make no comment about it. Just continue right on:

"You have done a great of acting in handling the breathing in the role of being hypnotized. Now, let's continue playing the role of being hypnotized in relation to solving the problem (whatever has been requested in the advance consultation) you came to me to help you solve. Act out your part in solving the problem, as I give to your subconscious these beneficial suggestions . . ."

Present whatever suggestions are needed to solve and/or correct the problem. Such handled, let the suggestions sink in and then directly ask the subconscious to arouse the client when what is desired has been accomplished.

As client arouses, comment, *"You did a great job in acting the role of being hypnotized, and without the need of being hypnotized you have mastered what you came to me for help to have mastered. You go on your way now, well and fine."*

THE SESSION IS THUS CONCLUDED.

Note to Hypnotherapist

Resistance to being hypnotized is often an ego (or a fear) matter. Some people like to feel they are in conscious control of everything they do. Of course they are not, but they like to feel that way. Critical mind says, "I can't be hypnotized. By agreeing, critical mind is bypassed in acting out the role, and selective thinking is established in the subconscious of the client, and the beneficial results accomplished. This is a subtle method, and mind can sometimes be tricky in doing exactly opposite from what it is told consciously to do, ala to doze off into hypnotic sleep when it is specifically told, "Do not go to sleep."

Always show care for your clients. They deserve your trust.

Chapter Forty-Three
Quotation Hypnotherapy

Generally speaking, the more the hypnosis induction method fits in with client's hobby interest, the more readily will it be accepted and go into affect. This method works well with clients who have an interest in quotations.

Consultation completed, and ready to commence the induction of hypnosis, go with client into your session room where it is quiet. Place a blindfold over client's eyes while he or she relaxes in a comfortable chair or lies upon a couch. Tell them they may effortlessly drift away into hypnosis, as they relax all over, and that you are going to read to them a treasury of valuable quotations they will enjoy. Tell them that every one of the quotations has been carefully selected, and they are to concentrate their attention upon the quotation, and contemplate upon the wisdom given. Explain that you will allow some space between each quotation for this purpose. They are to feel the meaning and drift into the quotation; as they drift into the quotation they will drift into hypnosis, and very possibly into somnambulistic sleep.

Tell relaxing client that when they understand the deep meaning of the quotation, their right forefingers will lift and then relax again. Understand! (Get this spontaneous subconscious signal response.)

START SOME SOFT DREAMY MUSIC IN THE BACKGROUND. READ THE QUOTATIONS, HERE GIVEN, IN A MONOTONOUS TONE OF VOICE. READ SLOWLY, AND TAKE YOUR TIME. MAKE THE MEANING OF EACH QUOTATION CLEAR.

Read quotations to client:

"What a wonderful thing life is. It is a miracle that you are alive."

> PAUSE FOR CONTEMPLATLON TIME.
> WHEN FINGER SIGNAL IS GIVEN, PRO-
> CEED ON AND READ NEXT QUOTATION.

273

"Humor brings in sunshine to what is said."

PAUSE FOR CONTEMPLATION TIME

"Corporations have neither bodies to be punished nor souls to be condemned. Therefore, they do as they like."

PAUSE FOR CONTEMPLATION TIME

"Early to bed and early to rise makes a man healthy, wealthy, and wise."

PAUSE FOR CONTEMPLATION TIME

"Think like a wise man, but express yourself like the average person."

PAUSE FOR CONTEMPLATION TIME

"Glories, like glow-worms, afar oft shine brightly, but looked at too near have neither heat nor light."

PAUSE FOR CONTEMPLATION TIME

"I was so much older then. I am so much younger now."

PAUSE FOR CONTEMPLATION TIME

"I used to think my trifles were important."

PAUSE FOR CONTEMPLATION TIME

"Woe is me, if I ever think I am becoming a god."

PAUSE FOR CONTEMPLATION TIME

"The secret of being a bore is to tell everything."

PAUSE FOR CONTEMPLATION TIME

"In nature there is no blemish but the mind. None can be called deformed but the unkind."

PAUSE FOR CONTEMPLATION TIME

"A faithful friend is the medicine of life."

PAUSE FOR CONTEMPLATION TIME

"Superstition sets the whole world in flames. Philosophy quenches them."

PAUSE FOR CONTEMPLATION TIME

"I am I plus my surroundings, and if I do not preserve the latter I do not preserve myself."

PAUSE FOR CONTEMPLATION TIME

"A slavish bondage to parents cramps expanding growth."

PAUSE FOR CONTEMPLATION TIME

"If we had keen vision and feeling of all ordinary human life, it would be like hearing the grass grow and a squirrel's heart beat, and we would walk on the road which lies on the other side of silence."

PAUSE FOR CONTEMPLATION TIME

"The beautiful have no enemy but time."

PAUSE FOR CONTEMPLATION TIME

"In dreams begins responsibility."

PAUSE FOR CONTEMPLATION TIME
ALWAYS WAIT FOR CONFIRMATION
UNDERSTANDING SIGNAL (OF LIFT
ING FINGER) BEFORE PROCEEDING
ON TO NEXT QUOTATION.

"How wonderful it would be if it were possible that we might hold a day's conversation with the dead."

PAUSE FOR CONTEMPLATION TIME

"A painful pleasure often turns to pleasing pain."

PAUSE FOR CONTEMPLATION TIME

"Sincerity is a jewel which is pure and transparent, eternal, and of great value."

PAUSE FOR CONTEMPLATION TIME

"One that strives to touch the stars, oft stumbles over a straw."

PAUSE FOR CONTEMPLATION TIME

"Physicians are like kings – they brook no contradiction."

PAUSE FOR CONTEMPLATION TIME

"Enjoy the honey-heavy dew of slumber."

PAUSE FOR CONTEMPLATION
TIME HYPNOTHERAPIST PAUSES IN
GIVING FURTHER QUOTATIONS TO
CLIENT, AND SPEAKS DIRECTLY TO
RELAXING CLIENT:

"You are doing fine. Your subconscious finger signal has shown each time when you comprehend the quotation given, You enjoy the contemplation, and it makes you drowsy and sleepy, and you effortlessly drift away – down deep into hypnosis. I will give you some more quotations to contemplate upon, but just allow your subconscious to cogitate upon them, as you drift into sleep. Sleep. Go to sleep, as you please."

"What lasting joys a man attends who has a faithful female friend."

PAUSE FOR CONTEMPLATION
TIME CONTINUE IN SAME MONO-
TONOUS RHYTHM GIVING QUOTA-
TIONS. FINGER SIGNAL OF COM-
PREHENSION CONTINUES EVEN
THOUGH CLIENT HAS MOVED
FROM CONSCIOUS COMPREHENSION
TO SUBCONSCIOUS COMPREHEN-
SION.

"Suffering can sometimes be called an initiation into a higher state of BEING."

PAUSE FOR CONTEMPLATION TIME

"People want peace so much that one of these days governments had better get out of the way, and let them have it."

PAUSE FOR CONTEMPLATION TIME

"Nationalism is an infantile sickness. It is the measles of the human race."

PAUSE FOR CONTEMPLATION TIME

"The stupid never forgive nor forget; the childish forgive and forget; the wise forgive but do not forget."

PAUSE FOR CONTEMPLATION TIME

"They never taste who always drink. They always talk who never think."

PAUSE FOR CONTEMPLATION TIME

"A scientific faith is absurd."

PAUSE FOR CONTEMPLATION TIME

"Science without religion is lame; religion without science is blind."

PAUSE FOR CONTEMPLATION TIME

"The past is but memories that will never happen again. The future may never happen at all. There is only the here and now."

PAUSE FOR CONTEMPLATION TIME

"Less and less try to make things happen and more and more just let things happen."

PAUSE FOR CONTEMPLATION TIME

"Enough is enough."

PAUSE FOR CONTEMPLATION TIME

Note to Hypnotherapist

Enough, Enough, Enough. Stop the quotations now. Your client will long since have gone into hypnosis. Your client will even seem to have gone to sleep. Breathing will have deepened and once in awhile a snore. Sometimes the finger signals continue right along, and sometime they cease too. Your client, in contemplating the quotations has enjoyed what they enjoy, and in this enjoyment of quotations has moved into the realm of sleep. But it is a somnambulistic sleep, and all the while the subconscious has been active. A mere suggestion, *"Subconscious mind give your attention to me now and turn into beneficial reality for my client what has been requested"* is all you have to do proceed right along with your prescribed session, as initiated in the consultation.

Chapter Forty-Four

Computer Hypnosis

Computer Hypnotherapy is a contemporary form of hypno-therapy. To understand it, appreciate that your brain functions like a biocomputer. It operates and directs your client's functions and behavior (equally yourself). A biocomputer is constructed of organic material, while a conventional computer is inorganic in construction. This is not difficult to understand, as we live right in the midst of the computer age.

Observe yourself and you will be observing your clients. As a biocomputer, you are far greater than any computer yet pro-duced. A good computer on your desk may have 800 million connections.

Your brain biocomputer has more than two billion. Its potential has been but scarcely touched.

Observe how like a computer we are. Be as technical as you wish in your examination. Computer devotees relate to that.

BRAIN is the biocomputer inside the head, within which are found the "memorybanks" of learning and experience. Also, within the biocomputer is found "the mind's eye" which can be linked to the computer's screen.

MIND is the keyboard, operated by SELF (consciousness). Through MIND the biocomputer is programmed.

HYPNOTHERAPY is the technology through which MIND can program the biocomputer brain.

PRANA is the cosmic electricity which provides the energy to make the biocomputer run.

Computer Hypnotherapy Induction Technology

Have client take a seat in a comfortable chair. Hypnotherapist and client gaze into each other's eyes until eyes feel heavy and fatigued. Then, tell client to close and roll his eyes backwards (under closed eyelids) as though he is looking into his biocomputer brain.

Then, tell client his biocomputer will be turned on to operate by bringing the vitality of PRANA into themselves. This cosmic electricity is brought in through deep breathing.

Have client take six deep breaths in rapid succession. This completed, tell client to relax more and more by continuing to breath in deeply in slow progression from this point onward. Tell client that with each breath he takes in this slow rhythm he will find himself becoming more and more sleepy, more and more relaxed, and more and more drifting down into hypnosis.

Tell client that now that he has his biocomputer in operation, he will quickly drift down into profound hypnosis.

Tell client, as he knows, the most advanced of modern computers are using verbal speech to program the computer.

Tell client that you will use this most modern approach. As you give him instructions verbally, he is to repeat them *silently* inside his biocomputer inside his head.

We are ready to go into operation now.

HYPNOTHERAPIST VERBALLY REPEATS THESE SUGGESTIONS TO CLIENT, IN THE FIRST PERSON, FOLLOWING WHICH THE CLIENT REPEATS THE SAME SILENTLY WITHIN HIS MIND.

> "My eyes are tired. My eyes are closed. I am becoming relaxed all over. I am drifting into hypnosis."

Client repeats this silently to himself. Do not rush client. Allow time for these suggestions to sink in.

"My eyes are tired. My eyes are closed. I am becoming relaxed all over. My biocomputer brain is now in full operation, and I am programmed to drift down deep into hypnosis.

"My biocomputer brain is now in full operation, and I am programmed to go deeper and deeper into hypnosis with every breath I take."

Client repeats this silently to himself.

"My eyes are closed, and they have become so relaxed now that I cannot open my eyes no matter how hard I try. I am programmed to be so relaxed, I cannot even open my eyes when I try. So I do not try . . . I just drift and drift down into hypnosis."

Client repeats this silently to himself.

"I am so relaxed and sleepy that my head is dropping forward onto my chest, and I sink into deep hypnosis."

Client repeats suggestion to himself. As head falls forward, hypnosis has been induced.

Hypnotherapist now moves from first to second person in presenting further programming to client.

"Good. Your biocomputer mind is operating to perfection. I will take over now and program it from this point on. All you have to do is relax more and more, and go deeper and deeper into hypnosis, as I beneficially program your biocomputer brain, of great benefit to yourself.

"I program into your biocomputer's memorybank this valuable wisdom to become your way of life. Let this wisdom always be with you for perfection and mastery of your mind and body. As this wisdom is programmed into your biocomputer brain, you will continue going down deeper and deeper into hypnosis. In this process, the fingers of your hands will function as the keyboard, and when the associated finger is pressed upon, that wisdom will come forth and shine in brilliance upon your SCREEN OF MIND to become your personal reality."

When your right forefinger is pressed upon, this wisdom will shine forth upon your `screen of mind,' and become your very own:

"You will less and less try to make things happen and more and more just let things happen."

PAUSE FOR SOME MOMENTS

When your right second finger is pressed upon, this wisdom will shine forth upon your "screen of mind", and become your very own:

> "In everything you do, you will always respond in practical action. You will always act and react in a way of greatest benefit to yourself."

PAUSE FOR SOME MOMENTS

When your right middle finger is pressed upon, this wisdom will shine forth upon your "screen of mind", to become your very own:

> "You will become a witness to everything you do in life. You will stand back and observe yourself. Then, you will be able to always improve your action."

PAUSE FOR SOME MOMENTS

When your right ring finger is pressed upon, this wisdom will shine forth upon your "screen of mind", to become your very own:

> "You will observe yourself as you truly are, and not as you imagine yourself to be. Then, day by day, in every way, you'll become better and better."

PAUSE FOR SOME MOMENTS

When your right little finger is pressed upon, this wisdom will shine forth upon your "screen of mind" to become your very own:

> "You will know that when your mind is under control, your mind becomes pure like crystal reflecting equally, without distortion, the perception, the perceiver, and the perceived. It is through such mind that your consciousness of yourself is known."

When your left first finger is pressed upon, this wisdom will shine forth upon your "screen of mind" to become your very own:

> "Know that your mind and body act upon each other in a continuous circling of both conscious and subconscious reaction."

When your left second finger is pressed upon, this wisdom will shine forth upon your "screen of mind" to become your very own:

> "Be like a log drifting down the stream, and the things you bump into often will prove to be your treasures of full living."

When your left middle finger is pressed upon, this wisdom will shine forth upon your "screen of mind" to become your very own:

> "The best way to learn to anything is to start right in and learn how to do it. Then do it."

When your left ring finger is pressed upon, this wisdom will shine forth upon your "screen of mind" to become your very own:

> "The past is but memories that will never happen again. The future may never happen at all. There is only the here and now."

When your left little finger is pressed upon, this wisdom will shine forth upon your "screen of mind" to become your very own:

> "When something of value happens to you, say `Thank You' to your inner SELF."

Allow it all to happen – the wisdom given to you in this time and space is now programmed into the memorybank of your biocom-pu-ter.

When you wish to prepare yourself to arouse from hypnosis, just press upon your right thumb. Following this, when you wish to be fully alert from hypnosis, press upon your left thumb, and you will arouse feeling wonderful and fine.

Note to Hypnotherapist

Remember always this "keyboard" of your fingers to bring forth the wisdom implanted in your biocomputer. In *computer hypnotherapy* the term "biocomputer" is substituted for "subconscious" – know forever that a "rose is still a rose by whatever name it is called".

Chapter Forty-Five

Transcendental Hypnotic Induction

In 1987, I wrote the book *Seeing The Unseen* which was published by Crown House Publishing Ltd in UK. The book revealed a past life through hypnotic regression. To this book, my esteemed friend, Martin Roberts PhD added an extensive foreword and postscript. Then, an appendix was added presenting for the first time my personal transcendental hypnotism induction method. As this is my original and a method I have frequently used, I include it – in complete detail – in my autobiography. A gift to you.

*This technique provides the hypnotized person with insights into his or her divine nature and immortality of *being*.

Often a person will consider his body as himself, and that is not the truth. Man is not just a body at his roots. He is an individual *consciousness* and, through his mind, his consciousness becomes known. A body is but an instrument used to conduct our affairs in the physical world. Transcendental hypnotic induction brings about this realization.

Have the subject take a seat in a comfortable chair, place his feet flat on the floor, and rest his hands in his lap so that they do not touch. The light in the room should come from behind the subject directed towards yourself, as the hypnotist. Give these suggestions:

> "As you sit quietly in the chair, relax every muscle of your body. Just let yourself go. As you do this, direct your attention to my eyes: look deeply into my eyes, and keep your complete attention fixed upon my eyes, until I tell you to close your eyes.

> "As you stare deeply into my eyes, notice how your perception of my eyes begins to change. It begins to seem that, instead of focusing upon my eyes, the point of focusing moves through my eyes – to the other side of my eyes – to a point far beyond my eyes. You will find that you are no longer looking at my eyes, but that you are looking through my eyes into myself. It is

as though my eyes become windows through which you look directly into the space which is inside myself. You are becoming aware that you are looking through the windows of my eyes out into the vastness of space – in which the stars of the heavens pulsate and shine.

"Let your entire body completely relax now, and send your BEING through the windows of my eyes and project your BEING into that vast space which spreads before you.

"As you look deeply in this manner while relaxing your body completely, your eyes become so heavy and completely relaxed that you can no longer hold them open, and your eyes close. So close your eyes. (Eyes close.) It feels so good to close your eyes now, and relax completely all over. Your eyes are closed now and are so relaxed that you cannot open them no matter how hard you try. Try as you wish, but you cannot open your eyes. So try no longer, just relax into the vast space which you see spreading before yourself even now that your eyes are closed.

"Now . . .

"You feel yourself sinking down into this vast space which spreads before you infinitely. But your eyes are closed, so you are no longer looking into my space . . . the space you now witness is your own space. Deeper and deeper you sink down into this vast space of yourself. Every breath you take sends you down deeper and deeper, down into this vast space of yourself which is independent of the physical world. Your breaths are deepening, and every breath you take sends you down deeper and deeper into this vast space . . . far, far down beyond even a vestige of consciousness of the physical world.

"Drift. Drift. Drift. You find yourself drifting in space. A mind free of its body in this space . . . drifting down ever deeper and deeper into space.

"Now ask yourself some questions as you drift down into this vast space. Are you the one who is called by a certain name in the physical world? Are you the person who lives at a certain address? Are you the person who possesses a certain bank account and holds a certain position in the world? Experience how you feel right now in this vast space in which you now experience yourself . . . this vast space which is beyond the physical world. And all the things that you thought you have suddenly come to have no meaning at all . . . for you are now a free mind drifting in free space. You are none of the things that you thought you were, and yet you are still YOU.

"As a free mind, you are drifting down deeper and deeper into this vast space. And to where do you experience yourself drifting? You are drifting down to the very center of this vast space; you are drifting down to the very center of yourself.

"You are drifting down, down to your SELF . . . going deeper and deeper into the vast space of yourself. You see your SELF before yourself, and you ask a question: 'How can this be . . . for I am here in space drifting down to myself?' And suddenly you realize what you really are – you are the consciousness of your SELF, and you appreciate and recognize this fact with great joy in at last knowing – in full awareness – what you really are. You are an individual consciousness, and you appreciate and recognize this fact with great joy in at last becoming fully aware of what you really are – that the SELF you see before you, in this vast space, is the real YOU, while the you which you had previously thought was yourself is but the mind which that SELF uses. This insight comes upon you like a bursting of stars . . . and suddenly you feel utter blissfulness, utter peacefulness, utter happiness . . . and you find yourself dropping down directly to that CENTER OF YOUR BEING, which is your SELF.

"You go on down, down into your SELF, and you merge as one BEING. In doing this, you experience complete rest, for now you are home. Now you know what you really are and what you are meant to be. Now you know what you really are: YOU are the mind of this SELF – the consciousness of this SELF – through which YOU manifest.

"Now . . .

"Even this realization begins to melt and fade away as you melt into yourself . . . and you experience no longer a separation of yourself as being mind on the one hand and as being SELF on the other . . . for your mind and your SELF have become one, as pure consciousness. Each is part of the other which combine as consciousness. NOW YOU KNOW BEINGNESS. And along with this experiencing of your BEINGNESS you also experience your relationship of oneness expanding to include oneness with all that is the universe. Suddenly you KNOW THAT YOU ARE PART OF THE TOTALITY: that a part of that totality is YOU . . . that YOU ARE THE TOTALITY . . . YOU ARE ONE WITH THE INFINITE.

"This experiencing of SELF that you now know completely changes your relationship to the physical world in which you live at this moment, in here and now, and that, of course, includes your body. It gives you a control over your body that you never before imagined you possessed – for now that you as mind and you as self work together as a team in complete unity, the SELF takes over control of the mind, as it manifests in the physical world. And the mind now under control of the SELF makes you a master of your mind – a MASTERMIND which can bring perfection to your body, as is your wish.

"With this control which you now have, you can make of yourself whatever you desire. You can heal your body, you can keep your body in perfect health, you can reform its habits, you can make your body perform to a perfection beyond your wildest dreams. You can master ALL that is about yourself, and achieve whatever you desire to achieve. You have discovered yourself and, fusing mind with SELF, you have established SELF as the controller of mind, and you become THE MASTER SELF.

287

"Now . . .

"You have discovered who you really are, and you can cause all concerns and worries to vanish and disappear forever, as is your wish. You are now in complete control of yourself, and you have the power to make of yourself exactly what you wish to be. From this time on, you will control yourself always from your CENTER OF BEING . . . and you will make of yourself the perfection which it is your right to be.

"This which you now know as truth, from having personally experienced this truth, will stay with you always. Every breath you take into your physical body automatically reinforces this truth, and causes it to become your realization. You know yourself as being in perfect control of your health and well-being.

"I bring you back now to the here and now on a joyous returning to the physical world with this blissful KNOWING burning within you like an everlasting flame."

Part Four

Entering the Esoteric

Chapter Forty-Six

Oriental vs. Occidental Hypnotism

The Eastern version of a hypnotism show is much different from a Western version. So you will understand; I will tell you of my observation of "Oriental Hypnotism", as I witnessed it performed in India.

In an occidental hypnotism show, volunteers are invited to come on stage and be hypnotized, while the audience watch the demonstrations. There is applause and laughter throughout the show.

In an "Oriental Hypnotism Show" silence reigns. No special volunteers are invited to participate, as the entire audience attending an Eastern version of a hypnotism show are the participating volunteers. It is considered a privilege for an Eastern hypnotic master to invite you to attend the performance.

There is no stage. The show is presented to all spectators exactly where they happen to be seated for the show takes place within the minds of the spectators, not something that is observed from without. The show commences with a "Magic Circle" being drawn by the hypnotist around the entire audience. Only those seated within the "circle" will see any performance.

The experience of each person attending the "Oriental Hypnotism Show" will vary with the individual. There occurs to consciousness the most thrilling hypnotism show that ever was. Personal, experiential. Forever it will be vividly remembered.

I must emphasize that the invitation to attend an Oriental Hypnotism Show is a treasured gift.

As explained, in Oriental Hypnotism the entire audience (those who wish to be included) is surrounded with a "Magic Circle", which the hypnotist draws with a stick upon the ground. Anyone attending who is outside the "circle" agrees to be silent. For those who agree to remain inside the "circle", all demonstrations are enjoyable and instructive, but no attempt is made to control the will of any attendee. It is within "The Magic Circle" that, for example, the legendary "Hindu Rope Trick" is performed (witnessed is a better word). There is absolutely freedom of will to remain within the "circle" and participate or not. Those who wish to remain form an agreement between the Hindu Hypnotic Master and themselves: they will allow hypnosis to ensue by following all the instructions carefully and seriously concentrating on the hypnotic experiences provided in the show. *Actually, it is more an allowing of the show to happen.*

Recently, I have presented an occidental presentation of oriental hypnotism, titled, "A Journey Into the Arabian Nights" based on the theme of Aladdin and his magic lamp, in which wishes are granted by the Genie. The results have been enchanting.

THIRTEEN HINDU METHODS OF HYPNOTISING

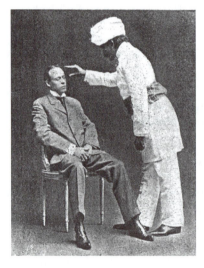 

Method No. 1.–The operator extends his hands with the fingers spread out and waves them around the head of the subject, whose eyes gradually close in sleep. The process may be varied by blowing on the subject's forehead between the eyebrows.

Method No. 2.–The subject is seated comfortably, and he is told to repeat a short monosyllable in a low voice, while the operator makes passes before his eyes. This soon results in a heaviness of the eyelids, followed by deep mesmeric sleep.

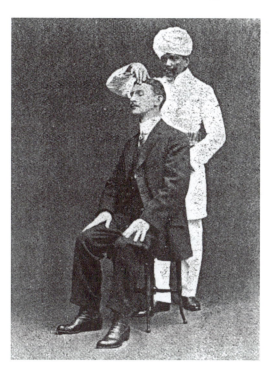

Method No. 3. – Here the operator places his right hand on the head of the subject, who is seated in an erect position.

If now the hypnotist makes passes with his left hand over the patient's spine, sleep will soon be induced with a sensitive subject.

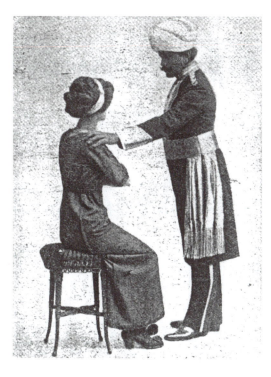

Method No. 4. – In this case hypnotic sleep is produced by gazing intently upward. A very little suggestion from the operator will then be needed to produce the effect.

Method No. 5.–A book may be handed to the subject, with the request that he will read each word very carefully and spell it. The effect should be produced before he has read a page.

Method No. 6.–The operator strikes a metal cup with an iron rod one hundred times, the patient being informed that she will fall asleep at the hundredth stroke.

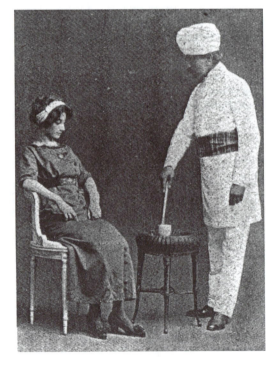

Method No. 7.–When the subject has closed his eyes, the operator touches them lightly with his index finger, at the same time suggesting that they will remain closed.

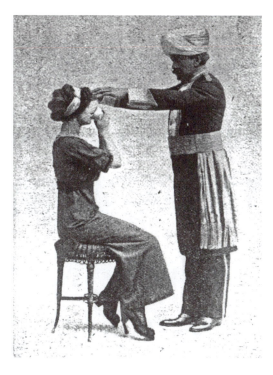

Method No. 8.–The operator makes passes over a glass of pure water placed before the subject, who is told that if she drinks it, she will fall asleep. When she has taken a draught and a few passes have been made over her, she soon passes into the hypnotic state.

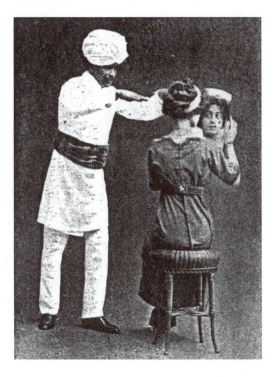

Method No. 9.–The subject is instructed to gaze intently into the reflection of her own eyes as seen in a mirror which she holds in her hand, at a distance of 8 or 10 inches. This will generally produce deep hypnotic sleep.

Method No. 10.–In India, one of the best methods of inducing hypnosis is for operator and subject to stare into each other's eyes until the latter becomes hypnotized.

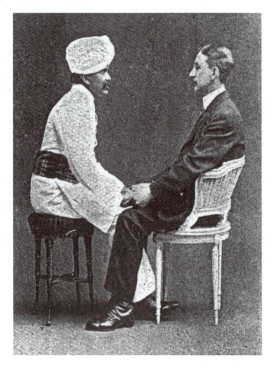

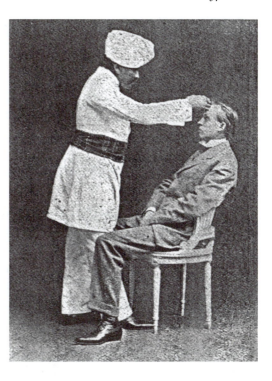

Method No. 11.—The operator places the palm of the right hand on the head of the patient, telling him that the hand will gradually become so heavy that he will be obliged to close his eyes.

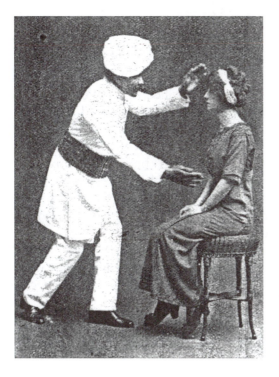

Method No. 12.—Another theory in India is that, if the subject closes her ears with her fingers, she will hear sounds as of pieces of glass falling at a great distance. Concentration upon this idea and appropriate suggestion by the operator will gradually induce hypnosis.

Method No. 13.—Let the subject close her eyes; you then place a bright light close to her eyelids, removing it slowly the next moment. This process repeated several times will put the patient to sleep.

Presenting Oriental Hypnotism

So you will understand:

Oriental Dynamic Hypnotism is the Hypnosis of Experimenting with Experiencing

To achieve it, follow these directions:

1. As the drone of Theta/Delta Resonance Sound comes in, close your eyes and relax comfortably in your chair. Enter into the sound, as it floods the room.
2. As directed, with eye still closed, take six deep breaths – in succession – while thinking of the breaths bringing in prantic energy, which you store in your solar plexus.
3. As it is described, visualize a "magic circle" being drawn around the entire audience – unifying the group.
4. Open your eyes as the Resonance Sound fades away, and concentrate your attention on the candle flame burning in front of the stage. Now, while gazing at the candle, everyone performs the OM mantra (pronounced AUM) three times. By repeating the OM mantra you are making a cosmic connection.
5. Then, as instructed, lock your hands together "The Om Mantra Way", and lift them high above your head into the increased energy in the room. Let happen what is suggested, and you will find your hands have become locked together so firmly you cannot separate them. Tug as hard as you will. They will separate immediately when the candle is blown out. You have taken a quantum leap from mental to physical control of your body.
6. Then, close your eyes and mentally affirm to yourself *eagerness* to come up and join the group on the stage to learn the art of pretending . . . which moves from pretending to believing . . . which moves from believing to reality, as you experiment with experiencing in this show. (*Better come up fast if you want to get a seat on the stage.*)
7. Enjoy every moment with elation, as you become the master of your mind . . . making it think *when* you want it to THINK.

Making it think *what* you want it to THINK. Making it *stop, thinking* when you want it to become SILENT. With such control of your mind, you become a MASTERMIND.

ON WITH THE SHOW

Chapter Forty-Seven

My "Ladder of Colors" Hypnotic Induction

In Eastern belief, a person is regarded as having a psychic nervous system in addition to the visible physical nervous system. It is held that the spinal column provides an invisible channel in its center called the *"sushumna"*. On either side of the *sushumna* flows a current of *prana* (vitality of life), of positive and negative types, the two currents passing through the substance of the spinal cord.

The two currents of *prana* which flow along the channel of the spinal cord have distinctive Hindu names: the current which flows on the right side being called *"pingula"* and is the positive current. The current that flows on the left side is called *"ida"* (pronounced *"ee-daa"*) and is the negative current. Spaced along the *sushumna*, in specific parts of the body, are special energy centers called *"chakras"*. The term *"chakra"* means wheel, disc or whirling-around-object, and is stimulated into activity by rising psychic energy (termed *"kundalini"*) ascending the channel of the *sushumna* from the base of the spine. It is claimed that there are seven main chakra centers along the channel   of the *sushumna*:

1. *The muladhara,* the lowest *chakra* located in the base of the spine.
2. *The svadhisthana,* the second *chakra*, in ascending order, located on the spinal column in the region of the reproductive organs.
3. *The manipura,* the third in ascending order, located on the spinal column in the region of the solar plexus.
4. *The anahata,* the fourth in ascending order, located in the spinal column in the region of the heart.
5. *The visuddha,* the fifth in ascending order, located on the spinal cord in the region of the throat.

301

The Seven Main Chakra Centers

6. *The ajana*, the sixth in ascending order, located on the spinal column in the regions of the pineal gland within the head (frequently referred to as "the third eye").
7. *The sahastrara*, the seventh in ascending order, located at the top of the head (the Hindus refer to this as "the thousand petalled lotus").

Each *chakra* center is associated with a specific color which when visualized within the mind is said to produce a vibratory frequency which stirs into activity the operation of the *chakra* associated with it. The colors are:

Red	Stimulating to the first *chakra*
Orange	Stimulating to the second *chakra*
Yellow	Stimulating to the third *chakra*
Green	Stimulating to the fourth *chakra*
Blue	Stimulating to the fifth *chakra*
Violet	Stimulating to the sixth *chakra*
White	Stimulating to the seventh *chakra*

This color is used to form the white light of projection about the subject.

When these colors are visualised within the mind, in sequence upwards from red to white such is called "The Ladder of Colors". Using this technique increases the influence of mind upon the body.

I give you here my personal version, developed while teaching hypnotherapy.

The "Ladder of Colors" Method

Sit in a comfortable chair with hands resting loosely in lap. Rest your feet flat on the floor. Now, relax and take a deep breath. Exhale slowly. Do it again; this time while inhaling visualize the color WHITE (color of the *Sahastrara Chakra*) coming into nostrils and filling the lungs with WHITE LIGHT – entering your body and spreading throughout your entire nervous system. Just sit quietly with eyes closed. Breathe comfortably feeling WHITE LIGHT forming an aura of purity about your SELF. Visualize it as a beautiful experience.

REST A FEW MOMENTS

Now, with eyes still closed, visualize – within your mind – the color RED. Fill your head with the color RED. Visualize RED in anyway you please: a red rose, a red apple, anything that is RED.

REST A FEW MOMENTS

Now, go up to the color ORANGE. Visualize the color ORANGE within your mind. See ORANGE anyway you please: a bowl of oranges, a glass of orange juice, a Buddhist monk in an orange robe. Visualize the color ORANGE anyway you please. See ORANGE with your mind's eye inside your head.

REST A FEW MOMENTS

Now, go up the ladder to the color YELLOW. Visualize YELLOW. Fill your head with YELLOW. Picture it anyway you please: the YELLOW yoke of an egg, the YELLOW center of a daisy. A blazing YELLOW sun.

REST A FEW MOMENTS

Now, go up the ladder of your spinal column, and visualize the color GREEN. See GREEN inside your head. Fill your head with GREEN. See GREEN as you wish: green grass, green leaves, a glowing green emerald.

REST A FEW MOMENTS

Now, go up the ladder and visualize the color BLUE. See BLUE clearly with your mind's eye: a blue sky, a blue lake. Use whatever image you like to visualize the color BLUE.

REST A FEW MOMENTS

Finally, go up the "Ladder of Colors" and reach the color VIOLET. Visualize VIOLET LIGHT filling your head. Possibly mentally see a bunch of violets, anything you wish as long as it fills your mind with the color VIOLET.

Allow yourself to submerge into the color VIOLET. LET VIOLET BE AS A MIST YOU DROP INTO.

"The Ladder of Colors" is a remarkable prelude to all forms of hypnotic inductions (both self and heteros). Submerged in violet, hypnosis is readily induced.

Practice "The Ladders of Colors" anytime and as often as you wish. It trains you in the ability to effectively visualize.

Note to Hypnotherapist

I often use "The Ladder of Colors" to commence a hypnothera-peutic session. It provides a mutual process you and your client can both do together. It is an interesting way to start a session: establishes rapport and produces a state of mind receptive to som-nambulism (profound hypnosis).[3]

---

[3] Ormond McGill, 2003, *The New Encyclopedia of Stage Hypnotism*, Crown House Publishing Ltd, Carmarthen, UK, p. 171.

Chapter Forty-Eight
Abundance Hypnosis

The "Mastermind Principles" of how to use creative mind in relation to magic was presented in Chapter Twenty-Eight, "The Greatest Magic in the World". It is presented here in relation to hypnotic phenomena. Abundance hypnosis provides a way to create in the universe using the power of your mind. Through the process you can get what you think you want out of life: wealth, love, success, whatsoever. The power is within you, but remember it is a two-edged sword that can conquer or destroy. Always use the power for the benefit of good.

There is nothing mystical about abundance hypnosis. It is a scientific method. Some call it "The Magic of Believing", others "The Power of Positive Thinking". Still others call it "Creative Visualization". And behind it all stand mind and consciousness. Mind and consciousness operate together; you can't have one without the other. You should have some understanding of both.

What is Mind?

Mind is nothing tangible. Mind is like walking. You know you have a mind just as you know you can walk, but after you walk where is the walking? It would probably be more understandable if mind were called "minding", – for mind is a process for producing thoughts, and thoughts are a form of energy. Mind can be likened to an instrument for thinking, and when properly used under the control of consciousness has tremendous power.

What is Consciousness?

The only way you can understand consciousness is in relation to yourself – *it is your awareness of your being,* i.e. your awareness that you are. That is to say, it is recognition of your SELF within yourself.

307

Please try to understand: it is not your outside self which you can see reflected in a mirror; rather, it is your inside self which you cannot see at all, but which you instinctively *know* is there. And that SELF can directly create in the universe. It is the God power. Surely you have heard, "God Is Within You".

What are Thoughts?

Thoughts are things. In other words, thoughts are energy taking form. Thought is a force in nature just as gravitation is a force in nature. When your consciousness uses your mind to pattern that force, it passes out as thought. The more you use your mind to power the thoughts the more you can directly create in the universe. It is the God power which is your heritage.

The Modus Operandi of Creation

It has been expressed (in age-old Eastern concepts) that to each particle of matter a particle of mind can be attached, in much the same way that fog can cause itself, by its moisture, to attach to the particles of dust in the air. In the same way, one might say, a little particle of "mind stuff" is attached to every atom in the universe so that every atom has its own particular "atom consciousness", as it were. When those atoms are bound together in, say, the form of a starfish, then you will have starfish consciousness. Or, if bound together, say, in the form of a bird you will have bird consciousness. Or, if bound together in the form of a man or woman, then you will have man or woman consciousness. Consciousness (awareness) of its creation makes it so (reality).

Everything in existence exists to the degree of being what it is in accordance with the consciousness of being what it is. The more consciousness becomes conscious of itself, the higher the evolutionary form of matter of which it is composed.

In the process of creation by mind, the objective is perceived and is then formed into the objective conceived. This is the initial process of visualization. In this process, the particles of "mind stuff" are agglomerated, thus forming different units of consciousness. This concentration consists of getting more of these particles into one place. That is, if you can condense them to a point, you have absolute unity of concentration at that point, just as a magnifying glass will focus the sun's rays at a point. It is then through concentration that the basis of matter (akasha) can be molded by creative mind to become reality in the physical universe.

Direct creating in the universe by mind takes energy, and the basis of energy is called *"prana"*. *Prana* is all pervading. The entire universe is manufactured from its subtle material (akasha) by the power of *prana*.

Prana comes into you through the breath, and certain ways of breathing bring in greater quantities which is exceptionally important when your mental efforts are directed to *create in the universe* what you want to create for yourself. Your consciousness directs your mind with the purpose to produce "thought desired" which when energized by *prana* becomes creative mind.

Creative Mind

The entire universe stands as proof of creative mind. As Jesus so aptly expressed it, "God is Within You" – which is to say that each person has his/her share of creative mind within himself, and can use it at will to create in the physical universe.

Creative mind is a combination blending of imagination (the creative center of the mind) and will (the directing of thoughts for specific purpose). It is accomplished through visualizing (Image Principle) what is desired to be created in the mind, and then by an effort of will projecting the mental image upon the *akasha* (Material Principle) while energizing the mental form with *prana* (Energy Principle), so as to create in materializing form the reproduction of that which your consciousness causes to be imagined in the mind.

In summation, three mental powers are used to create in the universe: the power of visualization, the power of affirmation, the power of projection. To effectively use these mental powers requires the ability to throw the mind blank, one-pointedness of concentration, and vivid imagination.

Your subconscious phase of mind instinctively knows how to manifest these powers. Using self-hypnosis or hetero-hypnosis tell the subconscious to put them into operation for you, under your conscious direction.

Chapter Forty-Nine

A Message from Delight

Delight gives you here a peek of what you will experience when you make the transition (that is when your physical body dies, and you have to vacate it).

Of course, as is always the case, the precise experience of each individual will differ. However, this message from Delight will give you a general idea of what to expect in life beyond death.

When your physical body dies and it can no longer "house" you, your soul (individual consciousness of yourself) pops out of the dead body via the crown chakra (top of your head). Sometimes you can actually sense the "popping" - much like the popping of a cork out of a bottle.

On vacating the dead physical body, you immediately enter a body most often referred to as "The Astral body". In appearance it is very much shaped after the pattern of the physical body you have just vacated, however, is of an entirely different frequency (vibratory rate).

If the astral body were to be described in the scientific terms of physics, it could be said that it is composed of a most tenuous condition of matter existing at a highly accelerated rate of vibration to that of the condition of matter in the physical universe. The rate of vibration of this body is so rapid as to be imperceptible to normal sensing (however, some persons are sensitive enough to perceive it).

When you first enter this astral body form, having just left the physical, many experience a bewildering effect, as your new body seems more restricted than the physical body you have vacated. That is, it cannot move physical things. It cannot be seen or heard by average sensing, by those still in physical body. It seems limited in what it can do. Of course, for you now exist in a realm of entirely different vibrations.[4] Now, come to know your guide.

---

[4] Ormond McGill, 1995, *Grieve No More Beloved: The Book of Delight*, Anglo American Book Company Ltd, Carmarthen, UK.

You will know who your guide is. In fact, if you have been the least bit sensitive you have known your guide all through your span in the physical body. Pause a moment, think and recall. You have known all your life.

People of all ages, from time immemorial, who are sensitive to such things have recognized that "something" or "someone" watched over them, something which is beyond themselves. Some refer to this as "the teacher"; some refer to this as their "guardian angel". Your "guide" is such an angel (sometimes male and sometimes female).

What is a "guardian angel?" Search inside yourself and you will know, for it has been a friend with you all your life on earth, a figure, being, entity, the still small voice within, call it what you will that has as its assignment YOU.

Possibly some will not choose to take this "guardian angel" concept seriously – whatever you wish. When you make the transition you will know!

Experiencing the "Reveries"

The "reveries", often as directed by your guide when passing onward provide a review of your life (just left behind), so you can face up squarely to how you have lived, and can prepare for a catharsis which you will experience within the Shadow land (which the Tibetans refer to as "The Bardo"). Just follow your guide on this, and consider it an opportunity of learning about the true nature of your SELF.

You will recognize many mistakes you have made, and recognize many things you could have done better, but you are not criticized for them. If you are wise you will profit from your mistakes and not make them again. "Experience the Reveries" and benefit yourself. Used constructively it provides a great opportunity. But unfortunately most are so "asleep" they only get confused by this review of their life and learn very little. Your guide will help you in every way if you accept this help.

What is "The Veil?"

The "veil" stands as one of the great esoteric mysteries of all time. The ancients likened it to a "still river" which you crossed from the shore of one world to the shore of another. Persons who have returned from near death experiences report it in various ways, as a sort of barrier, a grey mist, the doorway between earthly life and the next life. Whatever the imagery of the "veil" is, it can best be likened to a place and yet not a place where the borders of two worlds (Existences) of different frequencies meet and cancel out each other. On the one side of this "doorway" lies the physical world, and on the other – bordered by the reflective Shadowland (Bardo) – lies the astral world and/or mind world.

Is all this real or just imagination for you, as an onward passing soul? *It is assuredly experience and what more can you say about reality than that it is experience* (experienced)? We are so devoted to placing everything in spatial relationships that it is difficult not to consider anything unless it is "somewhere". If the "veil" must be conceived as being somewhere, place it as being universally close whatever the position in space, as it will be experienced following your transition.

It is through the "veil" that one passes in the astral body during the experiences of both birth and death. It is the "veil" which divides one side from the other, and at birth hangs like a "curtain of forgetfulness" on the individual in the physical world. There is wisdom in this fact, for in the forgetting of past lives the immediate one is given precedence for full experiencing. There is no need for a mystical explanation of this amnesia effect. Nature does not operate in supernatural ways but always in accordance with the natural laws, even if some are surprising.

The memories of past lives remain buried within the subconscious of each person, and by probing can sometimes be recalled. "Awakened ones" can remember their births and deaths without interruption. In unenlightened man, the "curtain" is not lifted (except by special techniques) from the mind until making the transition frees it, and permit an ever expansion of consciousness. Most seemingly do it so slowly taking lifetime after lifetime, but actually it can happen in a flash of "enlightenment" this very instant.

When you look at it objectively, the experience of dying is remarkable. Oriental people seem to understand this better than do most in the Occident. Death of the physical body must be looked upon as being simply a time of transition from the human plane of consciousness to a heightened (transcendental) plane of consciousness, and it would be well accompanied by solemn joyousness at the climax of the life just lived.

Delight expresses it like this: "Truly, if you look upon death as a gift package you have been waiting for expecting all of your life, when it comes you will receive it with gladness rather than sadness."[5]

[5] Ormond McGill, 1995, *Grieve No More, Beloved: The Book of Delight*, Anglo American Book Company Ltd., Carmarthen, UK.

Chapter Fifty

Thoughts on Reincarnation

The return of the formless into form is called reincarnation. Some believe in it and some do not. Belief or unbelief is irrelevant. It is the way of the universe. Everything is patterned on birth, death, rebirth. The very stars, vast galaxies, follow this pattern. So, I accept this truth, "There is not a living person in the entire world who has not returned from death to live life after life."

Here are some thoughts on reincarnation to mull over.

We have all died many deaths before we came into this immediate incarnation. What we call birth is merely the reverse side of death, like one of the two sides of a coin or like a door which we call "entrance" from the outside of a house and "exit" from the inside. The argument of a person who assumes that because he has no conscious memory of his many births and deaths proves that reincarnation is untrue is scientifically untenable. The field of man's perception, as is easily demonstrated, is extremely limited. There are objects he cannot see, sounds he cannot hear, odors he cannot smell, tastes he cannot taste, and feelings he cannot feel.

With the senses of the physical body so obviously limited, it is really astonishing that anyone should question the possibility of reincarnation just because he cannot remember his previous lives, and thus conclude he has had no previous existences, for in like manner no one remembers his recent birth, and yet no one doubts that he (or she) was born.

It was not so many years ago that evolution was a theory believed in by a few. Today it is accepted by the majority. What is evolution but the evolvement of the physical body, while reincarnation is the evolvement of the soul. Both are concurrent and are interrelated. Body after body, or more properly expressed, life experience after life experience, must be engaged in for the growth of the soul.

In the Bible, Christ says, "Except that a man be born again, he cannot enter the Kingdom of God." That is from the English retranslation, and Christian doctrine has interpreted "born again" as meaning a spiritual rebirth. The original Hebrew text however has it written as "born again and again". In the Koran, it is written, "God generates beings and then sends them back over and over again till they return to Him."

Many of the world's great minds have given credence to reincarnation. Voltaire wrote, "After all, it is no more surprising to be born twice than it is to be born once. Everything in Nature is resurrection." Nietzsche states, "Live, so that thou mayest desire to live again – that is thy duty. For in any case, thou wilt live again."

You can unravel the matter for yourself, if you reflect upon concepts which place as truth only one lifetime in the physical world which at the most (currently) rarely exceeds 90 years, and then balance it against an eternity on the other side. Such beliefs paint a very unbalanced picture of nature indeed. Likewise, the idea that one's behavior during that minute "droplet in time" in the great ocean of Eternity determines one's status in relation to God for the remainder of each soul's existence for the aeons which lie ahead is equally incongruous.

How long will the process of reincarnation continue for the soul from the formless to form and from form to formless in repetition? For an answer, suppose we say, "For as long as there is yet much to learn, much to desire, and much to experience in the physical side of life. As long as the desires for the physical world are there, the soul will reincarnate." Yet, the process is not endless. Eventually, enlightenment comes to every soul, and the cycle of rebirth is broken.

The importance of reincarnation cannot be over-emphasized if a full comprehension of soul growth is to be understood. Incarnations in the physical world are experiences in which the soul is gradually burnished to become a thing of beauty. This is enlightenment, which is a recognition of one's true SELF, one's true Status in relation to existence. It can take many, many lifetimes – in both the physical world and in the mind world – for some to reach that realization . . . that realization that some call "nirvana" and others "Oneness with God", and yet it is possible to achieve it this very moment. Birth and death are not phenomena which happen only once in any given human life. Such occur uninterruptedly. At every moment, something within us dies and something is reborn. The understanding of reincarnation is but an extension of this continuous fact.

It is of great importance that understanding and appreciation of reincarnation is today being given more and more credence by Western cultures, for when that long-awaited agreement among all people as to the truth of the matter occurs, there will no longer be doubt, no fallacious argumentation directed towards the truth of the immortal (divine) nature of ourselves. Then will Occidental man awaken from the slumbers of ignorance which have been hypnotically induced by a mistaken orthodoxy and concur with his Eastern brother.

Here are the sentiments regarding reincarnation as expressed in the Hindu sacred text, *The Upanishads:*

"As one's desire is, so is their destiny. For as their desire is, so is their will, and as their will is, so is their deed, and as their deed is, so is their reward, whether good or bad. For a person acts according to the desires they treasure. After death the person goes to the next world bearing in mind the subtle impressions of these deeds, and after reaping the harvest of their deeds, they return again to the world of action. Thus, one who still has the desires of the earth continues subject to rebirth. But he or she who does not have earthly desires, who has discrimination, whose mind is steady and whose heart is pure, and who does not desire to be reborn, reaches the goal, and having reached it, is form no more, and remains amongst the hosts with God."

Chapter Fifty-One
Yogi Pranayama Practices

As I have promised to give you secrets of my lifetime in this Autobiography, I am motivated to give you how to practice Pranayama. As Pranayama has assuredly been a treasure in my life, I will devote a chapter to this study, as Pranayama is definitely of value to body, mind and spirit. As you are that trinity, the practice of Pranayama belongs to you.

By means of arousing into activity the power of *prana*, the Yogis are able to direct the *pranic* energy, by the use of the will, into the various parts and organs of their bodies, thus strengthening them to a great degree. By similar methods, they are able to revitalize others and perform various forms of mental healing which is regarded as one of the magics of India.

Also the *pranic* energy is used in various psychic phenomena, such as telepathy, mental influence, etc. The Masters teach that all students of the magical power should add to their knowledge all methods of the arousing and projection of *pranic* force, in which the practice of "rhythmic breathing" plays an important part. I will now give you the very essence of this instruction.

Nadi breathing exercises

The *nadis* are psychic nerve channels which extend to all parts of the body in countless number, and which serve to carry the *prana* to every organ and part thereof. The Yogi teach that these channels of the *nadis* must be kept open and free, so as to allow an uninterrupted flow of *prana* through them. They have designed special exercises for this purpose. There are specifically three of these: "The Nadi Purifier", "The Nadi Stimulator", and "The Nadi Vibrator".

1. The Nadi Purifying Exercise

This exercise should be used at the beginning of any practice of rhythmic breathing as it clears and cleanses, purifies and rends free the channels of the nadis, and thus allows for an excellent flow of prana through the system. It is performed in this fourfold process. It is YOGA practice.

A. Assume the stable and easy Asana (seated with body upright and spine straight).

B. Inhale a deep breath, using both nostrils during the count of 6 units.*

C. Retain the breath for 3 units.

D. Shape your lips as if you intended to whistle, and then silently whistle out the breath through your pursed lips, using considerable vigor and propelling force in doing so. Perform this special method of exhaling the breath during the count of 6 units.

Repeat this exercise seven time without haste. Then rest for five minutes before undertaking any other breathing exercise.

NOTE: In addition to its employment as a preliminary to rhythmic breathing, this Nadi Purifier Exercise will be found helpful when you are fatigued. Then continue with "the Nadi Stimulator Exercise".

* Units are heart-beat counts: one beat = one unit

2. The Nadi Stimulator Exercise

This exercise should be used at the conclusion of any practice of rhythmic breathing as it stimulates the entire nervous system, and the body in general. Like the foregoing Nadi Exercise, it is accomplished through a fourfold process:

A. Stand erect, with head, neck, and back held straight, shoulders thrown back, abdomen slightly drawn in, and legs straight and stiff.

B. Inhale fully for 6 units.

C. Retain breath for 3 units as you perform this "muscular movement", i.e., extend both arms straight out in front of you, on a line with the shoulders, fists lightly clenched in an easy straight position: now, slowly draw your clenched fists back to your shoulders, contracting the arm muscles, as you do so.

So when the arms reach the shoulders the arms will be stiff and taut. At this point in the exercise . . .

D. Exhale the breath for 6 units, while you snap arms forward out in front again. Repeat the exercise seven times in a leisurely manner, then rest for a few moments. A little practice is necessary to acquire the knack of the peculiar "snap" as muscle movements. The exercise has a bracing tonic effect.

3. The Nadi Vibrator Exercise

The "Nadi Vibrator Exercise" stimulates both mind and body. The exercise tends to shake up the whole system. It's vibrating influence removes stagnation from the circulatory and nervous systems. It is performed in this manner:

A. Assume the stable and easy Asana (same position as in first Nadi Exercise).

B. Inhale during the count of 6 units, but instead of drawing the breath in the regular manner as a steady, continuous inhalation, inhale in a series of short, vigorous sniffs.

C. Retain the breath for 3 units.

D. Exhale the breath in a long, deliberate restful "sighing" breath for a count of 6 units.

Repeat the exercise seven times, then rest for a few minutes. This peculiar "vibrating effect" of this exercise removes all sluggishness.

Mantram Vocal Meditation

A mantram is a religious/magical recitation used by the Hindus. It is repeated over and over in rhythm. The Yogis place great emphasis on the beauty of the voice and cadence in such performances.

Swami Vivekananda has this to say on the matter: "By right practice a beautiful rite will come to you. The Yogis are noted for their wonderful voices, which are strong, smooth, and clear, and have wonderful trumpet-like carrying power.

Among the numerous breathing exercises employed by the Yogis for developing the desired quality of voice, the most famous is known as *the Mantram Pathfinder*. This exercise is practiced as follows: 1. Assume the stable and easy *Asana*. 2. Inhale as usual for 6 units, and 3. Retain the breath for 3 units.

Opening the mouth as in singing, exhale through the opened mouth for the usual 6 units, at the same time sounding the notes described below.

Repeat the exercise seven times, avoiding haste and overtiring your voice. Then rest for a few minutes before practicing further.

The sounds or notes used during the exercise consist of seven droning or humming sounds produced with the exhaled breath; one sound for each exhalation. The drone or hum produced is like a whirring sound, and the concluding humming sound of m-m-m-m-m-m-m must always be quite marked and persistent. The vowel sound of the hummmmmmm is varied with each of the seven repetitions of the exercise, as follows:

1. Sound "Hah" followed by the "m-m-m-m" hum so as to sound like Hahm-m-m-m-m-m-m-m.
2. In the same way sound "Haw" followed by the hum, as "Hawm-m-m-m-m-m-m.
3. In the same way sound "Hee" followed by the hum, as "Heem-m-m-m-m-m.
4. In the same way sound "High" followed by the hum, as "Highm-m-m-m-m-m-m.
5. In the same way sound "Hoe" followed by the hum, as "Hoem-

m-m-m-m-m-m.

6. In the same way sound "Hoo" followed by the hum, as "Hoom-m-m-m-m-m-m.

7. In the same way sound "Hum" followed by the "m-m-m-m-m-m-mm-m," thus making the full sound of 'hum-m-m-m-m-m-m-m-m-m.

The droning or humming sound of "m-m-m-m-m-m-m-m" will easily follow the vowel sound in each instance then you close your lips after making the latter, and continue the hummmmmn with closed lips. With practice, "The Mantram Pathfinder" will bring you a beautiful voice.

Yogi Ramakrishna suggests another vocal exercise used by the Hindus which will cultivate an outstanding voice. You can use this exercise in combination with the foregoing, if you wish. The exercise consists of puckering up the mouth as if you were about to whistle through it (or to say "Whew") and then, while holding that position of the lips and face, sing naturally through the puckered lips, sounding the notes through them without disturbing the position of the lips. Practice this exercise a little each day, and note how your speaking voice improves.

The Grand Yoga Breath

This is a popular form of *pranic* breathing in India. The Yogis practice it in order to call into activity the whole nervous system and centers of the body, and to distribute the *prana* to the plexuses which serves its natural reservoirs and "storage batteries of *prana*." In "The Grand Yoga Breath Exercise" the various *chakras* are aroused to activity, and, at the same time, the *nadis* are stimulated and energized. In it, also, the power of creative mind is invoked and applied in an effective manner. The exercise is performed as follows:

A. Lie down flat on your back, keeping the head, neck, back, and legs in a straight line. The position must be easy and natural.

B. Perform the usual cycles of rhythmic breathing as you have learned, i.e., inhalation for 6 units, retention for 3 units, exhalation for 6 units. Perform these cycles of rhythmic breathing for seven times, with a few moments of rest between each cycle. Now accompany each inhalation, in turn, with one of the following mental exercises, in the order given, the first with the first cycle, the second with the second cycle, and so on until the seven have been performed, one with each cycle, viz.:

1. Visualize the breath as entering the body through the bones of the legs and then exhaled through them. Try to "feel" as strongly as possible that this action is really occurring.
2. Visualize the breath as entering the body through the bones of the arms, and then exhaled through them. Accompany this with the "feeling" as above instructed.
3. Visualize the breath as entering the body through the top of the skull, and then exhaled through it; accompanying this with the appropriate "feeling".
4. Visualize the breath as entering the body through the stomach, and then exhale through it; accompanying this with the appropriate "feeling".
5. Visualize the breath as entering the body through the reproductive organism, and then exhale through it; accompanying this with the appropriate "feeling".
6. Visualize the breath as entering the body through the base of the spinal column, and then exhaled through it; accompanying this with the appropriate "feeling".
7. Visualize the breath as entering the body through every pore of the skin all over the whole body, from head to toe; accompanying this with the appropriate "feeling".

Having rested for a few moments following this first stage of "The Grand Yoga Breath Exercise", you are now ready to perform the second stage of the exercise, which is as follows:

A. Lie on the back in the same position, and with the same care, as in the first stage of the exercise.

B. Perform seven more cycles of rhythmic breathing, following the same rhythm, i.e., Inhalation 6 units; retention 3 units; exhalation 6 units. During each inhalation perform the visualization (and accompanying "feeling") of sending the *pranic* current to each of the *chakras*, in turn, one with each exhalation, in the order chanted. At the same time, use the will to "will" that the current will go where it is directed (where it is visualized as going and is "it" as going).

By this procedure, each *chakra* is energized and stimulated by the flowing *prana* thus directed to it. Here is the list of *chakras* to be reached in the way just instructed, in the order in which they are to be aroused in the exercise:

The "Nadi Purifying Exercise should be used at the beginning of any practice of rhythmic breathing as it clears and cleanses purifies and sends free the channels of the *nadis*, and thus allows for an excellent flow of *prana* through the system. It is performed by this fourfold process:

1. Assume the stable and easy Asana.
2. Inhale a deep breath, using both nostrils during the count of 6 units.
3. Retain the breath for 3 units.
4. Shape your lips as if you intended to whistle, and then silently whistle out the breath through your pursed lips, using considerable vigor and propelling force in doing so. Perform this special method of exhaling the breath during the count of 6 units.

Repeat the process seven times without haste or overexertion. Then rest a few minutes before undertaking any other breathing exercise.

In addition to its employment as a preliminary to further rhythmic breathing, this "Nadi Purifier Exercise" will be found very helpful when you are tired or fatigued in any way; in which case, it will be well to continue it with the "Nadi Stimulator Exercise" which follows.

This exercise should be used at the conclusion of any practice of rhythmic breathing as it stimulates the *nadis*, and accordingly stimulates the entire nervous system, and the body in general. Like the previous *nadis* exercise, it is accomplished through a fourfold process:

1. Stand erect, with head, neck, and back held straight, shoulders thrown back, abdomen slightly drawn in, and legs straight and stiff.
2. Inhale fully for 6 units.
3. Retain the breath for 3 units as you perform this "muscle move-

ment": extend both arms straight out in front of you, on a line with the shoulders, fists clenched – not stiffly, but in an easy straight position; slowly draw your clenched fists back to your shoulders, contracting the arm muscles as you do so, so that when the fists reach the shoulders the arms will be stiff and. At this point in the exercise . . .

4. Exhale the breath for 6 units.

Repeat the exercise seven times in a leisurely manner, then rest for a few moments. A little practice is necessary in order to acquire the knack of the peculiar "snap" of the muscle movements. The exercise has a bracing, tonic effect.

The "Nadi Vibrator Exercise" is employed when you feel an apathetic condition of mind and body. The exercise tends to "shake up" the whole system, and its vibrating influence removes stagnation from the circulatory and nervous systems. It is performed as follows:

1. Assume the stable and easy Asana.
2. Inhale during the count of 6 units, but instead of drawing the breath in the regular manner as a steady, continuous inhalation, inhale in a series of short, vigorous sniffs, just as if you were sniffing a pungent substance.
3. Retain the breath for 3 units.

"Asana" is a Raja Yoga (physical Yoga) term for assuming the proper posture when pranayama is practised. The rule is: whatever posture is the easiest for the particular person is the posture for that particular person to use. Most it is to assume an upright position of the sitting body, with head, neck, and chest in as nearly a straight line as possible.

1. "The Muladhara Chakra", situated at the base of tilt-spinal column.
2. "The Svadisthana Chakra", situated at the base of the reproductive organs.
3. "The Manipura Chakra", situated in the center of the trunk, just back of the Solar Plexus.
4. "The Anahata Chakra", situated in the region of the heart.
5. "The Visuddha Chakra", situated in the region of the throat.

6. "Tile Ajna Chakra", situated at the brain, just back of the center of the eyebrows.
7. "The Sahasraha Chakra", situated on the top of the head, at its center.

C. "The Grand Yoga Breath Exercise" should be concluded by "visualizing", "feeling", and "willing" a great current of *prana* to sweep over the entire body, reaching every outer and inner part breathing every organ, center and region with a great flow of *pranic* power and energy, and thus vitalizing the whole physical system, in its entirety.

The Living Battery of Prana

The real East Indian magicians in producing their mysteries, require the employment of *prana* in connection with the creative mind, feel the necessity of regarding their body as "a living battery, of *prana*", and keeping that battery well charged. To this end, they perform the following *pranic* exercise:

1. Assume the stable and easy Asana, with the following variation, i.e. place your feet close together, side by side, so as to close the circuit at its end. Also close the circuit at the other extreme of the limbs (the arms) by locking the fingers of each hand in the following manner, viz., by placing the palm of one hand over and facing the other palm, the tips of the fingers of each hand resting hooked into the closed fingers of the other hand: the thumb of each hand touching the outer edge of the opposite hand just below the little finger on each. The position of the hands is simple to achieve once you try it.
2. Retaining this position, practice rhythmic breathing in the regular cycles, i.e., inhalation 6 units, retention 3 units, exhalation 6 units. Make your rhythmic breathing easily and naturally without effort.
3. While performing this rhythmic breath, "visualize," "feel," and "will" that the *prana* you are absorbing with each breath will be distributed in your closed circuit of "the living battery" in your body as well as by all the pranic enters, *chakras*, and *nadis*.

The oriental magicians frequently sit in this attitude for sizable periods at time thus charging themselves with Pranic energy in this closed-circuit exercise. They also employ these general principles for controlling emotions, removing unwanted stress and establishing desired flows. The method for this consists simply of practicing the rhythmic breathing exercise, with its proper Asana and characteristic "6-3-6" units of rhythm, during which process the magician "visualizes", "feels" and "wills" himself to experience the opposite emotion to that which he desires to master.

For example, if it is the emotion of fear or dread that one wishes to overcome, then the emotion of courage is visualized to supplant it. All undesirable emotions are negative in character, and the way to kill most negative is to concentrate upon the opposing position which, when used in conjunction with the *pranic* rhythm of breathing, has a powerful effect in such regard. You can use the method exactly as the magicians do to master your own emotions.

Imparting Pranic Energy Together

The skilled magician is not only able to charge himself with *pranic* energy, but, as desired, is able to charge other persons with the power as well. The following two methods are effective in this regard, the first of these is as follows:

1. Have the other person seated before you with toes touching yours, and hands clasped in yours.
2. Both yourself and the party to whom you are imparting *pranic* energy must practice rhythmic breathing in harmonious unison, observing the same rhythmic unit and "breathing in time with each other"; you setting the time measure according to your own pulse beat.
3. During the performance of the rhythmic breathing in unison, you must "visualize", "feel", and "will" the flow of *prana* as passing from out of yourself and into the other person—picturing, feeling, and willing it to flow through your hands into his or hers.

The second method for this purpose is to have the other person seated back to back with you; the two spinal columns touching each other, each person assuming the Asana position as used in "the living battery" process which you have studied. Then breathe "in unison", precisely as described in the first method while projecting the *prana* into the other person by "visualization", feeling, and "willing" it to flow from one spinal column to the other.

Either of these two methods of imparting *pranic* energy to others may be used, and are employed by the magicians in helping the other person use these psychic methods to gain physical improvement, circumstances, etc. In all such cases (which the magicians refer to as "treatments by *prana*"), the thought of the desired improved condition is projected along with the flow of *prana*, by "visualizing, feeling, and willing".

Pranazing Water

The magicians also practise a technique of charging water with *prana*, the water in turn being drunk by persons in need of a higher charging of *prana* within themselves. This method is particularly useful in the treatment of ill persons.

In this practice, the glass or cup of water is held in the left hand, letting the bottom of same rest in the hollowed palm of the right hand. Rhythmic breathing is then performed as has been instructed, the right hand is then held over the glass or cup in the process of this breathing; gather the fingertips together over the water, then shake them gently toward the water as if one were trying to throw from the fingertips little drops of water that had gathered on them. After a few moments of this "shaking", open the right hand and pass the palm slowly around the top of the glass or cup, about 6 in. above it. Perform this pass above the glass in a circular motion seven times. Through all of this process of pranazing the water, "visualize", "feel", and "will" the flow of prana into the water. The Hindu magicians state that when pranazed water is drunk by the individual, such will act in charging the person with the needful prana.

While we are dealing with the subject of *prana* healing methods, I will give you a more careful magic of this form of real magic practiced in India. Yogi methods of this *prana* healing is applied in three general ways, (1) by the use of the eye; (2) by the use of the breath; (3) by the use of the hands.

Healing by the Eye

In the *pranic* treatment by the use of the eye, the Yogi healer practices rhythmic breathing, while at the same time, gazing fixedly into the eyes of the patient, and "visualizing", "feeling", and "willing" that a powerful flow of *pranic* energy will pour into the body of the patient, reaching the affected parts and restoring them to normal functioning; accompanying this projection is the thought and "mental picture" of the organ in question being normal in every respect.

Healing by the Breath

In the *pranic* treatment by the rise of the breath, the Yogi healer practises rhythmic breathing, and in his exhalations he breathes directly upon the affected and ailing pains, or upon the surface of the skin directly above such. In some cases, the healer exhales his rhythmic breath upon a piece of flannel or cloth which is then placed over or upon the affected and ailing region of the body. This method produces a sensation of warmth and a general soothing effect upon the patient. During the process the healer constantly "visualizes," "feels," and "wills" the flow of *prana*, together with the desired result. Healing by "the *pranic* breath" is a very old form of healing. It was practiced in India for thousands of years. In certain temples in India, the priests cure diseases by this method of breathing upon the patients; and thousands of cases are carried to the temples each year, often from points hundreds of miles distant. As I have mentioned, psychic healing is one of the magics of India.

Healing by the Hands

Pranic healing by the use of the hands is unquestionably the most commonly found form of healing of this kind, both in India and other lands. It is known in many countries as "the laying on of hands".

In many cases, the treatment merely control "laying in the hands", accompanied by rhythmic breathing and appropriate visualization, etc., but there are several other forms of applying and directing the *pranic* force which I will now describe. In all of them the rhythmic breathing accompanies the use of the hands, combined with the "visualization", "feeling", and "willing" mental processes which the Yogis say are essential to the success of the psychic treatments.

In general, making healing passes with the hands are used in this method of healing for the distribution of *prana*. One method is to extend the open fingers of each hand, like the sticks of a folding fan. Hold the opened bands about one foot from the body of the patient. Then raise them above the patient's head, and bring them down along the body in a slow, sweeping motion from his head to his feet. When the pass is completed, move the hands side wise, making a motion as though you were "flicking" water from them. Then close the fingers together, and bring the hands up in a swinging movement along the sides of the patient's body until they extend above his head. Then repeat the passes, and so on until you feel that the treatment has been continued long enough, and the patient is sufficiently charged with healing *prana*.

All downward movements of the extended hands are soothing; all upward movements of the extended hands are invigorating. Sidewise passes of the extended hands have a "stirring up" or "loosening up" effect which is helpful in cases of congestion, etc.

Sometimes a rotary pass is found stimulating and helpful; the hands being rotated in front of the body of the patient, in the direction of moving the hands of a clock. Sometimes a "boring movement" of the extended forefinger is employed to increase the flow of blood to an area in need of cleansing. Letting the palms rest on the affected surface for a time also produces a healing effect; many Yogi healers employ this method almost exclusively. Others gently stroke the body with the extended fingers; the stroking always being in an outward and downward direction. Another variation form is "the vibration method", in which the fingers are placed firmly over the affected part, and a vibrating movement then manifested by the hands.

In India, a Yogi will frequently "pranaze a handkerchief," using the same method as was given for pranazing a glass of water; the charged handkerchief is then worn by the patient over the affected part.

The Yoga teaching holds that all forms of mental or psychic healing of all kinds, no matter under what name applied, are in reality accomplished by this same method via the projection of thought and will accompanied by *prana*. Swami Vivekananda has this to say on the subject: "We see these in every country who have attempted the control of *prana*. In many countries of the world I have heard of this power being used under many different names, such as oydic force, animal magnetism, faith healing, etc., but if we analyze the different processes we shall find that the background of each is this control of *prana*, whether they know it or not. If you boil down their theories, the residuum will be the same. It is all the one and the same force they are using, only unknowingly. They have stumbled on the discovery of a force, and do not know its nature, but they are unconsciously using the same powers which the Yogi uses, and which comes from *prana*. All manifestations (if power arise from this control). Many men do not know of this secret of the Yogis which is one of the most ancient of all, but this is the true explanation. These are among the various functions of pranayama."

Prana is by no means only used in healing, it is the energy source of the manifestation of all forms of mental magic. Remember always this law (if the great magicians" Thought, Will, and Prana constitute The "Threefold Powers").

The Science of Pranayama

Ever since my return from India, I have practiced pranayama, so it definitely deserve a place in the Autobiography of my life.

Pranayama is the Yogi method of bringing vitality into your body. It is a sustainer of life. The Yogi regard *prana* as basic to the magic of living. So, the term "magic" is frequently used in connection with pranayama. *Prana* provides that power in charging "the magic twins" of imagination and with directive power. Over the centuries, the Yogis have developed a science of charging the mind and nervous system with *prana*, through techniques of life-giving breath. The breath is not the *prana*, but *prana* enters the body through the breath.

Pranayama in definition is the science of the regulation of breath for the purpose of controlling, directing, and applying the *prana* or vital/energy force. Pranayama is largely concerned with rhythmic breathing consisting of stages of inhalation, retention, and exhalation of the breath in prescribed rhythm. Pranayama is a feature of the great school of Yogi teaching known as "Raja Yoga", and is regarded by Hindu Sages, as well as by their students, as a very important part of their magical instruction.

Before proceeding to instruct you in the precise technique of "Hindu Rhythmic Breathing", I shall describe the Hindu teaching concerning the physical mechanism which is employed in the processes of pranayama (the control of prana).

In addition to western physiological knowledge concerning the two great branches of the nervous system, the cerebrospinal nervous system and the sympathetic nervous system, the Hindu Sages teach an additional knowledge concerning man's nervous system, a knowledge that has long been held secret, it is the knowledge known in India as Kundalini, "the serpent power".

For an understanding of this power, the Yoga teachings hold that in each human body there is stored up a supply of *prana*, and that this supply is constantly in touch with the universal supply of *prana* which abides throughout all space. Or, to phrase it in the quaint manner of the East, the human body is regarded as a little inlet of *prana* which is connected with the great ocean of *prana*, front which an infinite supply may be drawn.

The figurative illustration of the tiny inlet and the great ocean of *prana* mentioned above, is part of a favorite Hindu philosophy. It aptly pictures an apparent separateness, but also shows the real connection of contact of individual existence with the Universal Existence, and of the power which abides in each. In this the Yogi feel that he has "all the *prana* therein" to draw upon when he needs a greater supply; such is affirmed by the highest of orient teaching.

Let us now take a general view of the Yoga teachings of existing psycho/physical mechanism over and by means of which the *prana* operates the process of Pranayama. (For the continuity of this text I am somewhat repeating here what was given in Chapter Forty-Seven.)

First, it is held that the spinal column is the seat of a unique arrangement which is still to be appreciated by western science. The spinal cord, is regarded as having an invisible channel in its center called the *sushumna*, either side of the *sushumna* flows a current of *prana* – the two currents passing through the substance of the spinal cord.

At the lower end of the *sushumna* (the base of the spinal cord) is found subtle invisible substance, a tenuous form of *akasha* in the shape of a triangle. This triangular shaped substance is known as "the Lotus Chamber of the Kundalini", and is the reservoir or storage center of a certain very powerful form of *prana* which is called Kundalini". *Kundalini* is often referred to as "the secret energy" or "the serpent power" in Hindu teachings. It is regarded as of the greatest importance, and is held as the key performed in man's magical performance.

The two currents of *prana* which flow along the chamber to its spinal cord known as the *sushumna* have distinctive Hindu names. The current that flows to the right side being called *pingula*, and is the positive current. The current that flows on the left side being called *ida* pronounced, *idah* and is the negative current. The terms *pingula* and *ida* also apply to the respective channels over which these currents flow, as well as to the currents themselves. Each of these currents has its own distinctive quality and importance, and produces its own effects. They also constitute important elements of Pranayama.

Another important element of Pranayama is that of the *sushumna*. These are great centers of *prana* which are located in certain places along the channel of the *sushumna*. These "lotuses" or centers ar as follows:

1. The *Muladhara*, or lowest lotus, located at the base of the spinal column.

2. The *Svadhisthana* the second in ascending order, located at the spinal column in the region of the reproductive organs.

3. The *Manipura*, the third in ascending order, located on the spinal column in the region of the solar plexus.

4. The *Anahata*, the fourth in ascending order, located on the spinal column in the region of the heart.

5. The *Visuddha*, the fifth in ascending order, located on the spinal column in the region of the throat.

6. The *Ajana*, the sixth in ascending order, located on the spinal column in the region of the spinal gland within the head.

7. The *Sahastrara* highest in ascending order form and substance even outside of the head and above it; as the Hindus express it, "brooding over the crown of the head like a bird over her nest".

These seven centers (lotuses) are called in Hindu teachings the *Chakras*.

The term "chakra" in definition means wheel, disc, or whirling around object. This term is applied to these centers because the latter manifests a peculiar vibratory, whirling activity when aroused into motion by the *kundalini* ascending the channel of the *sushumna*. In addition to the seven great *chakras*, there are also various minor *chakras* located in various parts of the body, but these do not especially concern our present study.

The *chakras* are not physical organs of the nervous system but are psychical ones. In other words, they are composed of astral or etheric material. The Hindu teaching considers them as "psychic centers of power".

When not aroused and energized by the ascending kundalini, the masters say the *chakras* are motionless and rest like drooping flowers. However, when they are pranazed, it raise themselves like sunflowers facing the sun and their motionless condition is transformed into one of a rapt whirling motion.

As was mentioned, the function of the lowest *chakra* (the *muladhara*) is to act as the storehouse of the *kundalini*, that potent form of *prana*. It is the function of the highest *chakra* (the *sahastrara*) to distribute the *kundalini* to the brain. In its entirety, the *sushumna* may be considered as a great battle of psychic force and power, and each of its *chakras* has its own special function in the generation and distribution of certain forms of *prana* within the nervous system.

Of such is the psychic/physiological system of these tenuous organs within the human body. In Pranayma, the practice of the correct rhythmic breathing, there is set into action the forces of the *sushumna* and its associated *chakras* in the direction of arousing, releasing, and directing the *kundalini* or serpent power. Thus by the oriental system of rhythmic breathing the magician releases and directs the potent *kundalini* according to his will, and in this process produces the power for his performance of the real magic of India.

Every person is the possessor of these psychic/physiological organs of power, and as such, is a potential magician, but in the average individual the *sushumna* channel is almost entirely closed. It is in the degree of the psychic or occult development of the individual that this channel is opened, and, in direct ratio to that opening, is measured the magical abilities of the person. Despite some repetition, so important is this to your developing skill as a magician that I want you to have a description of this important psychic process in the actual words of the Hindu Sage, Sadhu Parimal Bandhu, exactly as I recorded them:

"In the lotus of the *kundalini*, there is the power of the *kundalini* coiled up. When that *kundalini* awakes, it tries to force a passage through that hollow canal running through the spinal cord called the *sushumna*. As it ascends the *sushumna*, the *kundalini* rises step by step, and, as it were, layer after layer of the mind becomes opened, and all the different powers of Yoga become manifested. When it reaches the brain, the Yogi becomes the master of mind arm body. He finds himself free, and filled with power.

"In the rhythmic breathing of Pranayama comes a tendency of all the molecules of the body to flow in the same direction. And when mind changes into will, these currents change into a motion similar to that of electricity in exact manner that the nerves show polarity under the action of electric currents. For your understanding, this shows that will evokes within the nerve currents an action very similar to electricity. Indeed, it is intimately related to electricity.

"When all the motions of the body have become perfectly rhythmical, the body will have become, as it were, a gigantic battery of will. This is the true 'will power'. This tremendous will is exactly what the Yogi wants. In this is the physical explanation of the importance of the breathing exercises of the Yogis. They bring about a rhythmic action in the body, and help us, through the respirator, centers to control other centers. Thus the aim of Pranayma here is to arouse the coiled-up power in the *muladhara*, which is called the *kundalini*.

"All the sensations and motions of the body are being sent to the brain, and sent out of it through the wires of the nerve fibers. The column of sensory and motor fibers in the spinal cord are the *ida* and *pingala* of the Yogis. They are the main channels through which the afferent and efferent currents are traveling. But why should not the mind send the news without any wires. Taking the analogy of electricity, we find that man can send a current only along a wire; but nature requires no wires to send her tremendous currents. Indeed, your Western science will eventually find the means of transmitting electricity without wires. Mind can do it now. This proves only that the wire is not really necessary, but that only our inability to dispense with it compels us to use it. The Yogis say that if the mind can send the news without the wires of the nerve fibers, then one has removed the bondage of matter.

"If you can make the current pass through the *sushumna*, you have worked the problem. The mind has made the network of the nervous system, and has to break it, so that no wires will be required to work through. Then alone will all knowledge come to us and there will be no more bondage of body; that is why it is so important to get control of the *sushumna*. If you can send the mental current through that hollow canal, without any nerve fibers to act as wires, the Adepts acclaim you have solved the problem, and it is also spoken that it can be done.

"The *sushumna* in average persons is closed up at its lower extremity, thus no action comes through it. The Yogis propose a practice by which it can be opened, and the nerve currents made to travel through it. The center where the residual sensation are, as it were, stored up, is called the *muladhara* which is the root receptacle within which is the coiled-up energy of the serpent power (*kundalini*), ready for action when it is aroused. Now, if this coiled-up energy is aroused and made active, and then consciously by will made to travel up the *sushumna* canal, as it acts upon center after center (the *chakras*), a tremendous reaction will set in. And when it reaches the metropolis of all sensations, the brain, the whole brain will react, arid the result is the full blaze of illumination.

"Whenever there has appeared any manifestation of supernormal power, magic, or wisdom, such inevitably must have been the result of some current (even if in small amounts) of the *kundalini* having found its way into the *sushumna*, for such is the power of all magic no matter what its form. Many such practices set free a minute portion of the coiled-up energy of the *kundalini* purely through happenstance. Only in the practices of the East Indian Masters in Yoga is the true potential realized."

As I have pointed out to you in this consideration of the science of Pranayama, the arousal of "the serpent power" is the great aim of the Yogis. Thus aroused, the *kundalini* ascends and mounts in spiral movement like the wriggling of a snake, upward along the channel of the *sushumna*. Until aroused, the *kundalini* is a sleeping serpent which remains coiled-up and inert. It is not dead, however, but merely sleeping or hibernating like a snake during winter. It remains static until aroused into dynamic action by the proper methods or stimuli.

There are several reasons for the *kundalini* being called "the serpent power" by the Hindus. In the first place, the "coiled-up" position of the inactive *kundalini* is akin to that of the serpent. Again, the "wriggling motion" of the ascending kundalini, in its spiral mounting of the *sushumna*, closely resembles that of the moving serpent. In its dormant, sleeping state, the *kundalini* is sometimes represented by the familiar occult symbol of the serpent holding its tail in its mouth, or having swallowed its tail.

In this symbolic representation, however, the Hindus have no intention of ascribing an evil character to *kundalini* power in showing it as a serpent. On the contrary, they employ the serpent as a symbol of wisdom and power, and it is abundantly active in high states of consciousness, or, as it has been called by esoteric scholars in the West, COSMIC CONSCIOUSNESS.

There is wisdom and knowledge expressed in this phase of antiquity, "Be ye wise as the serpent".

Part Five

Literary Endeavors & Other Things

Chapter Fifty-Two
Literary Endeavors

I have always considered books to be the greatest bargain in magic and hypnotism. You can learn so much from books. I have enjoyed writing books. To me the printed word is often more durable than the spoken word. The spoken word can vanish with the speaker. The printed word remains long after the writer is gone.

The first writing in association with magic I did back in 1937, when I wrote a column for "TOPS", titled *The Psychic Circle*. It was a discussion of psychic phenomena to give magicians thumbnail knowledge of such things of possible usefulness as patter themes for mental magic. The column appeared in the first 12 issues of the original "TOPS" when Percy Abbott started it. "TOPS" continued on through the years as one of the top magic magazines exclusively for magicians.

Following *The Psychic Circle*, I did another column for the 1938 issues of TOPS: *Hypnotic Comments*. The continued respect this series has enjoyed through the years speaks volumes for magicians' interest in mental magic, which Ted Annemann referred to as the most adult form of magic. Such interest is but natural, for the whole art of conjuring is based on a love of performing the impossible and knowing the unknowable.

My next literary effort in magic was writing *Radio and Night Club Mindreading*, when Dunninger on radio was in ascendance. It was published by Thayer's Studio of Magic in 1944.

Also in 1944, I wrote *How To Produce Miracles*. Although written in 1944, it was not until 1976 that it appeared in print: first published in hardback by A.S. Barnes Co., Inc., and subsequently in paperback by Signet Books. I did the decorative illustrations for this book in surrealistic art style. The famous magician, Eugene Berger, once paid me the compliment that *How To Produce Miracles* was a book written much ahead of its time. I have never forgotten.

In 1953, I did two works on hypnotism for Dr. Rexford North: *A Better Life Through Conscious Self-Hypnosis* and *Dental Hypnosis*. These were published by his Journal of Hypnotism Company. That original little company and magazine are advanced today, under the direction of two of Dr. North's youthful employees – Dwight Damon and Elson Eldridge, Jr. – into the National Guild of Hypnotists, Inc. and the prestigious *Journal of Hypnotism* published bimonthly by NGH. What started as an acorn with Dr. North has advanced into a giant oak tree which covers the world as one of the largest hypnotic organization upon the planet.

In 1959, following our return from the Orient, Ron Ormond and I co-authored the *Into the Strange Unknown*. It was published by the Esoteric Foundation of Los Angeles. The original manuscript recounting our adventures was so massive for the varityping method of printing at the time that I had to remove some chapters. These I later formed into a book titled *The Secret World of Witchcraft*. This book was published by A.S. Barnes and Company, Inc. fore-runner of the current giant Bordon Books chain of bookstores. This book in 1973 was distributed for the American Market by Barnes and Co., and by Thomas Yoseloff, Ltd. for the UK. This book has become rare. The contents are bizarre.

In the pages of this book will be found, at one and the same time, redblooded adventure fare for the "chills and thrills" seeker and a serious discussion of sorcery and witchcraft, and related fields of supernatural activity such as psychic phenomena, haunts, divination, miracle healing, and extrasensory powers.[6]

These subjects are presented for consideration in an extensive introduction that provides background for the reports on witchcraft, some of which are personal experiences, others those of close associates – which range around the world. The reports tell of personal brush with witchcraft in the Philippines which sends a chill up one's spine. Before the dozen or so reports are finished, the reader has explored examples of witchcraft by way of New Guinea and Hong Kong to Southeast Asia, India, Tibet, Africa (Northern Rhodesia and Zaire) and Brazil. In the process the reader is shown the universality of the phenomena of witchcraft, fully documented and illustrated.

---

[6]I have been told that the book has been used as a text in anthropology classes.

The dust jacket of the book depicts a member of the Leopard Society of Africa. It is not a benign society. Its members dress in the skins of leopards and kill in the manner of that animal, using steel talons and fangs. It is hard to repress a shudder.

Back to the writing of books on magic, in 1950, I wrote three other books which were published by Abbott's Magic Company: *21 Gems of Magic, Fooling the Public*, and *Psychic Magic*. Also, during the 1950s my science fiction *Atomic Magic* was published by Magic, Inc. of Chicago. This book suggests science fiction themes for magic, with appropriate tricks included.

In 1976 A.S. Barnes & Company published my book, *The Mysticism and Magic of India*. This book might well be called the "textbook" of genuine Hindu Magic and Yoga practices I learned during my adventures. Later Westwood Publishing Company purchased the rights and republished the book under the title of *The Hypnotism and Magic of India* (still in print).

To me, writing books is like eating peanuts. Once I start I can't stop.

Book after book keep rolling along. Likewise, audio cassettes, videos and CDs. Of all my books, my favorite is the one channelled by Delight *Grieve No More, Beloved*. To me it is my most important work as it tells of personal immortality. However, booksellers probably prefer my book, *The New Encyclopedia of Stage Hypnotism*, which has become a best seller.

Also By Ormond McGill

A Better Life Through Conscious Self-Hypnosis (NGH Books, Inc.)
Abundance Hypnosis (Booklet published by NGH Books, Inc.)
Advertising For the Independent Businessman
Art of Stage Hypnotism, The (out of print) (Border Books, Inc.)
Atomic Magic (Ireland Magic, Co.)
Balancing Magic and Other Tricks (Millbrook Press)
Chalk Talk (A Tribute to Harlan Tarbel)
Dental Hypnosis (NGH Books, Inc.)
Dream Doctor Cases, The
Encyclopedia of Genuine Stage Hypnotism, The (Abbott Magic Co.)
Encyclopedia of Stage Illusions (Burling Hull – co-author) (First Books)

Entertaining With Magic (Barnes & Co, Inc.)

Everything You Want to Know (Shelley Stockwell – co-author)

Fooling the Public (Robert Bernhardt – co-author) (Abbott Magic Co.)

Fun of Collecting Cinderella Stamps and Labels (unpublished)

Grieve No More, Beloved: The Book of Delight (Anglo-American Book Company Ltd.)

Hypnotism and Meditation (Westwood Pub. Co.)

How to Book of Hypnotism, The (Tom Silver – co-author) (Silver Publications)

How to Plan Successful Suggestion Formulas (Booklet published by NGH Books, Inc.)

How to Produce Miracles (Barnes & Co, Inc.) (Paperback published by Signet Books Co.)

Hypnotism and Mysticism of India (Westwood Pub. Co.)

Hypnotism and Yoga (Booklet published by NGH Books, Inc.)

Hypnotism Questions and Answers (Tom Silver – co-author) (Silver Publications)

Instantaneous Hypnosis Techniques (Booklet published by NGH Books, Inc.)

Into the Strange Unknown (Esoteric Books)

Magic and Illusions of Lee Grabel, The (Patrick Martin – co-author)

Soap Bubble Magic (Hades Magic Co.)

Many Lives of Alan Lee, The (Irvin Mordes – co-author) (NGH Books, Inc.)

Mind Magic (Millbrook Press)

Mysticism and Magic of India, The (Barnes & Co. Inc.)

New Encyclopedia of Stage Hypnotism, The (Crown House Publishing Ltd.)

Paper Magic (Millbrook Press)

Pomés Hypnosis (NGH Books, Inc.)

Pre-life Regression Therapy

Professional Office Hypnotherapy

Professional Stage Hypnotism (Westwood Pub. Co.)

Psychic Magic (Abbott Magic Co.)

Real Mental Magic (Hades Magic Co.)

Religious Mysteries of the Orient (Barnes & Co. Inc.)

Science Magic: 101 Tricks You Can Do (Barnes & Co. Inc.)

Search for Cosmic Consciousness, The (Shelley Stockwell – co-author) (Creativity Unltd.)

Secret World of Witchcraft, The (Barnes & Co. Inc.)

Seeing The Unseen (Crown House Publishing Ltd.)

Secrets of Stage Mindreading (Crown House Publishing Ltd.)
Successful Suggestion Formulas for Hypnotherapy (NGH Books, Inc.)
Three New Hypnotherapy Techniques (Booklet published by NGH Books, Inc.)
21 Gems of Magic (Abbott Magic Co.)
Voice Magic (Millbrook Press)

Chapter Fifty-Three

Hypnomeditation

While we are in the section of my Autobiography dealing with Literary Efforts, it provides an opportunity to tell you how I came to write the book *Hypnotism & Meditation*, which was published by Westwood Publishing Company in 1981. It all began with my learning about Tantra Meditation while in India, in 1958. A long while back, but just a drop in the bucket compared to the original text on Tantra Meditation that Devi did some 3000 years ago. As legend tells it:

Devi was the consort of Shiva who gave her the 112 methods of Tantra Meditations which are regarded as the full gamut of all the forms of meditation existing in the world. Devi described these two methods in her book, *Vigyana Bhairava Tantra*, which has become a Holy Book to the Hindus of the stature of "The Bible" to Christians and "The Koran" to Mohammadans.

In Sanskrit, *Vigyana* means consciousness. *Bhairava* means divine love, and *Tantra* means techniques. Tantra is concerned with what you can become, not with what you are. Tantra has no ideal for you. Your unknown ideal is hidden within yourself, and only you can find it by becoming aware. That is why Tantra is meditation.

Shiva gave these Tantra Meditations to Devi as an act of love.

I had commenced writing a book on Self-Hypnosis describing practical methods of using the power of the mind to master unwanted habits via subconscious reconditioning, when a flash came in, why not use the process of hypnosis to establish the Tantra Meditations in the subconscious of individuals? It seemed to fit right with the so-called "New Age". So I changed direction and wrote this book instead. When completed, I sent the manuscript to my friend, Gil Boyne, who operated a hypnotism training institute and the Westwood Book Publishing Company in Glendale, California. Gil had always adhered to the academic in the books he published, so I was really surprised that he accepted it. I am sure it was an act of friendship. Possibly no one was more surprised than

Gil at the reception the little book had. The book is still in print.

Some Thoughts on Hypnomeditation

Hypnotism and meditation are opposites of the same. Hypnosis is motivated to achieve a certain goal; meditation is not motivated and has no goal to achieve. Hypnosis entails a constriction of consciousness. Meditation entails an expansion of consciousness. Hypnotism and meditation will be seen as diametric to each other. To understand, look at a coin: on one side you see heads and on the opposite side you see tails – both appear entirely different yet they constitute the one coin. It is easy to see how I originated the word "hypnomeditation" for the process. Hypnomeditation merges the attributes of hypnosis and meditation into each other.

Hypnomeditation moves one into the realm of what is called "Enlightenment" (which is an instinctive knowing of what existence is all about and your place in relation to existence). Using Hypnomeditation will help you find your so called "Center of Being" which deep inside oneself is felt as serenity and peacefulness. It is then that you discover existence is not your enemy but is your friend. It is then that you discover the wisdom of turning your attitude towards life into a festival. Shiva was so right when he told Devi, "Live your life as on a playground not as on a battlefield."

Appreciate These Attributions of Meditation

Meditation is a state of being – it is not a state of doing. There are many ways of meditating. They all function as pathways to discover meditation. Meditation will transform you when you discover that about yourself which is immortal. That is why the process of hypnomeditation is so important; for unless you move in an altogether different dimension than that of intellect, you will find no answers. You can never find an answer to the real truth of your BEING in philosophies. You can ask a question and a philosophy may give you an answer which either satisfies you or doesn't satisfy you. If it satisfies you, you become a convert to the philosophy, but you remain the same. If it doesn't satisfy you, you continue on searching for some other philosophy to be converted to. But again you still remain the same; you are not transformed in coming

to know the true nature of your SELF, and your intimate relationship with existence.

Only actual experience can transform you. That is why hypnomeditation can produce a transformation in you, for its processes
are existential.

It can be looked upon that man is a duality by nature, he is inner and
he is outer. The outer is his surface life, the life he lives in the world,
the life he daily recognizes. Life in the world is constantly changing,
there is nothing permanent about it; it is but temporary, and is lived
over and over and over. The inner is the real SELF – it is ETERNAL.
It was the same at the beginning, if there was a beginning, as it will
be at the ending, if there is an ending. The inner is the soul of man;
it is not temporary – it is eternal, it is deathless. Unfortunately, man
is so asleep to his reality, that he is but very slightly aware of this
phase of his life at all. Only when he wakes up and becomes enlightened does he come to know this life, which is his true life. Meditation
can bring in a knowing of this true life. Using Hypnomeditation
presents a pathway that shows you the way to recognizing your
divine nature. But remember, meditating is not meditation . . . meditation is a way of living, it is even a way of dying and living life
beyond death. To experience that way of living is Enlightenment.

The practice of hypnomeditation

To practice Hypnomeditation one must have a process for inducting
hypnosis in oneself, and then decide what form of meditation one
wishes to establish in the subconscious. I will give you one of my
favorites in this chapter. First learn how to use this hypnotic induction
technique for yourself.

The self-hypnosis method you can use for hypnomeditation

To use an analogy, the subconscious phase of mind possesses power
to destroy us or improve our life. This technique of Self-Hypnosis
works excellently for use with hypnomeditation – proactive of
bringing into being the state of meditation as a positive state of
mind.

It will be recognized that Hypnomeditation commences a circular process which is self-perpetuating. The subconscious aspects of mind simulate the meditative aspects of the individual while the meditative aspects stimulate the subconscious aspects. Also, the process is self-operative once it is commenced as both subconscious activity and meditative activity are below the threshold of consciousness.

You are now ready to prepare conditions of conducting this Self-Hypnosis session.

If possible, conduct your Hypnomeditation sessions in the same room each time – a room that is private, quiet, and which you can darken. Make these sessions exclusively your own.

Place a burning candle on a table in front of a comfortable chair. Concentrate your attention upon the candle flame, as you relax in the chair. Just allow your mind to drift, allowing whatever thought that comes in to just pass through it.

Now, breathe deeply through your nose, hold the breath for about 5 sec, then exhale very *slowly*. Repeat this three times. As each breath is inhaled visualize energy moving into your body and down your back to the base of your spine. As each breath is released visualize all negative energy and tension moving up from the base of the spine, and out of your body.

When you complete the three breaths, allow your eyes to close and with every breath you inhale and exhale become aware of the energy moving in and out of your body, and with this energy relax away every tension. Start at your feet and think of how relaxed they are becoming. *Think it and you will feel it*. Now move your attention up your legs relaxing the muscles in your legs; move on up through the muscles of your torso relaxing the torso muscles. Now, think of relaxing your hands and arms. Now, think of relaxing your shoulders, up your neck and over your face clear up to the top of your head. Every muscle of your entire body has been progressively relaxed. In this process, let all sensations that come in be exactly what they are and do not try to change them.

Now in this relaxed condition, continue being with your body and visualize all feelings, tensions, emotions as flowing out of your body from your fingertips and toes. And along with this discharge of energy, think of how each breath you take is causing you to become more relaxed and sleepy. Continue to think of how very sleepy you are. How very, very sleepy. How deep and full your breaths are becoming. How relaxed and comfortable your whole body feels. There is a wonderful peacefulness stealing over your body. You are sinking down, down, down towards sleep.[7]

This is the time in your voluntarily induced condition of self-hypnosis in which the "outcroppings of the subconscious" occur most markedly. This is the psychological moment to implant *hypnotic suggestions*[8] into your subconscious to deepen its own hypnotic conditioning. It is a compounding process.

Slowly lift your hands and place the palms over your ears, pressing the hands flat against the head, then repeat and *speak out loud* hypnotic inducing suggestions, such as these[9]: *I am so relaxed, so drowsy, so sleepy that I am sinking down, down, down deep into hypnosis, I am sinking deep inside of myself, I am reaching through directly to my subconscious mind. Every suggestion that I give myself goes directly into my subconscious mind like seeds falling upon the ground to take root there and blossom into beautiful being. I am sinking down, down, down, in deep hypnosis, and every suggestion that I give myself goes directly into my subconscious and automatically goes into effect, automatically becomes reality. I am in deep hypnosis and every suggestion which I give myself goes deep into my subconscious mind and becomes part of my*

---

[7] Suggestions of sleep are almost invariably associated with the induction of hypnosis, as you are aware. Ideas of sleep and/or going to sleep carry associations of relaxing the body and placing the mind in a passive condition. Actually, since attention is being applied in the process of giving suggestions of "sleep", a normal sleep state is not produced; rather a state of consciousness is manifested which while outwardly appearing much like sleep inwardly is of an entirely different nature: this is the state of mind known as hypnosis—in which state suggestions will powerfully influence the subconscious mind.

[8] As the mental state you are in this time is foreign to alert reasoning, it is well to have committed to memory this series of hypnotic suggestions; then you can let them flow out without having to think about the exact words (expressing the ideas) much as you would in reciting a rhyme.

[9] The process of repeating your "suggestion-meditation-formula" out loud to yourself with your hands pressed over your ears will cause the suggestions to *rrrrring* through your head with power. The procedure gives your verbalized suggestions a humming-ringing forcefulness that seems to echo inside your very brain. Autosuggestions presented in this manner are very powerful in producing subconscious effects.

being. I can feel my breaths deepening and every breath I take sends me down deeper and deeper into hypnosis. My subconscious mind is now ready and receptive to receive into it and act upon every suggestion which I give it in relation to meditation. My suggestions automatically go into action making these meditation suggestions part of my Being, part of my very Self. My subconscious mind knows the truth of my Being and implants these wonderful suggestions deep in my Being which suggestions heighten my consciousness and increase my awareness of my real Self which dwells inside my body at my Center of Being. I relax now down in deep hypnosis and my subconscious mind is ready and waiting to receive and put into action all meditative suggestions which make me aware of my true nature; which make me realize my real Self as the Divine Being which I am. I await now these meditative suggestions which bring me the realization of my inner Self. After I receive these meditative suggestions I will sink down passively for a few minutes deep in hypnosis while the suggestions become my very own, from which lassitude I will gradually awaken to full awareness ready to resume my daily activities feeling splendid and well. Come in now meditative suggestions, and go deep within my Being.[10]

You can give the suggestions to yourself as explained below, or put them on a cassette. Then, passively be receptive to the instructions. As the suggestions come in make no effort to think about them especially, just allow yourself to continue to sink deeper into the hypnotic condition becoming yet more relaxed, more drowsy, more sleepy as the suggestions come in: indeed, as the meditative suggestions come in, it will seem that you scarcely heed them at all, as they bypass your conscious mind and go directly into your subconscious mind.

Start some meditative music in the background if you wish. Then, place your hands over your ears, and repeat the gist of the meditation formula or listen to a tape with the formula. It is powerfully influencing of subconscious receptivity. Here is a Hypnomeditative Formula I like.

---

10. At this point in the induction process, you are in hypnosis ready and receptive to receive whatever "suggestion-meditation" formula you wish to give to yourself; allow your hands to drop into your lap thinking that as they drop into your lap it deepens your hypnosis and now you eagerly await the implanting of the meditation suggestions.

The White Light of Protection Meditation

The strongest force in the universe is love. That is which is meant when it is expressed "God is love". But all that is has its opposites, for opposites have to be. In the case of love it is hate. In the case of what is named God is a named Devil. Positive and negative. Such is the "yin and yang" nature of existence. Recognizing this, is why practising meditation brings one to their "Center of Being" (Soul, if you will) and advocates that aspects of love be emphasized when meditating techniques are used. The good in the universe is symbolized by white while the opposite is symbolized by black. So, in this process of meditation a WHITE LIGHT OF PURITY is visualized as surrounding the individual. This is protective meditation. It can bring you much benefit, as it symbolized love in the universe. Understanding this, you are ready to implant this meditation in your subconscious. The self-hypnosis state you have induced in yourself prepares your subconscious phase of mind to be receptive. Use a tape or memorize the gist of this meditation-formula, and repeat it to yourself, speak out loud to yourself with hands over ears:

"My inner Being is surrounded at all time with the White Light of Purity. As I accept the White Light into my Inner Self I become a source of love. This White Light symbolizes the strongest force in all the Universe that of love. This White Light protects me from all harm, from all invasions of outside influences, and forms a wall of protective love around me. It is my Armour.

"I have become a source of love, and henceforth I have but to repeat these words: I accept this *White Light of Protection Into My Inner Self*, and the phenomenon of transcendental protection of myself will automatically spring into action covering me with an Armour of Love ever protecting me in every way. I am protected by God."

As you repeat this meditation to yourself, you will very likely find yourself, during the process, becoming more and more lethargic and sinking deeper and deeper into hypnosis.

As this occurs, just let yourself go, and sink deep inside yourself.

Even go to sleep if you wish. Gradually you will begin to arouse. You will feel refreshed and relaxed, and you will realize an inner sense of protection that is beyond all the beauty you have ever known. The experience will awaken you, and you will realize the wonderfulness of life, as it really is. Hypnomeditation will bring you that state of Enlightenment about which the masters have spoken and which many people have sought, but which few have realized. It is given as a treasure to you.[11]

---

[11]Refer to *Hypnotism and Meditation* for specific "Meditation Suggestion Formulas".

Chapter Fifty-Four
Inventions & Innovations

The Love Clock

Recently, I turned my attention to inventing/developing "The Love Clock". This clock says, "I Love You" on telling the hour instead of just a Rrrrrring! Also, it repeats those "Three Little Words" on every hour while the clock is running.

I hold an 18 year patent on "The Love Clock". It will be interesting to see what develops. Now, I am working on a patent for a total Subliminal " I Love You" message included in the clock.

The Energy Room

I also designed an energy room, based on electrified crystal energy (from an Atlantean memory), for a private school. The school operators were enthusiastic and reported excellent results.

Use of the Energy Room

The person in need of revitalizing enters The Energy Room, and takes a 20-minute rest within a crystal induction energy field. They enter the room and relax upon a couch while being *bathed* in crystal energy augmented by low-voltage electrical current. I use this in association with my "Vitality Hypnosis Process" described in Chapter Thirty-Nine.

In they go, all tired and low on vitality. After resting 20 minutes in The Energy Room, they come out revitalized and raring to go back to work or to anything else that requires their attention.

It is my hope to help those who need such help. Every school, hospital, industry, and even private home could use this special room invention.

Symbiotical Resonance Sound

I developed this invention with the help of my computer expert friend, Joe Worrell. Contemporary paradigms in the therapeutic use of sound is remarkable. Here is the hypnotherapy of the future which you can use in work today. It is based on the vibration resonant nature of sound.

When you listen to music, it can change your mood and emotionally affect you. Actually, it is not the music that moves you, but, at its roots, it is the particular vibrational matrix that resonates or harmonizes with your inner matrix and produces those stirs.

Sound vibration can be very powerful. Everything is in a state of vibration, different rates and intensity. The vibrational matrix of the sound produced by Symbiotical Resonance Sound tends to correlate and unify thought pattern in the brain, in turn affecting the mind to the point of stillness. Once this is accomplished the hypnotic program is given, and when accepted by the subconscious phase of mind becomes part of the inner matrix of correlated thought; thus, the mind accepts new thought patterns therefore affecting a behavior change.

To understand the effective operation of Symbiotical Resonance Sound appreciate that your brain functions as a remarkable biocomputer with its wires (your autonomic systems with its sympathetic and parasympathetic divisions) going to every part of your body. Your brain is the control center, and suggestions presented in the hypnotic state cause your subconscious mind to affect your biocomputer to operate in accordance with how you desire to affect the behavior of yourself or your client, thus integrating the new behavior with conscious mind. Symbiotical Resonance Sound places your biocomputer in a receptive state to be receptive to programming suggestions.

The combination of brain activity of Theta and Delta is the hypnotic state of mind (hypnosis) in which suggestions for desired behavior will be subconsciously activated. Symbiotical Resonance Sound is a scientific combination of the frequencies of Theta and Delta, which cause your biocomputer to be receptive to such conditioning.

While using "Symbiotical Resonance Programming", I use symptom-removing direct suggestions. I let my client express precisely that which is desired to be accomplished.

The Symbiotical Resonance Sound Hypnotic Induction Session

Arrange to have your audio Resonance Sound cassette (or CD) in your session room played very softly before client enters. Subdue lights in the room. Make the room pleasant and comfortable. Then invite client into your session room, and hold your consultation with the soft sound frequency surrounding the client in the background. With low volume it will be unobtrusive. During consultation learn exactly what client wishes to accomplish.

Consultation completed, have client recline in session chair or lie on couch. Position body comfortably and close eyes. The Symbiotical Resonance Sound is then increased in volume to a higher, yet pleasant level. You can determine this by adjusting the volume of the sound to what is pleasant to yourself, as the Theta/Delta sound is listened to. It is much like a continuous oscillating drone.

At this point, inform client that you will leave him (or her) alone in the session room, while they become absorbed in the vibratory sound matrix. They are just to let their mind drift free of all effort, and just peacefully listen to the sound, thereby become one with the sound. Often they will experience a sensation of "floating".

After 5 minutes or so of this solitary sound absorption, you re-enter the room and quietly seat yourself beside client and induce hypnosis by your favorite method. Lower the volume of sound a bit so when speaking to somnolent client your suggestions are clearly heard.

Having placed client in hypnosis, now present your direct "suggestion formula" to client. The client's absorption will advance as

Theta/Delta Frequencies advance the effectiveness of your suggestions, as the sound, itself, will have produced a hypnotic (responsive) state of mind. That is to say, client will tend to have entered hypnosis even prior to your induction process – you will have produced a mental condition of hypnosis upon hypnosis. The effect is compounding producing of *profound hypnosis*.

The following is for your convenience. It defines the levels of brain function and their frequencies.

A Listing of Brain Wave Frequencies

This listing of brain wave rhythms is useful in gaining an understanding of brain wave activity in your computer brain during the induction of hypnosis. It shows that brain waves in hypnosis are more similar to normal awareness than the slower brain wave of natural sleep.

Gamma 41-100HZ   *Gamma Rhythm*
Wakeful state of brain, high Stimulation.

High Beta 21-40 HZ   *Beta Rhythm*
Beta 16-20 HZ   Normal wakeful state of brain activity.
Low Beta 13-15 HZ

Alpha 8-12 HZ   *Alpha Rhythm*
Relaxation sets in. Brain Activity lessens.
Readinesss for hypnosis enters.

Theta 4-7 HZ   *Theta Rhythm*
Reverie. While in profound hypnosis
(somnambulism).

Delta 1-3 HZ   *Delta Rhythm*
Brain activity during sleep, or less
unconsciousness.

The unconsciousness of natural sleep gives mind and body a break – a chance to get away from it all, as well as to recover vitality. This is very important if life is to continue in the body. It is also important to an understanding of hypnosis. Outwardly hypnosis appears like sleep but inwardly it is different. Yet the two states are obviously related as both are brought about by relaxation, and suggestions of "sleep" are common to hypnotic inductions.

Bringing in "The Force"

This is an innovation of mine.

George Lucas in his famous "Star Wars" movies brought public attention to "The Force". There is nothing new about "The Force". It has been around for time immemorial. It is the vitality of the universe. The force is cosmic energy, which can be directed by your mind. In my performances, I show audiences how to experience the power and generate it for their personal use.

Modus Operandi for Bringing in "The Force"

Stand erect, alert, and at attention. Allow your arms to hang by your sides 6 inches out from your body. You are turning yourself into an antenna to receive the force.

Now, commence breathing deeply three times, and with each inhalation affirm: "I bring the cosmic force into myself (hold the breath) asking for strength, guidance, and protection (exhale)."

Repeat the process three times. Then wait. You will experience THE FORCE enter you like a tingling of electricity in your hands.

Try it and experience!

Chapter Fifty-Five

Concluding My Autobiography

I am not ready to pass onwards yet – too much to do!

Somehow "passing onwards" seems more accurate than the conventional way of stating that a person who as died has "passed away". The fact is that nothing in the universe passes away. It changes but it does not pass away. The entire universe (and that includes you and me) is constantly subjected to the state of change, yet it is always there. Life and death are like that.

Time marches on, and I just turned ninety. I suppose that makes me an old man, but honestly I don't feel like an old man at all. People often ask me how it feels to be an "old man" of 90 years?

Frankly, I scarcely know what they mean. I don't feel a bit different inside myself than I did at 39, as Jack Benny used to say.

Age is pretty much an attitude of mind. Think young and you stay young. Outside the body can get a bit creaky; it takes longer to pick things up when they drop on the floor; the legs are not as fleet as once they were, *but inside you're as young as you feel.*

To me, so-called "old age" is great – the best years of my life. As Maurice Chevalier expressed in it the movie *Gigi*, "I am glad I am not young anymore as there is no more aggravation." How true that is: the stress and strain of younger years filled with ambition to do this or that is gone, and you feel fine.

At 90 years, I can just be myself. It's great!

The genius, Charles Steinmetz (1865–1923) made the statement, "Man's next frontier (even greater than his exploration of outer space) will be the exploration of his inner space (the realm of mind)." In relation to my Autobiography, I have currently given attention to the study of this frontier. It is a continual effort without effort, day in and day out, and even some at night that keeps me continuously busy appreciating the miracle of existence.

I have condensed various concentration and consciousness advancement exercises into ready performance. I have found these useful to myself. Also, I have presented them as exercises that others, who are of such interest, can find them easily performable and useful to themselves. That, of course, is entirely up to the individual.

This exploration of our inner space provides quite enough to keep me busy before I make the transition. When will that be? I have not the slightest idea. I suppose it will be when I have completed what I have to complete on this 3-D planet. I have many dear friends who are still here with me; even more have already made the transition to the other side. Slight difference, as the other side and this side are "paper thin" between.

How nice it will be to rejoin Delight. However, there is no hurry, as there is no time in eternity.

As to what adventures lie ahead for me, so I can write an additional Chapter to my Autobiography. Your crystal ball is as good as mine, in such regard.

Why try to spoil the fun by guessing what new adventures lie ahead? Just let them happen on their own by less and less trying to make things happen and more and more just letting things happen. As Buddha puts it so bluntly, "Nothing need be done."

On concluding my Autobiography up-to-date I sincerely say, "May the pursuing of my life's story have value to the pursuing of your own."

Appendix One

Become a Thoroughbred

At 90 years of living (and still living), I have written my Autobiography telling of events, and things that have been created by me, and of events and things that have come to me, as gifts that I have treasured.

It seems that there are still some things to share that I have learned in this lifetime that yet must be recorded. So I add these Appendices to what has gone before; to what is currently going on in my here and now. The dictionary definition of an Appendix is "supplementary matter added to the end of a book that details with ever greater understanding an appreciation of that which was previously given." In such regard, I have added this text.

I call this Appendix "Become a Thoroughbred", which relates to a pedigreed horse of excellent quality. The dictionary refers to a thoroughbred as a breed of horses marked by high-spirited grace. Practices the assortment of exercises given you here. They will add to your high-spirited grace.

So, come with me and munch upon the green grass and we will graze together.

I have cultivated various exercises in concentrating attention a la Advancing Consciousness, as they are important to me. Life is so exciting when one becomes fully alert to their perception. Enjoy every moment, for the truth is that every moment is full of miracles. Indeed, it is a miracle that we are.

The magic of thoughts

Man (which term is used to include both genders of the human species) can be looked upon as having a trinity of awareness: self, mind, and thoughts. Self is our consciousness which uses mind to produce thoughts, and thoughts are the way we think, which is the way we are in the physical world. "As a man thinkest in his heart so is he."

Mental equilibrium

Mental equilibrium is mental discipline, which is a paramount factor in life's achievements. In mental equilibrium all things (whatsoever) are met with calm detachment, being free of judgments either for or against. Mental Equilibrium is the balancing of thoughts.

Logical thinking

Logical thinking is scientific concentration. Logical thinking prevents one from making mistakes and often leads to success. Always remember, the beginning of success is the knowledge of one's faults.

The hurry habit

Much of the way of the modern world is the way of hurry, hurry, hurry. Hurry becomes a habit that is often the source of accidents and mistakes. Hurry causes a ceaseless agitation. Hurry is a matter of time, and there is no time in eternity. So slow down; remembering you have eternity for doing whatsoever you have to do. Without hurry you will actually get more done than if you hurry.

The way of optimism

Mind has an instinctive Center of Right Knowledge. Knowing what you know is right is optimism. Optimism is like a bright light that removes the shadow of doubt.

The demise of doubt

Doubt is the opposite polarity of knowing. To dwell in doubt undermines your confidence. Use Mental Equilibrium, Logical Thinking and Less Hurry to make it disperse.

Mentally picture the way you want to be

When you become at peace with yourself you become at peace with the world. A peaceful mind brings serenity and creative mind-power. Just let it happen without trying to make it happen. All the inner operations of your body function of their own accord. Allow your mind that freedom. Just form mental picture of the way you want to be, and let it be.

Thoughts on self-control

Thought Control is Self-Control, and vice versa. Use your Will to achieve this strength of character. Freedom of Will is a divine gift. It has great power. Use it wisely to control your thoughts, for thoughts are forms of energy – and energy makes things happen.

Using the psychological moment

Psychology is a study of the mind, and mind is the creator of thoughts. Psychology is really instruction in mental discipline. There comes a moment in every thought when it has its greatest impact. Such is known as "the psychological moment". To become consciously aware of these moments is part of the mastery of mind. How? Learn by experiencing.

Scientific concentration

Science aims to explain and make things logical so such can be use-ful in organized ways. Concentration is mental attention. Combine with science to make forms of mental effort become an act of pleasure that you enjoy. Do it. Do it. Do it until it becomes a habit of the constructive way you use your mind.

The power of imagination

Imagination is the creative power of the mind. Everything that is first started in imagination. It is well you understand this power, for it can be both productive and destructive depending on how it is used. Understand this: every thought we think starts a matrix in space leading to is physical creation (its creation depending upon the concentration and which is placed upon the thought). As imagination is the creative power of the mind its use should be constructive – in which is formed as a matrix in space heading to become a physical reality.

Claiming what is your own

Whatever you elect to create by your thoughts is your own. Your thoughts belong to your private world, unless you choose to share them. They are exclusive – they belong to no one else but thyself.

As Emerson expressed it: "Whatever in nature is thine own Floating in air or pent in stone, Shall ride the hills and swim the sea. And like thy shadow follow thee."

Appendix Two
Advancing Your Senses

Awareness is a synonym for consciousness. The more aware you are the more fully you live life to the hilt. So many live life as though they were half asleep. Wake up! The way to wake up is to advance your consciousness, and put your conscious (which is your SELF) in everything you do. If you wish, you can regard such awareness and/or consciousness as concentrated attention. Here are some exercises in concentrated attention that will advance your consciousness.

Start by paying deliberate attention to your relatively unimportant acts, so that you can better concentrate full attention upon important acts. In other words, break the habit of doing so many things while scarcely being aware you are doing them. Reverse that and become deliberately aware of everything you do. That is advancement of consciousness. Do this . . .

Deliberately pay attention (concentrate attention) while you are dressing, brushing your teeth, taking a shower, while combing your hair.

Concentrate your attention on your food while you are eating. Deliberately become aware of the taste of the food, how it masticates in your mouth, and experience the swallowing. When you eat put full attention upon your eating, and do not distract your attention.

Put attention while you are walking. Feel the brushing of your clothes upon your legs. Feel the rippling of your muscles while you walk.

Concentrate your attention (become conscious of) while enjoying recreation. Enjoy fully your recreation and keep your mind free from pressing matters while you recreate.

An important point in these exercises for advancing consciousness is to do one thing at a time. Concentrating only on what you are immediately doing is the way.

Relaxing mind and body

Appreciate fully that mind affects the body and likewise that body affects the mind. Learning how to relax and let things *go* while you relax is a first essential in concentrating attention without distraction. To do this, learn how to still your senses (seeing, hearing, tasting, smelling, feeling); become quiet, suspend confused mental activity. That is what is meant by "entering the silence"–it is then that your mind can fully exert its power and produces the thoughts you wish produced under your deliberate control. The rule is to discipline your mind so it produces thoughts you wish it to think.

Attention brings into your reality that which you most strongly think about. To deliberately be able to control what you think about is a great skill. It is based upon concentration of attention. Concentrated attention is attention to definite objectives. This power of concentration can be trained to a high degree of perfection viz.:

Concentration of attention = increasing awareness
Increasing awareness = advancing consciousness

Now, on occasion perform these exercises in your private room.

Subdue the light in the room. Lie outstretched upon your back on your bed. Stretch your feet down as far as they will go. Next stretch your arms out, as though reaching for the ceiling. Be sure your head is level with your body. Raise your head and let it fall back on the bed, as though it did not belong to you. Do this three times.

Now, raise your right arm, and let it fall back upon the bed, in the same loose and natural manner, as you did with your head. Do this three times. Do the same with your left arm. Do the same with your right leg. Do the same with your left leg. Now, just relax and let your mind drift, without control – just allow it to go wherever it wants to go, entirely of its own choosing.

If you find you must think, just think, "I am resting. I am resting. I am resting."

Simple. Easy to do. Very pleasant. You are starting on your way to become master of your mind. Make it a joy to do.

When you wish to, you can proceed on to performing this exercise in concentrating attention:

The perception of details

(Note the time you start this exercise)

Chose any small object such as a pencil, pen, key, matchbox, any small object (it makes no difference what) that you can hold in your hand.

Commence now examining the article – in every detail – with great care. Do not hurry, just take your time. Suppose the small article you have elected to hold is a pen. Note with care . . .

What kind of a pen is it? How well does it write? What firm manufactured the pen? What color and general shape is it? Are there any scratches or blemishes upon it? How do you like the way it writes? Etc. Go over every detail. When your careful examination is complete, note the time, and affirm how long your examination has taken. As your powers of concentration advance, your full consciousness of the object will advance and you will find your examination takes longer and, yet, to your sensing time seems more condensed.

You will find this mental exercise of real value. It will train your observation of everything you perceive. It will advance your consciousness.

When you perform this exercise sit quietly still. Choose a fresh article each day for your mentally detailed examination.

Sometimes the exercise will possibly make you sleepy. If it does, just be drowsy. It's perfectly okay.

Concentrating on your senses

Now, let's move on in this training to becoming more conscious of your senses. Remember always that concentration of attention intensifies the power of the senses to a remarkable degree. We will start with the sense of smell, as it is your most-close-to-nature sense, and being close to nature is to recognize the divine nature of yourself.

Advancing your sense of smell

A great part of people take their sense of smell for granted, and make no effort to advance it. Yet, Masters of the Mind place great importance upon it. In the East, for instance, the Yogis flood their chambers with fragrant incense. Aromatherapy is becoming popular in the West. The advancement of your sense of smell is directly related to advancing your consciousness.

Deliberately acquire a state of mind of analyzing the different odors that assail your sense of smell. In other words, concentrate your attention upon your sense of smell. Animals have far keener sense of smell than does mankind.

An excellent exercise is to walk through a forest while giving attention to picking up the great variety of smells that are natural to nature. Getting close to nature will give you a tremendous boost in awareness.

Such practice, from time to time, will greatly increase your power of attention. Practice daily describing different odors – their character, intensity, and their affect upon your*self*.

Advancing your sense of hearing

This exercise will advance your sense of hearing by concentrating on it. If you practice it daily, your hearing will become more and more acute.

Get a clock with a loud tick. Or, if you wish, use a Metronome such as musicians use in practicing. Any music store can supply one.

Place the ticking-device in your private room. Have things quiet and alone, so just the ticking sound stands out. Then, gradually walk backwards in the room – very slowly – away from the source of the sound. While doing this, listen attentively to the ticking sound.

As you find that ticking grows fainter, walk even more slowly backing away from the sound. And when you reach the spot where you can no longer hear the ticking of the clock, take note of the place where you are standing. This gives you a chance to experience how your hearing is advancing, as you reach a more distant spot ere long. Always maintain the original source of the sound.

The most important point in this hearing advancement exercise is the listening attitude. You must keep your ears on the "stretch", as it were, for the sound of the tick, and – very important – never allow yourself to think of any other thing but the tick. That is, concentrate intently upon the ticking sound. As much as possible do not let your mind wander while practicing these consciousness advancing exercises.

The exercise in advancing your sense of hearing continues.

Go outside and take a slow walk. As you quietly walk along listen to the great variety of sounds that come into you. As you are able, identify the sounds and the location of the source from whence they originate.

Then, from amongst the many sounds, pick out one sound and concentrate full attention upon it for a few minutes. Doing this outside walking exercise in picking out selected sounds will benefit your auditory sense.

Advancing your sense of taste
You can advance your sense of taste by concentrating on the taste of the food you eat. Center your full attention on the taste of the food, and experience it fully. Many people do not. Fully enjoy your sense of taste. Eat slowly: never in a hurry.

To really appreciate your sense of taste *slow down*.

Concentrating upon the taste while eating excites the salivary glands, thus aiding the process of digestion. In your practice, also note the different parts of the tongue giving different sensations of taste. Experiment to determine what part of your tongue produces the greatest intensity. Note, also, that the central part of your tongue has no sensation of taste. Try this:

Put a grain of sugar or salt in the center of your tongue, and you will note that you can detect no sensation of sweetness or saltiness. In general, children have a keener sense of taste than adults. The middle part of the tongue of a child produces sensations of taste which are absent in the adult.

With practice the sense of taste can be developed into a profession. There are expert tea and wine tasters who are paid big wages for their cultivated skill in tasting. The more you put your consciousness into tasting, the more you will develop this skill.

Always remember, the ultimate aim of these exercises is to advance consciousness, i.e. advance attention and concentration via effort without effort.

Advancing your sense of touch
The Sense of Touch can be advanced to a great degree. An interesting touch experience which advances attention is to try to detect the cold on back of the hand, or on the cheek or brow. Try this:

Take a pencil with a blunt point and draw it gently over the palm of your hand. As you draw the pencil slowly over the palm's surface, every here and there, you will experience a sudden sensation of cold. These parts are the "cold spots" on the hand.

There are also "warm spots" on the palm of the hand. You can detect them by dipping a steel knitting needle with a blunt end in warm water, then wiping it dry and drawing it over the palm's surface. The "warm spots" will be found to have less intensity than the "cold spots".

You can advance your sense of touch by touching articles in the dark, or with your eyes closed. The more you practice "seeing with your fingers" in the dark, the more you will advance your sense of touch.

Advancing your sense of sight
Get a sheet of blank paper and with a black pen mark a spot about the size of a dime in its center. Pin the paper on the wall. Stand back ten feet. Now gaze at the spot. The paper pinned to the wall should be at eye-level.

Continue gazing at the spot steadily with your body free of all movement . . . gaze at the spot steadily and mentally count slowly up to one hundred. Allow your eyes to blink as much as desired; the object is to concentrate your mind on the counting. As much as possible, make your mind free of all other thoughts; just concentrate on the counting. Breathe naturally while counting.

Perform this exercise twice a day. It will advance your sense of sight.

Concentrating on the nerves
In your quiet room lie about your bed and relaxed. Now direct your concentrated attention upon your prone body. Try to become conscious of your heart beating, the murmuring in your ears, the sound of your breathing. Concentrate exclusively on the sounds of your body, while not paying the slightest attention to other sounds of an outside nature.

Next concentrate upon various parts of your body such as your head, your feet, your arms, your legs. Then go inside your body and concentrate on your lungs, your heart, your bowels, your liver, your kidneys, and other bodily organs and/or functions.

While concentrating on these various parts of your body, visualize the blood flowing and carrying life and health to each and every part. Try to make your thinking so vigorous, so real, that you can actually feel the blood coursing through your body.

Now place your hands over your ears, and say out loud to yourself: "I am alive; every cell in my organism is filled and thrills with life; every part of me is filled with vitality." Let your hands drop from your ears and relax all over mental-picturing yourself standing up in perfect health; strong of mind and strong of body. Now, let yourself doze off, if you so wish, while literally realizing it with all intensity of your mind/soul. This is a grand exercise to take, just before going to sleep and before rising in the morning. Not only will it improve your concentration powers, but likewise benefit your health. You will find a realization, as you advance the consciousness of yourself that your body is a reflection of your mind.

Advancing your attention
Take a column in a newspaper, and commencing at the top, cross out with a pen or pencil every letter O you come across. Go faithfully from the top of the column on down. It seems simple at first, but you will soon find you grow weary and your attention will wander away from what you are doing. You must try to prevent this by the effort of your will. When you succeed in doing this, you are succeeding in advancing your attention. This will help.

Say to yourself every time you find your thoughts wandering, "My attention is directed towards marking out each letter O. I am not thinking of anything else." When you succeed in mastering this lesson in blocking out the O's, you have made a big stride in concentration.

You can practice this exercise daily as many times as you wish and wherever you are. Perform the exercise at first for just 5 minutes and keep track of how many O's you crossed out. If you keep a record of these, you will note real progress in the advancement of your attention.

An exercise in voluntary action
Sit back in your chair in your quiet room and twirl your thumbs. Do it slowly and keep your gaze fixed on your thumbs. Do not think of anything but the twirling.

If you find it difficult to prevents thoughts coming into your mind while you twirl your thumbs, continue the twirling and count slowly up to one hundred.

This exercise is very simple, yet it makes demands upon you, for you will find it difficult to keep your thoughts solely on the twirling. The more you learn how to do this, the more you will become master over your Voluntary Actions.

Concentrating on sleep
A very good exercise in concentration on sleep is the water method. Do this . . .

Put a glass of water on your table in your private room. Sit back in a comfortable chair, relax, and glaze into the depth of the water. If there is any light in the room, have your back turned to it. Simply gaze into the water and think of its cool, calm depth. It has a quieting effect upon you, much related to how your feel when you sit beside a stream of running water, out in the country.

Again, while gazing within the glass of pure, clear crystal water hold the thought in your mind that you are becoming drowsy and sleepy. This is the practice. It is unlikely that you will go to sleep, but very likely that you will become drowsy and sleepy. The object of the exercise is to simply keep the mind on a train of thought of sleep and quietness, so as to strengthen your entire nervous system. By being able to concentrate on sleep, you will be able to calm the mind and render it passive and quiet at the dictates of your will.

In the study of this method, you will note how close it is to the study of self-hypnosis previously discussed.

A consideration of the induction of sleep
For the induction of sleep as a deliberate mental process, we come close to the deliberate induction of the state of mind of hypnosis. For the induction of sleep several concomitant conditions are necessary, chief among which are an exhaustion of potential interest and the presence of monotony. The induction of sleep is the resultant of these joint conditions. Other conditions, of course, are more-or-less essential and conducive to sleep, such as a peaceful state of mind, a comfortable posture, and absence of external excitement, etc.

The faculty of imitation also helps bring sleep about. When we see others dozing we tend to follow their example. Talking about sleep tends to induce sleep, just as talking about food provokes hunger. Monotonous sounds, such as raindrops falling upon the roof, or the breaking of waves upon the seashore tends to encourage slumber.

Muscular repose is, also, a desired preliminary to sleep. The transition from the waking to the sleeping state can sometimes be sudden, but generally there is a noticeable gradation. And thus you go to sleep.

Sleep and hypnosis

How interesting it is that so often it is said, hypnosis is not to be regarded as sleep; that it is more an awaken state of mind that it is a sleep state of mind. Truly amazing! In producing hypnosis one prepares all the conditions for sleep and even tells the mind "Go to sleep!"–and then states it is more related to wakefulness than it is to sleepfulness.

Makes me smile.

Appendix Three

Exercises in Attention & Mental Discipline

Exercise one

Go into a room where a conversation is going on, and see how much of the conversation you can mentally block out. Take up a book and try to read, making up your mind that you will not listen to a single word of the conversation. Say to yourself, "I will not hear a single word of this conversation." How well were you able to accomplish this objective? Test it for yourself.

Read for 5 minutes while trying to block out the conversation mentally. Then try to see how much of the conversation you can write down. Never mind if it seems disjointed. Write down what you recall, even though it is just a few words. *Note*: This is not a memory exercise; it is an exercise in developing the ability to be mentally selective of what you do not want to come in. The more words of the conversation you can write down, the more the practicing of this exercise will be good for you.

At first, you will find this a difficult exercise in directed attention. But it is an important one, as when you learn how to direct your attention totally on where or what you want to give attention to, beyond outside disturbances, you are becoming more and more a master of your mind.

This exercise makes great demands on your concentrative powers, and is, therefore, very important. Practice it often, remembering to preface the exercise by affirming that you will not hear a single word of the conversation around you.

Exercise two

Lie down on your bed, stretch out and relax. After you have so rested for a few moments, try to make your mind a blank. To do this, as each thought comes into your mind, by an effort of will, try to reject it; that is, do not follow it up and allow a train of thought to be established. In other words, resolutely put each thought to one side, as it comes in. Do this consistently and you will come close to knowing what is meant by "blanking the mind".

At first it will seem almost impossible, but it is possible. This exercise is great practice in concentration for disciplining the mind. It develops both will-power and thought-control.

Be careful in your first attempts at this exercise. Practice it for only a short period and only once a day for the first week or so. When you can keep the mind blank for some three minutes, you will have developed remarkable control over your thoughts.

Exercise three

When you have learned how to make your mind blank, as in the previous exercise, you can perform this exercise.

Lie down and make your mind blank for a few seconds. Then, instantly commence to think of a subject (decide on what the subject will be before commencing the exercise).

Suppose, for example, health is the subject to be concentrated upon. In performing the exercise, think of the benefits of having perfect health; think of what it means to have perfect health. Affirm, in your mind, how wonderful it would be to have perfect health – continuously free from illness.

Then, when you feel you have well considered the subject, banish it by making the mind blank again. After a few seconds rise. The exercise is complete.

Perform this exercise each day, using a new subject each time to conjecture upon, such as Wealth, Power, Position, Prestige, Love,

Happiness, etc. Think also of any particular ideal you would have realized in your life. Reject negative thoughts.

Concentrate on the positive, as we tend to become that of what we think.

The main difficulty of performing this exercise is to keep the mind on the subject being considered. Keep control over it, and never allow it to wander from the subject. As you advance you can practice this exercise for 15 minutes or so each time. As soon as the exercise is over, banish the subject from your mind. Let it go blank. You are gaining in control over your mind.

Exercise four

This exercise further disciplines your mind. To perform it, take a simple word of three letters, such as MAY, CAN, PEN, CAR, TOP, HAT, etc. and write it on a blank sheet of paper in bold letters, using a black-marking pen.

Now, gaze steadily at the middle letter of the word you have written on the paper. You must try to obliterate out of your mind the idea of the word. Concentrate solely on the middle letter.

Suppose, the word you have written is MAY. Do not let the thought of MAY enter your mind – think only of the letter "A". You will find that the mind will struggle and it will want to take in the word as a whole, and will try to spell or pronounce the word mentally. As this is an exercise in directing attention, do your best to prevent such.

The exercise looks simple, but actually it is quite difficult. It cannot be done until you have first mastered the previous exercises of mind control. However, mastery will come with repeated practice. Try it on a series of words, 2 minutes on each, at different intervals during the day. This is an excellent exercise to concentrate attention and keeping the mind from wandering.

The Psychology of Attention

What is attention?

The mind is always busy. Thousands of messages are being sent to and from the brain every hour of our lives; some of them are rushed into consciousness and we become aware of them. This is awareness of attention. This form of attention is called "Non-Voluntary Attention", and is usually but momentary.

When we deliberately turn the stream of consciousness into a definite channel and attend to one object and/or subject, such attention is termed "Voluntary Attention". It is the kind of attention which chiefly concerns us in *concentration*.

"Voluntary Attention" is the mind's directive and selective power – the power to turn the stream of consciousness into definite channels of thought.

It is well to distinguish between the terms "consciousness" and "Attention". *Consciousness* is the state of mind which results whenever sensory impressions produce a mental experience. *Attention* is the state of mind which emphasizes the selective character of specific thoughts.

Captured Attention

Some things we do – both, mental and physical – automatically capture our attention.

Business
Business activity of any kind automatically compels our attention. Things that obviously need attention spontaneously capture our attention to be tended to:

Neatness

Cleanliness

Orderly Arrangement
Things well done, in orderly fashion, spontaneously capture our attention.

Expectation
Expectation for something to occur, forces us to attend to the expectation for it to occur.

Curiosity
Curiosity compels attention. In many ways, curiosity advances our perception.

The Unusual
That which is novel compels our attention. It combines with curiosity.

Movement
We are more inclined to pay attention to a moving object than one which is stationary.

Pleasure
When something, either mental or physical, gives us pleasure, it draws our attention with powerful force.

Experience
Experience with things we know how to do we spontaneously give attention to. The more the experience, the more attention can be given to it in perception without effort.

Interest
We give most attention to things and activity we are interested in.

It is well to know these motivation centers for attention, for in concentrated attention consciousness advances.

The Habit of Attention

Attention is a type of habit one wants to acquire. The habit of attention demands as its prime directive, an inclination to attend.

The easiest way to cultivate the habit of attention is found in repetition.

To keep attention, it must become a habit of riveting upon the objective. For practice, rivet your attention on any object for 5 minutes while determining the details of the object.

Further, to acquire the habit of attention practice the dismissal of irrelevancies. When trivial thoughts come in, refuse to entertain them.

Paying attention (being aware of) to your breathing coming in and out of your body is a masterful way to advance the habit of attention.

Finale to Attention

This Appendix on "Concentrated Attention" finalizes on developing physical strength (health) and mental force (mind control). Whatever contributes to health brings in the vitality of concentrated attention.

Health is largely a matter of constitution – it comes by Nature. Its maintenance is requisite.

Vitality
To add and store up vitality think and practice the numerous things, in such regard as *prana*, about which I have written in this, my Autobiography.[12]

Will
Will is the direction of mind under the direction of consciousness. Will is the cultivation of willing to be and do, under the direct command of the mind which you have learned how to control.

When you have learned how to discipline the mind via "Make your mind think what you want it to think; make your mind think when you want it to think; make your mind stop thinking when you want it to stop thinking; become a witness to your thoughts" you have become a "Master of Your Mind" ("Mastermind").

When one becomes a "Mastermind" one advances from Self-Consciousness to Cosmic Consciousness. It is an advancement from homosapiens to homosuperior – the next stage in human evolution.

---

[12] Refer to Chapter Thirty-Nine "Vitality Hypnosis".

Appendix Four

More Treasures from My Treasure Chest

Many seeks treasures outside of themselves, while their greatest treasures are to be found within themselves.

The more you practice these exercises and advance your consciousness the more fully alive you become. Here are further exercises in concentrating of attention I have frequently used. As they are important to me, I include them in this Appendix to my Autobiography. Gifts to you – increasing your control of yourself.

Concentration for Control of the Arms

Get a sheet of paper and in its center, using a black marking pen, make a black spot the size of a half dollar. Pin the paper on the wall of your room on level with your eyes, when you are standing. Then move back from the paper on the wall about 8 to 10 ft, and extend your right arm (if you are right handed; left arm if left handed) in the direction of the black spot on the wall, and point the second fingers out until it appears to exactly cover the spot to your vision.

Now, if you run your eyes along your arm to the fingers, just as in sighting when firing a rifle, you will notice if there is the slightest wavering of your second finger. Do not watch the hand, watch the tip of the second finger. If there is the faintest quivering of the arm the "fingertip" will show it.

What you must do in this exercise is to try to keep the fingertip exactly in the center of the distant black spot. At first you may find your arm unsteady, but with practice control will be gained over it. Gaining this control of muscular steadiness is the purpose of the exercise.

You will find this exercise tiring to the muscles of the arm, so at first do not practice it for more than a minute or so at a time. You can practice it several time each day, if you wish. You will find it will make your arm more and more steady.

This is an excellent exercise for those who wish to excel in shooting, penmanship, playing golf, etc. . . . anything where steadiness of the hand and arm is required. It is important to keep your breathing natural when performing the exercise.

An additional method

Take a cane and point it at some object across the room, and run your eyes along the stick so that the end of the cane covers the object to your vision. Concentrate on keeping the cane firm and steady while pointing directly at the object.

Try this exercise at different angles in pointing the cane towards a distant object. For instance, point to a star overhead; then at an object on the level of your height; then at some object on the wall. Try with first one arm and then with the other. Practice this exercise in private. Keep your mind firmly fixed on what you are doing.

This exercise develops eye/hand coordination. I have used it frequently in developing the ability to draw.

Exercise for Control of the Muscles of the Leg

Put a coin on the floor, and stand back from it about 2 ft. Stand upright with your hands by your sides. Then raise and extend your right leg until the toe of your shoe is over the edge of the coin – try to keep it exactly in line with the coin. Watch the toe, and see if you can detect any movement of the foot. This exercise will be found tiring to the muscles of the leg like the foregoing is to the arm muscles. Practice it only for a few minutes during the first week or so. When you gain control at the 2 ft distance, gradually extend (move further back from the coin) until your distance is close to 3 ft. When you are successful at this distance, then perform the following exercise:

Use the same paper you used for your arm exercise, and pin it to the wall about 3 ft above the floor. Stand away from the wall and raise your foot until the toe of your shoe covers the spot on the paper. As you practice, gradually heighten the paper until the spot approaches a level with your eyes. You will find the strain on the muscles increase as you heighten the spot. Avoid the strain by raising the height of the black spot gradually.

Practice this exercise with each leg alternately. Do not think of anything else when performing leg muscle exercises. Keep your mind fixed on what you are doing, and breathe naturally.

Exercise for Control of Muscles of the Head

Sit back in a comfortable chair, and gaze at the black spot pinned to the wall in front of you. Have it on a level with your eyes, while you relax back in the chair.

Gaze at the spot for 5 minutes (time it with your watch). It is okay if your eyes blink, but keep your head motionless, even when you look downward at your timing via the watch.

Concentrate on keeping your head absolutely still. Mentally repeat to yourself, "I must keep my head perfectly still and think of nothing else."

Pay attention to your breathing when performing this exercise. Your breathing should be deep and rhythmic. This is important.

The person who has perfect control of the muscles of the head and eyes introduces charisma into their personality. Practicing this exercise produces a feeling of calmness that will soon become habitual to you. Practice this exercise for 5 minutes the first week; afterwards extend it to 15 minutes.

Exercises in Concentration Applied to Special Purposes

Concentration applied to reading

Take a page in any book, magazine, or newspaper and read it carefully with a view of seeing if there are any misspellings. Read very carefully, spelling each word silently. If you do this exercise properly (slowly and carefully) by the time you have finished the page you will find that you have no idea of what you have been reading. Your entire purpose is to sort out misspellings. Test the accuracy of your work by going over the same material on the following day. Test it further by going over it again two or three days later. Then advance the test, by starting with the last word on the page and read it backwards – still looking for misspellings.

Do not confuse this exercise with being a "proofreader". It is entirely different. A "proofreader" must attend to the sense of what is being read, as well as look out for misspellings. You must concentrate solely on the misspellings.

You will find that this is a good exercise in concentration, for it makes demands on your powers of attention. Practice it for 5 minutes daily. The results obtained in reading concentration are surprising.

Concentration applied to memory

Take a detailed picture and look at it intently for 10 minutes. Note the subject of the picture. Note the details of the picture, and their respective position to each other. If there are human figures in the picture note how they are dressed, etc. As you do this, keep your mind intent on careful observation of the picture.

Do at least a full 10 minutes observation of the picture; longer if you wish. When your examination is complete, dismiss it from your mind, and proceed on to other activity.

The day following your careful observation of the picture (at about the same time) bring the picture back to your memory. Take a piece of paper, and draw a rough sketch of the picture (no talent is required).

Your drawing completed (good or bad) compare your recalled sketch of the picture, and note what details you may have omitted.

Again spend 10 minutes or so carefully observing the picture, then put it aside. Next day draw your sketch of the picture from memory. Check it with the picture, and see how much you have improved. Perform the exercise often – it is an excellent memory exercise.

Concentration on bodily sensations

In this exercise, you concentrate on various bodily sensations, Hunger, Thirst, Cold, Heat.

Lie on your bed, stretch out relaxed upon your back, and think of HUNGER. Try to think what it would feel like to be ravenously hungry with no means of satisfying your hunger. Picture being hungry in your mind until you actually experience the pangs of hunger. Feel it keenly. Then, turn your mind in the opposite direction, and think of yourself sitting down to a sumptuous meal. The dinner is delicious, and you eat and eat until all hunger is gone.

Next, concentrate on being THIRSTY. So thirsty that your mouth feels parched and dry. Then, concentrate on the opposite, as you enjoy drinking a glass of cool, clear refreshing water. All sensations of thirst are gone.

Next, concentrate on being COLD until you feel yourself shivering all over. Then, concentrate on the opposite; feel HEAT until you are aglow.

You will find this mastering of mental sensations becoming transformed into physical sensations in your body, a wonderful exercise. Not only does it advance your powers of concentration; it produces deliberate control of physical sensations in your body.

In addition, you will find this exercise heads you in the direction of controlling pain in your body via mental control.

Concentration on writing verses

Writing verses is an excellent exercise in concentration, plus adding to your vocabulary. In performing this exercise at first choose verses simple in construction. The concentration comes via the endeavor to find words that rhyme. Do not be concerned with trying to write poetry; all you are to concern yourself with is the rhyme; the subject matter is unimportant.

If you find, you cannot write complete verses, simply match words that rhyme together, such as: cat/mat, doll/poll, ferry/merry, etc. Proceed in this simple way, until your advance writing complete verses.

In performing this exercise, keep your mind centered, on the rhymes, concerned with the meaning of the words.

Concentration applied to breathing

This is an important exercise used by the yogis. It is used as a means of attaining perfect concentration.

Sit in a chair with your spine straight. Breathe deeply in your 'normal' fashion. Now, take a deep breath and press your forefinger against the right nostril closing it. Exhale the breath through the still open nostril. Again inhale deeply through the open nostril – draw in the breath slowly and gently. It should take 8 seconds to inhale. Next, hold the breath for 8 seconds, release your finger from the closed right nostril, and use it to close off the left nostril. Exhale the breath, this time, through the right nostril – take 8 seconds to do this.

Next, draw in your breath through the right nostril for 8 seconds. Hold the breath for 8 seconds. Release left nostril and close off right nostril, thus exhaling the held breath through the left nostril.

Continue this rhythm of breathing back and forth between the nostrils. Do this process of deliberate rhythmic breathing for 20 minutes, e.g., 8 seconds inhale . . . 8 seconds hold . . . 8 seconds exhale. This is a good rhythm to start on. As you gain more control of your breath, you can gradually extend the number of seconds for inspiration, holding, and expulsion. Do not alter the number of times you do it. Keep to 20. Also, avoid all movement, other than shifting in closing off one nostril and then the other, back and forth, when you perform the exercise.

In this exercise, concentrate your attention upon your breathing. This exercise has a beneficial effect on the nerves and respiratory system; it produces a cool, calm dispassionate feeling. It is one of the finest modes of concentrating that you can practice.

Concentration applied to self-reliance

This seems such a simple exercise, yet it often proves to be the most difficult for many people. The exercise is simply to learn to keep your mouth shut. Tight shut.

Just notice for one day all the people you meet, and observe how very few keep their mouth shut – tight shut.

Notice, also, the men and women how are of strong character and purpose – those who are self-reliant are those who have learned the wisdom to keep their mouth shut. Tight shut.

In other words, think before you speak. You will find that you will think more and speak less.

The fact is that if you practice this exercise regularly, it will increase your self-reliance. The exercise will be of great benefit to you.

We are so used to speaking without first thinking that, at first, this exercise will require concentrated attention, until the habit is acquired. Then you will do it naturally – automatically.

Concentrating on controlling the facial muscles

There are three positions from which to practice this exercise:

1. Sit upright in front of a mirror and try to avoid the slightest movement. Concentrate your gaze at the root of your nose. Breathe naturally.
2. Stand upright in front of a mirror and fix your gaze at the root of your nose from this position. Breathe naturally.
3. Stand upright in front of a mirror with your hands down by your sides. Stand motionless. Breathe naturally.

At first do not practice these position for longer than 5 minutes; gradually increase to 15 minutes. Watch your breathing carefully in each position. You will find the exercise will give you conscious control over your facial muscles.

The ability to control your facial muscles has great value, for these muscles are always trying to betray your thoughts to others. Bad news. Good News. Surprise. Fear. Joy, all employ the facial muscles to express themselves, and people judge you by these muscles as much as by what you say. Practice to control your facial muscles, and you advance the privacy of your thoughts.

Concentration applied to mastering unwanted habits

You can master unwanted habits for yourself by practising this exercise in concentration.

Habits enslave you because they seem to give you a required satisfaction, and we tend to do that which satisfies us. Reverse in your mind satisfaction for the habit to dissatisfaction for the habit, and the habit looses its power of satisfaction. Such an effective way for mastering unwanted habits.

Do this:
Lie on your bed and stretch out. Relax. Relax. Relax. Now, imagine yourself standing in front of yourself.

Suppose, for example, that you are an alcoholic and know full well that you must master the habit for your own well-being. Now, disassociate yourself from your imagined self, and directly tell this altered consciousness of yourself or the horridness of drunkenness. Let it be that you are speaking to an actual personality to whom you are affirming the disastrous effects of being an alcoholic. Then imagine you are giving this personality advice as to how to master this unwanted habit. Picture this person, who you have conjured in your mind, the benefits of sobriety, contrasted with the degradation of drunkenness.

Imagine you are trying to instill into him (or her) your own hatred and horror of drunkenness. Feel this horror, this hatred until your whole mind and body throbs with the feeling.

In this practice, you are forcefully making the habit of drinking intoxicating liquors not only an unsatisfying habit, but literally a horrifying one.

Tell your disassociated self that now that the habit no longer satisfies and is totally unwanted, how happy the personality will henceforth be at distancing from further drinking. And, how joyous are the benefits of good health and self-mastery that has been achieved.

End the self-induced session, by telling SELF (him or her) that the satisfaction for the habit has been replaced by distaste for the habit, and its existence is no more.

If the concentration in this exercise is intense, you will find an immediate turnaround from drinking to nondrinking. Not only drinking will no longer bring you satisfaction, but also your distaste for the habit is such that you couldn't drink further – causing drunkenness – even if you tried. Reported results have been remarkable as to the instant success of this method.

The same method of telling your alter ego distaste for further indulgence to an unwanted habit turns such habit not only to distaste for the habit, but also produces a positive hatred to the habit you wish to discard, such as smoking, overeating, etc.

Concentration on the power of faith

Faith is concentrated imagination. Faith is belief in something desired, even when there is no positive proof that it is so. Faith is an attitude of mind that produces positive results in the physical world. Faith is the transformation from imaginary to reality.

Perform this exercise in Concentrating on Faith by believing what you place your faith upon will occur in actuality.

Start by knowing precisely what your desire is. Go to your private room. Lie down and relax your body. As you relax your body, so does your mind relax–mind becomes quiet and receptive. Being receptive to something is to have faith in the occurrence.

Ready, set, go. Everything depends upon your FAITH definiteness. Sometimes it will occur in most unexpected ways.

Place your hands gently over each ear and speak out loud to yourself expressing to yourself your absolute faith that what you request will become reality.

You will find that according to your ability to concentrate, believe, and state clearly what you desire and have faith in its occurrence, it will occur.

Faith does not require intellectual understanding. Faith is based entirely on "the power of believing". Wishes are fulfilled with The Power of Faith.

In performing this exercise, in addition to intoning your desire-to-be-accomplished to yourself, simultaneously picture in your mind that the fulfillment of the desire has been accomplished. Let your body be still during this exercise and perform it frequently for 30 minutes at a time.

Mastering FAITH is a tremendous achievement.

Concentration applied to obtaining objectives in life

You will note how directly connected are the practices of the mind-controlling exercises I give you here to the self-hypnosis methods I previously presented. The mental power is the same. In these Appendices, I have condensed the processes into precise exercises you can perform. Perform the exercises, and the results desired will occur.

This particular exercise is closely associated with the Power of Faith previously presented. Every person has a basic desire to succeed in life, and the surest way to gain it is to have a positive objective of what you wish to occur and/or accomplish. For this purpose do this:

Sit at ease in your private room, and think about what you wish to be. Imagine you see your desired goal accomplished, and make clear in your mind the required steps to achieve it.

Picture to yourself the successful man or woman you wish to be. Imagine how you would act; how you would speak; how you would be when you become the successful person you wish to be. Repeat over and over to yourself – in your mind – the success in life you desire to be.

Then, say out loud to yourself (close your eyes when you speak to yourself): "I will become the kind of person I visualize myself becoming. Such will be me. I know the steps I must take to reach my goal, and nothing will hinder me from taking those steps. I know I will reach my goal of my personal achievement I SHALL! I SHALL! I SHALL!"

After you have concentrated in this manner, follow on and live the successful character you have conditioned yourself to become in your daily life.

Follow this plan for success in life. Make the effort to do it without effort. It takes no special effort. Just perform the exercise and affirm to yourself. I shall succeed. I know I will win. Nothing will deter my success. I know "I will reach my goal in life. So be it!"

This is a grand exercise in concentration directed towards an achievement purpose. Perform it for half an hour each time, you perform it. Perform the exercise in achieving your goal objective in life, as often as you please.

Appendix Five

Antiaging

I have applied two processes to my life that have been a help to me. I give them to you here along with three philosophical thoughts which have appealed to me:

1. Live life fully to the hilt at whatever chronological age you happen to be.
2. Less and less try to make things happen and more and more just let things happen.
3. The past is but memories that will never happen again. The future may never happen at all. There is only the here and now.

Here are the processes for antiaging.

Antiaging Process One

A mind gone wild can cause a lot of trouble. Learning how to control your mind will keep you plenty busy, and you won't have time to worry about how old you are. Use this discipline:

MAKE YOUR MIND THINK *WHAT* YOU WANT IT TO THINK.

MAKE YOUR MIND THINK *WHEN* YOU WANT IT TO THINK.

MAKE YOUR MIND *STOP THINKING* WHEN YOU WANT TO STOP THINKING.

BECOME A *WITNESS* TO YOUR THOUGHTS.

Be a witness to your thoughts? Why not. Most of them did not originate with you anyway.

Next, come to know that your mind has five main function centers:

1. The center of right knowledge

2. The center of wrong knowledge

3. The center of imagination

4. The center of sleep

5. The center of memory

If you would control your mind, learn how to use these mental functions well: *Advance* your Center of Right Knowledge. *Suppress* your Center of Wrong Knowledge. *Control* your Center of Imagination. *Use* properly your Center of Sleep. *Be cautious* of your Center of Memory.

Your Center of Imagination is the tricky one, as imagination is the creative function of the mind. Used properly it can make you a genius. Used improperly it can destroy you. Just remember, imagination is a two-edged sword. Wield it carefully.

Wow! Doing this, you sure won't have much time to worry about aging. And if you would have a peaceful mind hold four attitudes towards life and those you meet in life:

1. Congratulate the successful

2. Be compassionate to the miserable

3. Appreciate the virtuous

4. Do not dwell on evil

Remember that while *mind* is nothing tangible, it does have the power to produce thoughts, and thoughts are forms of energy produced by your biocomputer brain. Believe it or not that power definitely has physical aspects. Make a Mental Energy Meter and test it for yourself.

The Mental Energy Meter

Take a piece of medium-weight paper, about 3 inches square, and fold it diagonally from corner to corner. Then open it and make another diagonal fold so that there will be two folds (or creases) forming intersecting diagonals. Again open the paper, which will now present the appearance of a low, partially flattened out pyra-mid (like a little umbrella).

Next take a long needle and force it through a card, matchbox, or anything to form a base for the little apparatus, so it projects an inch or so out of whatever is used for its base. Place this on a steady table where it will be free of drafts of any kind.

Now, take the folded paper and balance its downside center on the tip of the needle point. You have designed a sensitive appara-tus that will revolve freely upon the needle point. It is ready to operate.

Operation

Place the open palms of your hands around the suspended paper pyramid, in a semi-cupped position. Keep the hands a half inch or so away from the paper so that it may revolve freely. Hold your hand still and concentrate your mental energy upon the paper pyramid, and mentally command it to revolve upon the needle point.

At first it will wobble – perhaps revolving in one direction or the other. Slowly at first, and increasing in speed as the mental energy continues. Keep your hands still throughout the experiment. Just use your mind (producing thoughts and thoughts manifest physi-cal energy).

With practice you can make it revolve – in response to your thought: in one direction ... stop ... then revolve in the opposite direction. It is quite remarkable. Success with the experiment depends upon the mental energy being projected by the individual.

Numerous explanation of what causes the paper to revolve have been offered, such as heat from the hands, breath currents, etc. If the paper resting upon the needle point revolved in only one direc-tion, then possibly one of the explanations could be accosted. But when a person, with a little practice, confidence, and concentrated "thought-energy" can cause the paper umbrella to revolve first in one direction and then in another, and stop on mental command, it is clear you are experimenting with a Mental Energy Meter that can measure the "thought-power" of yourself.

Make the simple device. Experiment with it. Then judge for yourself. Make it a game you play just for the fun of playing, and guaranteed you will stop worrying about aging.

Antiaging Process Two

Here's a process you can have fun with that brings in energy to your body. It will make you feel young all over. Do this:

Sit in a chair, extend your arms in front of yourself, and start shaking your hands vigorously. Shake them in any direction, anyway they want to go. Just shake them wildly, in absolute freedom. You start with effort, but soon the shaking will become effortless, and it will seem to occur almost by itself. As you do this, allow your mind to grow calm and experience yourself as the shaking. The time will come when it seems that it is no longer your hands that are shaking, rather it is YOU who are shaking – both inside and outside.

When you *become* the shaking rather than just doing the shaking, you will begin to feel yourself filling with energy, an energy that somehow seems both mental and physical, at one and the same time.

After you have become the shaking of your hands, and have had enough of this activity for awhile, relax your hands into your lap and rest a bit. You are now ready to perform another associated process which brings the shaking to your entire body in an automatic way, bringing you great quantities of vital energy.

Stand erect, close your eyes, and allow your whole body to vibrate. You will find this easy to do, as you have already started the energy flowing throughout your body. So, now just allow your whole body to become energy, allowing your body to melt and dissolve its boundaries. Just stand relaxed, loose and natural. You do not have to do anything; you are simply there waiting for something to happen; all you have to do is co-operate with it and allow it. The co-operation should not become too direct; it should not be a pushing; it should remain just an allowing. You will find that your body will start making movements on its own. What movements it makes depends on you; all persons are different. Possibly your head will twitch and your body will start shaking in different ways. Just allow it to take on the shaking freely, *and shake any way it wants to go.*

Possibly your body will make subtle movements like a little dance, your hands move, your legs move seemingly on their own, and your entire body starts shaking with subconscious movements all over, and all you have to do is allow the shaking to happen.

The energy is very subtle, so do not resist it. Just allow it to develop on its own, and, as it does, think of the shaking as being the energy of the universe coming into you. Age stands still when the energy of the universe comes into you.

Appendix Six

Review

A review of Ormond McGill's show at the McKinley Auditorium, Honolulu, Hawaii, February 6,1957
(Excerpted from *Famous Magicians of the World*, reviewed by Arnold Furst)

Ormond McGill has written many books about hypnotism and is one of the best known hypnotists presenting a full evening's entertainment. His most famous book, The Encyclopedia of Stage Hypnotism, is recognized as a standard text as are several others of the twenty-one works he has authored. His show has been witnessed by many hundreds of thousands during the past twenty-four years that he has toured the United States, Canada and the Hawaiian Islands.

"Mindreading Confidential" is the title of the show which was presented in the Hawaiian Islands for its world premiere. Incorporated in this show are many of the features of "East Indian Miracles" and the "Séance of Hypnotism" with which Ormond McGill is so often identified. The new magical illusions and demonstrations of mentalism make this one of the most outstanding mystery revues touring the world today.

The curtains opened on a simple setting of two large and very colorful tapestries which gave an oriental background to the performance. Ormond McGill walked to the center of the stage with an East Indian Carpet Bag in his hand. A sudden puff of smoke and flames burst forth from a brass urn sitting in the center of the stage. McGill grabbed a puff of smoke and threw it into the carpet bag. Reaching into the bag, previously shown empty, he slowly withdrew his hand with a burning ball of fire. This flaming coal was calmly carried across the stage and deposited in an elaborately carved brass container held by his assistant. Another flash from the urn in the center of the stage and another puff of smoke was tossed into the empty carpet bag and withdrawn as a bail of fire. This was continued for awhile but finally, instead of a ball of fire, McGill withdrew his hand from the bag and he was holding a burning cigarette. Additional cigarettes were produced from the air and the routine of cigarette manipulations was concluded with a production of a lit cigar and a smoking pipe.

An attractive young assistant brought forward a shining duck pan into which McGill poured some liquid and ignited with a match. The flames were covered for just an instant as they were replaced by a large white rabbit. McGill then invited a young lady from the audience to come up on the stage and assist him in hypnotizing the rabbit for what he termed an: "informal bit of fun". The rabbit was rested on its back by the use of a specially constructed cradle and remained in that position until given the proper command by the young lady. Informality is certainly the best word to describe Ormond McGill's manner which the audiences find so appealing. The lady from the audience was graciously thanked and sent back to her seat.

A small green silk handkerchief was slowly rolled into a ball and held tightly in his fist. When the hand was opened the handkerchief had vanished and in its place was an egg. McGill offered to explain this simple effect as he slowly withdrew the handkerchief from the artificial egg. McGill pushed the handkerchief into the hollow egg for a second time and then concluded his "explanation" (?) by warning the audience to never show the wrong side of the egg ... unless one was prepared to break the egg open and that is exactly what Ormond McGill did.

A piece of rope which had been dyed red was now shown and the performer explained that it represented the Hindu Line of Life. The rope was then cut and restored to its original condition as the simple story enfolded. Several playing cards were selected by various people seated in the audience as Ormond McGill presented the great magical classic of The Rising Cards. McGill presents this effect along mindreading lines as he mentally discovers the name of each selected card and then causes it to rise and finally jump out of the small water goblet.

Next, a young man from the audience was invited to come upon the stage for a "lesson in magic". This time a green handkerchief was taken from a glass casket on the table and when it vanished right in front of the man's eyes, it returned most mysteriously to the glass casket.

I think the audience enjoyed this routine a bit more than usual because the young man upon the stage was Bob Krauss from The Honolulu Advertiser newspaper and the most popular columnist in the Hawaiian Islands. He was up on the stage as the result of a publicity stunt which had been arranged several weeks previously. He wrote in his column on Friday, February 1st, that he would buy a new deck of cards and after mixing them up would remove one card from the pack and replace it back into the pack in a reversed condition so that all the cards faced in one direction and the chosen card faced in the other direction. It was arranged for Ormond McGill to do the same thing with a deck of cards he would be holding in California, over two thousand miles away. When McGill arrived at the Honolulu airport the two decks were compared and the single card reversed in each deck was found to be the Queen of Diamonds. As a consequence, Bob Krauss had agreed to allow Ormond McGill to hypnotize him or use him during the opening night's performance in the Head Burning Illusion.

At the conclusion of the Green Handkerchief routine, Bob Krauss was made to kneel in front of the apparatus for the Fire God Sacrifice Illusion. His head was encased in some large brass tubes and a lit torch was plunged down into the tubes. Flames burst forth and then the tubes were shown empty. However, after a few brief seconds of apprehension on the part of the audience, the head was seen to he intact on the body and Bob Krauss was dismissed from the stage with the admonition from the performer to "try not to lose your head in the future".

Another publicity stunt was culminated next as the house lights were turned up and two uniformed patrolmen from the Honolulu Police Force came up on the stage with a copy of The Hawaii Times and an envelope inside a frame which was completely covered with cellophane. Ormond McGill explained that he had been asked to predict the headline of the Japanese section of The Hawaii Times. His prediction had arrived a week previously, sealed in the frame, and it had been on display in a store window in Downtown Honolulu.

One of the policemen, who was of Japanese ancestry, opened the envelope and read the prediction which was compared with the newspaper the other policeman held for comparison. It corresponded exactly!

Standing in front of the curtain which had been drawn during the presentation of the Newspaper Headline Prediction Ormond McGill borrowed a gentleman's handkerchief and tied a knot in one corner. Instantly the handkerchief seemed to become "alive" and it danced about right over the footlights. The front curtains then opened and the handkerchief was dropped into a small cabinet which sat isolated in the center of the huge stage. The Spook Handkerchief routine which followed was the original creation of Delight McGill who travels with the show as the stage mistress and is in charge of the elaborate light and music cues.

Ormond McGill spoke briefly about the "most dangerous trick in the world". One of the assistants walked on in a military manner carrying a regulation army rifle. An attractive young lady walked on the stage from the other side and was induced to stand in front of a small piece of glass. Before continuing his presentation of Shooting Through A Woman, Ormond McGill paused to hypnotize the girl so that she would not feel any pain in the event that anything went wrong. Careful aim was taken and the rifle discharged. The girl screamed and the plate glass directly behind her was shattered. Next to show the path the bullet took, McGill pushed a huge shiny needle and several yards of red ribbon through the girl's body. I was amazed at the effectiveness of this illusion and I realized that it was due to the logical sequence of effects. The audience was certainly well impressed as the young lady walked off the stage, just a bit shaken by her ordeal.

One of the most beautiful effects in the show was a Color Changing Plumes which was especially designed and built for McGill by Horace Marshall. After the feather plumes were changed several times in a mysterious manner, they were suddenly transformed into a large and most colorful bush standing over four feet high.

Another feature presented for this opening night's performance was a demonstration of fire eating by George Ito. George Ito was born in Honolulu although he has spent the past six years in and around New York City. During that time he appeared in several Broadway productions and he performed on the Steve Allen TV show. He has the added distinction of having stumped the panel of the popular television program, "What's My Line?"

To close the first act of magic and illusions with an East Indian background, Ormond McGill held the audience spellbound with his routine of the Linking Rings. This perennial classic was presented using large brass rings. This is in keeping with the artistic effect that Ormond and Delight McGill try to maintain throughout their show of mystery. The rings linked and unlinked in the hands of the spectators as well as those of the performer and even after a careful explanation on the part of the magician, the audience ended up more mystified than ever.

The second act consisted of various demonstrations of mentalism and telepathy and it is from this act that the entire show gains its name. As an effect in Thought Control, McGill asked several spectators to write some numbers on a slate. The mentalist wrote a figure of several digits on a small blackboard and then when the numbers on the slate were totaled, they coincided with the sum predicted by the performer.

Lt. Albert Fraga, fingerprint expert with the Honolulu Police Department, was next introduced and invited up on the stage. A small goldfish bowl containing four hundred small fingerprint cards that had been supplied by the FBI was stirred up by a lady in the audience who then selected one of the fingerprint cards. This chosen fingerprint was handed to Lt. Fraga who was seated on the stage at a small table and he was asked to find the Identification Order issued by the FBI which would identify the person whose fingerprint had been selected.

As Lt. Fraga busied himself with this task, Ormond McGill asked those in the audience to think of some questions they would like him to answer. One of the attractive young assistants handed McGill a large crystal ball into which he gazed intently for a few moments. Two initials were called and when a person raised his hand, McGill told that person his name and the question on his mind and then gave him an answer either in a serious or humorous vein depending upon the mood of the individual. After about 15 questions were answered Lt. Fraga indicated that he had classified the selected fingerprint and had identified it with his file of persons wanted by the FBI. Thereupon, Ormond McGill proceeded to reveal the person's description, his criminal record and finally his name.

A committee was invited to come upon the stage to take part in a spirit séance. After they were seated in a large semi-circle, a young lady was introduced as the medium and she was locked into a packing case so that she would be unable to reach the objects which were placed on top of the case. However, when the packing case was covered by a cabinet, instantly, bells were rung, tambourines shook and other manifestations took place. The members of the committee were asked to write the name of a president of the United States who was dead. One of these was chosen and several blank artist canvases were shown and placed in full view on top of the packing case. Slowly a bit of coloring was apparent on the blank canvas and gradually it developed into a faint but easily recognizable portrait of George Washington.

Two ladies from the committee on the stage were asked to step forward and place their hands upon a small table. As Ormond McGill talked to the ladies, they began to feel a gradual movement in the table and it went from one side of the stage to the other until it actually went up in the air a few feet and seemed to be floating in spite of their efforts to hold it down. This was certainly a most remarkable demonstration of something we read and hear about so often and seldom see.

For the final number in this act Ormond McGill explained that he would attempt a demonstration of Materialization and Dematerialization.

The packing case containing the young lady's body was again covered with the cabinet which was supported at its four corners by four men from the committee on the stage. One of the young men assisting McGill walked into the cabinet and stood inside it with his head protruding. The young man called out "One, two" … and the young lady said, "three!" Obviously the young man's body had dematerialized and the materialized body of the attractive medium walked out of the cabinet in his place. The expressions on the faces of the committee men on the stage showed how deeply they were impressed by this most effective presentation.

The third act of the show consisted of the Séance of Hypnotism almost exactly as presented in every large motion picture theatre by Ormond McGill during the days when he was known as Dr. Zomb. In fact, his reputation as Dr. Zomb, the hypnotist, has compelled him to add that title to his billing and today in all of his advertising you will find after his name the line, "The Man Called Dr Zomb."

The background of colored lights and the carefully chosen musical selections are factors which contribute to the remarkable ease with which Dr. Zomb is able to handle a group of 20 or 30 volunteers from the audience who wish to experience the sensations of being hypnotized. Before inviting anyone to come up on the stage, Ormond McGill first spoke briefly of the power of suggestion and actually demonstrated that power in such a way that almost 90 per cent of the members of the audience were in some slight way influenced. Next everyone was assured that he would in no way be embarrassed or made uncomfortable by coming up on the stage. Those genuinely interested were invited to take the seats provided for them on the stage and on this particular evening there were a great many young men who were members of the Civilian Air Patrol who responded.

The entire committee was given a demonstration of the Hypnotic Meditation Test. Next one young man from the committee was caused to fall forwards and then backwards into an assistant's waiting arms.

Returning his attention to the entire group, McGill gave them several tests which the audience found most amusing to watch. The mood changed again as Solo Hypnosis was demonstrated on one subject and various forms of catalepsy were shown.

Next was the demonstration which often causes the most commotion. Dr Zomb demonstrated mass hypnosis on the entire committee on the stage and influenced many members of the audience who indicated their willingness to take part in the experiment. These people in the audience soon found their arms outstretched in front of their bodies and they were walking down the aisle towards the stage in the manner of a sleepwalker. These new subjects were invited to remain up on the stage for the hilarious fun that followed.

One of the men on the stage was given the posthypnotic suggestion that he would return to the audience and go back to sleep. Others on the stage were invited to an "hypnotic party" and given glasses of water to drink which caused them to feel slightly intoxicated. Another young man tested the hypnotic eyeglasses and this demonstration caused the audience to roar with laughter. The program became more hilarious as several other post-hypnotic suggestions were put into effect simultaneously.

Self-hypnosis was then explained to the entire group on the stage and through its process they were all induced to go back into the hypnotic trance. During this portion of the demonstration the subjects experienced the feeling of being very cold and very hot. Many began to remove parts of their clothing. Changing to an experiment in age regression, Dr Zomb had the volunteers on the stage behave as they did during the time when they were third grade students in Elementary School and during this sequence they felt the various emotions of children at a Saturday afternoon matinee of their neighborhood motion picture theatre.

With one final post-hypnotic suggestion for the entire committee, Ormond McGill dismissed them individually with thanks and so ended his séance of hypnotism which is perhaps one of the most carefully planned portions of his entire program in spite of its appearance of complete spontaneity. The routine is arranged so that the audience is held entranced by the demonstrations with the single subjects and then thrown into gales of laughter at the amusing antics of the entire group. In this way no single individual is ever embarrassed but the entire committee of volunteers are enjoying their experiences on the stage, both as spectators and active participants. I was pleased to note that at all times Dr Zomb spoke to each or the subjects with complete respect and sympathetic understanding.

The Hindu Basket Trick was next presented as the concluding illusion in this show of magic, mentalism and hypnosis which ran a bit more than two and a half hours. Verna Aveiro slowly descended into the basket which seemed barely large enough for her small body. Instantly Ormond McGill pushed long steel swords and bamboo rods into the basket so that they passed through all the sides. When the magician stepped into the basket the audience gasped and frankly I was startled myself. Quickly the swords and bamboo poles were removed and handed to Garry Aveiro as Verna emerged completely unharmed and the curtain dropped on this mystery revue with an East Indian setting.

USA, Canada & Mexico orders to:
Crown House Publishing Company LLC
4 Berkeley Street, 1st Floor, Norwalk, CT 06850, USA
Tel: +1 203 852 9504, Fax: +1 203 852 9619
E-mail: info@CHPUS.com
www.CHPUS.com

UK, Europe & Rest of World orders to:
The Anglo American Book Company Ltd.
Crown Buildings, Bancyfelin, Carmarthen, Wales SA33 5ND
Tel: +44 (0)1267 211880/211886, Fax: +44 (0)1267 211882
E-mail: books@anglo-american.co.uk
www.anglo-american.co.uk

Australasia orders to:
Footprint Books Pty Ltd.
Unit 4/92A Mona Vale Road, Mona Vale NSW 2103, Australia
Tel: +61 (0) 2 9997 3973, Fax: +61 (0) 2 9997 3185
E-mail: info@footprint.com.au
www.footprint.com.au

Singapore orders to:
Publishers Marketing Services Pte Ltd.
10-C Jalan Ampas #07-01
Ho Seng Lee Flatted Warehouse, Singapore 329513
Tel: +65 6256 5166, Fax: +65 6253 0008
E-mail: info@pms.com.sg
www.pms.com.sg

Malaysia orders to:
Publishers Marketing Services Pte Ltd
Unit 509, Block E, Phileo Damansara 1, Jalan 16/11
46350 Petaling Jaya, Selangor, Malaysia
Tel : +03 7955 3588, Fax : +03 7955 3017
E-mail: pmsmal@streamyx.com
www.pms.com.sg

South Africa orders to:
Everybody's Books CC
PO Box 201321, Durban North, 4016, RSA
Tel: +27 (0) 31 569 2229, Fax: +27 (0) 31 569 2234
E-mail: warren@ebbooks.co.za